"A treasury of facts debunking myths of aging and a collection of marvelous anecdotes of older individuals living out the best years of their lives. A delightful and informative must-read for people of all ages."

—Barbara Russell Chesser, Ph.D.,
Coauthor, *Chicken Soup for the Golden Soul*

"Whether you're 40 or 80, this book is for you."

—Moya Olsen Lear, author of
An Unforgettable Flight

"A must-read for anyone who thinks life is over at 55. Finally, an honest look at . . . the prejudices and half-truths that plague this wonderful season of life."

—Thomas Benjamin, President,
Environmental Alliance for Senior Involvement (EASI)

"Interesting and inspiring. . . . [*Funny, I Don't* Feel *Old!*] provides ample evidence that the enjoyment of life can intensify over the years."

— Rick Bowers, *Third Age News Service*

"Carter Henderson has an important message for you. Stop worrying. There's never been a better time to be over 50."

—Korky Vann, *The Hartford Courant*

"Without denying the difficulties of aging, Carter Henderson . . . points out with good humor the real positives that [we] like to keep our eyes and minds on."

—Meryl Thulean, Executive Director,
Institute for Learning in Retirement

"Baby Boomers and other older people in search of uplift, inspiration, and good news will find comfort in these pages."

—*Rotarian*

"A great gift. I gave this book to my mother and father after they turned 55 and they both enjoyed it very much."

—Amazon.com reader comment

About the Author

CARTER HENDERSON, former *Wall Street Journal* London Bureau chief and front-page editor, is the author of *Free Enterprise Moves East: Doing Business from Prague to Vladivostok, Winners: The Successful Strategies Entrepreneurs Use to Build New Businesses, The Energy Suppliers, 20 Million Careless Capitalists* (with Albert C. Lasher), and *White House Doctor* (with T. Burton Smith), and has written for numerous magazines.

Today, Henderson engages in a wide variety of work, including business and financial consulting, fundraising, speech-writing for Fortune 500 companies, developing minority businesses, and leading international fact-finding missions, in addition to regularly teaching and speaking. He has no thoughts of retiring.

Funny, I Don't Feel Old!

How to Flourish After 50

CARTER HENDERSON

 **PRESS**

Institute for Contemporary Studies
Oakland, California

This book is a publication of the Institute for Contemporary Studies, a nonprofit, nonpartisan public policy research organization. The analysis, conclusions, and opinions expressed in ICS Press publications are those of the authors and not necessarily those of the Institute or of its officers, its directors, or others associated with, or funding, its work.

Inquiries, book orders, and catalog requests should be addressed to ICS Press, Latham Square, 1611 Telegraph Avenue, Suite 902, Oakland, CA 94612. Tel. (510) 238-5010; Fax (510) 238-8440; Internet www.icspress.com. For book orders and catalog requests, call toll-free in the United States: (800) 326-0263.

Cover and interior design by Rohani Design, Edmonds, WA. Editing and photograph research by Melissa Stein. Indexing by Pat McKinley, Intelligent Imaging, Berwyn, PA. Printed by R.R. Donnelley & Sons Company. Bound by Dunn & Co., Inc.

0 9 8 7 6 5 4 3 2 1

Library of Congress Cataloging-in-Publication Data

Henderson, Carter F.
    Funny, I don't feel old!: how to flourish after 50 / Carter Henderson.
        p.   cm.
    Includes index.
    ISBN 1-55815-497-3 (hardcover)
    ISBN 1-55815-508-2 (paper)
        1. Aged—United States. 2. Aged—United States—Life skills guides. 3. Retirement—United States. II. Title.
    HQ1064.U5H43   1997
    305.26'0973—dc21   97-28690
                                                                                CIP

To Countess Vera Tolstoy, 94, granddaughter of Russia's great novelist, Leo Tolstoy, who fled Russia shortly after Tzar Nicholas II and his family were ordered murdered by Lenin, came to the United States following World War II, and whose extraordinary life is still in full bloom.

And to Douglas Leigh, 90, whose spectacular advertising signs turned New York's Times Square into The Great White Way during the 1930s and 1940s—and who's still at it, lighting some of Manhattan's premier skyscrapers.

CONTENTS

Introduction xi

Prelude xvii

1. THE EVER-VIGOROUS MIND 1

The Indomitable Leibowitz 4
"What's on Your Mind?" 5
Going Strong 7
The Amazing Mr. Bell 10
Raw Courage at Work 12
Keeping Your Mind Trim 14
In Search of Wisdom 17

2. LET THE GOOD TIMES ROLL 21

A Fashionable Maturity 22
Suddenly On the Outside Looking In 24
Retirement's Surprising Delights 25
The Kitty Litter King Whoops It Up 30
In the Name of Art 31
On the Road Again 33
"To Serve, Not to be Served" 35
Signing Up with the Peace Corps 39
Dangerous Men and Adventurous Women 42
Senior Cybernauts 44
"Ask Me About My Grandkids" 48
Reminiscing with Tolstoy's Granddaughter 51

3. GOOD HEALTH: THE ULTIMATE GIFT 55

Aging Is Not A Disease 57
Confessions of A Dancin' Granny 60
Turning On to an Energetic Diet 63
How Ronald Reagan Stayed in Shape 65
The Greatest Exercise on Earth 67
A Good Night's Sleep 70
Decompressing Stress 73
Cosmetic Surgery to the Rescue? 75
Triumphing over Age-Related Diseases 77
Exciting Advances in Prescription Drugs 82
A New Breed 85
A National Agenda for Research on Aging 86
Good Health in Print 88
A Dud at 70, A Stud at 80 91

4. THE JOY OF VINTAGE LOVE, ROMANCE,
     AND SEX 95

Relighting the Fires of Romance 96
A Garden of Delights 98
Leading Double Lives 100
The Plain Facts—and the Good News 101
To the Rescue! 102
Love's Unending Song 103
The Flourishing Dating Industry 106
Capitalizing on the Hunger for Love 110
Three Million Aging Gays and Lesbians 112
The Approach of AIDS 115
An Honorable Pact with Solitude 117
Finding New Freedom 120
The Golden Girls 121
Investing in Friendship 124

5. A PASSION FOR WORK 127

Secrets to a Long and Happy Life 128
A Bright Man 131
Vintage Achievers 133
Artists at Work 137
Entertaining Careers 140
To Retire, or Not to Retire 142
Keeping Our Eyes Open 146
A New Meaning for the Word "Homework" 148
Out of Retirement and into the White House 150
Spicing Up Your Life with a New Career 152
"It Ain't Over 'Till It's Over" 153
Starting a Business of Your Own 154
The Woman Who Wasn't Born Yesterday 156

6. THE AGELESS DOLLAR 159

"Where the Money Is" 162
Staying Solvent after Retirement 165
Time Dollars 167
Funny Money 168
All Older People Are Not Alike 170
Wooing Affluent Oldsters 171
Hunting for James Dean and I Love Lucy 174
Selling to Secure Adults 177
The Rising Cost of Modern Medicine: The Bad News... 181
...And the Good News 183
Whither Social Security? 186
Are We Entitled? 191

7. ADVENTURES IN FUTURE WORLD 195

Clearasil vs. Preparation H 198
Dawn of a New Millennium 200
Going Out with a Bang 204

An Electronic Whirlwind 205
Dream Homes of Tomorrow 207
All Wired Up 209
Conquering High-Tech Anxiety 212
Overselling the Future: A Word of Caution 214
The Comeback of Unconventional Medicine 216
Witch-Doctor Medicine 218
Bionic Mice, Pigs, and Goats 219
Mother Nature's Number One Priority 221
Dr. Tomorrow—Today 222

8. SEARCHING FOR PARADISE 227

Adventuresome Retirees 231
Dream Town—Or Tourist Stop? 233
The Adventures of Group Living 236
Roadmaps to Paradise 237
The Best Place in America if You're Old Old 239
Confronting Caregiver Burnout 240
A Nice Place to Visit, but... 243

9. INTO THE SUNSET 245

Rethinking What It Means To Be Old 247
A Philosophy of Aging 248
Suddenly You're the Family Historian 253
Methuselah Here We Come 255
Journey's End 260
The Secret of Immortality 262
Drawing Nigh 265
Evensong 267

Appendix: Resources on Aging 269
Additional Resources 276
Sources of Information on Investing 278

Index 285

INTRODUCTION

When I reached retirement age, I made up my mind that I would live this period as if my whole life were in front of me.

　　　　　　　　—Minna Keal, British composer

Old age ain't no place for sissies.

　　　　　　　　—Bette Davis, American actress

"Unbelievable!"

　　　　　　—George Bush at 72, after parachuting out of a plane at 12,500 feet

Americans 50 and older are redefining what it means to be in the prime of life, and we're having the time of our lives doing it. Thanks to profound changes in everything from finances to physical fitness, our best years have been moved up to the 50s, 60s—and frequently beyond.

We all know that ours is an age-conscious society. In the last few decades, age has been seen as something to be avoided at all costs by an aggressively youth-worshipping culture. Older people were practically banished from advertisements, movies, and television sitcoms, assumed to be on the fast track to decrepitude both mentally and physically. Perhaps most devastating of all, we were viewed as asexual beings whose "romance among the ruins" was seen as distasteful by those still in the bloom of youth. "Nowadays, the whole idea of age is considered obscene," concludes feminist writer Germaine Greer.

It seems as though the mainstream media, dominated by youthful reporters and writers, still hasn't gotten the message that the years from 50 on can be delightful for people in the homestretch of their lives.

A typical example: I was ready to leave my fellow exercise fanatics at the local gym and head down the road to the old folks' home after glancing through a recent series in the *Minneapolis Star Tribune* devoted to "the problems faced by older people and those who help them." The series featured twenty-five topics, beginning with: (1) Coping with crisis, (2) Survival checklist, (3) Financial crisis, (4) What if the money's gone, (5) Family troubles, (6) Emotional problems, (7) Health problems—and on and on. Can't you just see the *Minneapolis Star Tribune's* older readers trembling with anticipation as they awaited the next article in this series to be plopped on their doorsteps?

Fortunately, all that's changing at an astonishing pace. Said the late Bernice Neugarten, professor of education and sociology at Northwestern University, "We are living in an increasingly age-irrelevant society in which age-appropriate behavior is breaking down."

You'd better believe it. The years of celebrating youth are inexorably giving way to the growing power of older Americans, who constitute the nation's wealthiest and fastest-growing segment of the U.S. population—with those 85 and older growing the fastest of all. The first members of the 76 million-strong baby boom generation, including President Bill Clinton, have started turning 50. They will be "the best-educated, most affluent and healthiest generation in the nation's history," says the American Association of Retired Persons, "and are poised to rewrite the story of aging in America."

Households headed by people 50 and over have close to $1 trillion in annual income, control half the nation's discretionary income, own three-quarters of all financial assets, and have a net worth totaling a staggering $6 trillion-plus, an amount equal to the nation's annual Gross National Product. And don't overlook our irreversibly growing voting power, illustrated by the conversion of Social Security into the third rail of politics—touch it and you die.

In colonial times, half of America's population was under age 16 (as it is in many developing countries today). By 1990, that figure had risen to 32 years. By 2010, according to the Census Bureau's projection, it will be 39. And if the levels of fertility, mortality, and net immigration decrease in the coming years—a distinct possibility—an astonishing 40 percent or more of the U.S. population will be 50 or older by the year 2050.

Advances in technology are helping older people, including doctors, scientists, architects, and other professionals, to keep pace with their younger colleagues, just as the recent flood of new scientific insights into the aging process (and how to decelerate it) is revitalizing the lives of senior Americans.

To begin with, there's the appreciation of how exercise, a sensible diet, and an active lifestyle can slow the aging process, and how youth-enhancing hormones, skin-smoothing elixirs, and cosmetic surgery can improve it. Then there are the biotechnology breakthroughs which are using the promising curative power of the body's own gene pool to successfully arrest devastating age-related illnesses. Such developments have helped push life expectancy in America to 75.7 years and climbing, according to the National Center for Health Statistics. And if you make it through to 65, says the

Metropolitan Life Insurance Company, men can look forward to reaching a record 80.5 years, and women 83.9 years.

But just look in any bookstore: the shelves allocated to the topics of "Aging and Retirement," usually hidden in some out-of-the-way corner, are bursting with facts and figures about deteriorating health and loss of independence. It's about time we gave the brighter side of aging its due—that's why this book brings together up-to-the-minute research, success stories, and truly *useful* information about how to make the most of our later years.

All spheres of life are filled with examples of those who are actively creating, living it up, and giving what they can well into their golden years, and it's high time we celebrated them. These seniors, some of whom are well known, and others just like you and me, show that there are certainly no preset age limits to accomplishment and full enjoyment of life. The following is just a small sample of those whose inspiring stories populate this book:

Diminutive and frail Mother Teresa, who won the Nobel Peace Prize for her work in founding hundreds of shelters and clinics for the poor in India and elsewhere, lived well into her 80s, and her reputation as a no-holds-barred fund-raiser was undiminished by age. After the Knights of Columbus honored Mother Teresa with a medal and check for $100,000, New York's Cardinal John J. O'Connor thought to himself as he introduced her to his bishops, "You'll learn to count your fingers after you shake hands with her."

Hollywood film star Jack Palance astonished millions of viewers watching the Oscar Ceremonies when he got down on the floor—after being handed a gold statue for best male supporting actor—and at age 73 did three one-armed push-ups.

Businessmen Bill Koch, who's worth several hundred million, got interested in yacht racing, and plunked down $65 million for a fast custom-built boat. He joined the San Diego Yacht Club in his 50s, and challenged and beat world champion Dennis Conner, winner of the famed America's Cup.

Then there's Lavina Steineck of Colee Cove, Florida, who lives in a rental cottage on a tight budget and has never seen a movie star or a racing yacht up close. Yet she too leads an exciting life, and when she turned 100 the other day she was still having a ball tending her vegetable and flower garden, doing a little cooking, watching a new television friends had given her, and fishing in the canal in back of her house using a cane pole. "I've caught some wonderful catfish," she says, "and one day I even hooked an alligator."

Yes, millions of older Americans have never had it so good, and it's about time we see ourselves for what we are: the most fortunate group of 50-plus men and women in our nation's history—if not the world's.

PRELUDE

A Sure Thing? Don't Bet on It!

M any more people are living to age 100 and beyond these days, as 47-year-old Frenchman Andre-Francois Raffray discovered to his sorrow when he made an unfortunate bet. Raffray agreed to pay 90-year-old Jeanne Calment 2,500 francs (about $500 a month) until her death, upon which he would inherit her sumptuous flat in the lovely town of Arles where Vincent Van Gogh painted some of his masterpieces.

Trouble is, Raffray died on Christmas Day 1995 at age 77, while Calment was feasting on foie gras, duck thighs, cheese, and chocolate cake. "I'm afraid of nothing, and I don't complain," she said on February 21, 1996, when she turned 121—making her the world's oldest living person, according to the *Guinness Book of World Records*.

The next day, a Paris production company released a four-track CD titled "Time's Mistress" in which Calment recounted her memories over a musical score of rap, techno, and a regional dance tune called farandole. Calment donated her share of the record's proceeds toward the purchase of a minibus to take her retirement home neighbors on outings.

And what does the unfortunate widow of the man who bet he'd outlive Calment say about all this? "In life, one sometimes makes bad deals," she lamented, as she continued writing those $500-a-month checks to Calment, who passed away on August 4, 1997 at the ripe old age of 122.

1

THE EVER-VIGOROUS MIND

Age is a thing of mind over matter. If you don't mind, it don't matter.

—Anonymous

Most notions about aging and the brain are based on folklore rather than fact. If you really study aging carefully and look at it in the absence of disease, there is no reason to believe that aging per se leads to decline and loss of cognitive and intellectual activities.

—Dr. Zaven Khachaturian, research director,
National Institute on Aging

It's a man's own fault, it is from want of use, if his mind grows torpid in old age.

—Samuel Johnson

Every Saturday night, some of the best informed experts on investing can be seen on the CNBC-TV program, *Strictly Business*. The show is hosted by a young hotshot CNBC staff person, who is joined by somewhat older Wall Street superstars who come and go—plus a white-haired regular, 69-year-old Bill Wolman. Wolman, chief economist for *BusinessWeek* and CNBC-TV, has a grasp of financial markets that usually has the younger panelists eating his dust. They voice their opinions on investing, the economy, and politics, and then Wolman says, "The fact of the matter is...." and that's usually that.

Strictly Business is immediately followed by *The McLaughlin Group*, hosted by 70-year-old John McLaughlin, who manages his panel of much younger Washington-based pundits with an iron hand. McLaughlin first asks each panelist for his or her opinion on the most pressing question of the day, usually (but not always) waits for a reply, and then bellows, "The answer is....," drawing the discussion to a close.

Ken Olsen, who founded Digital Equipment Corporation and built it into a $14 billion global megafirm, and inventor Michael F. Lamorte, who has created everything from solar cells to computer chips, have also taken on new, mind-challenging projects late in life—projects that would intimidate most men half their age.

Ken Olsen and a small group of colleagues have created a new company called Advanced Modular Solutions, offering customers a kind of computer time-sharing. The firm grossed about $4 million in 1994, but expects to reach $16 to $24 million by the end of 1997. Michael Lamorte has launched Applied Engineering Software, Inc., a company that gives engineers a revolutionary way of using mathematics to imitate nature so they can solve problems designing planes, developing drugs, or even finding oil. Respected scientists have called Lamorte a crackpot, but early applications of his new method have had some success, and he's forging ahead.

When writing a book like this, particularly when you're a contemporary of Olsen and Lamorte, you quickly learn that age is a nonstarter when it comes to creativity. Time and time again I've been impressed by the work of men and women who just keep getting better as the years roll by. These people are forever thanking their lucky stars that they're still productive, and members in good standing of the workaday world.

I remember hearing about Doris Eaton Travis when she was pushing 90 and had been on a wild ride. She had been a Ziegfeld Follies girl for three years, and had appeared in several Hollywood movies, including *Whoopee!* with Eddie Cantor and *The Very Idea* with heartthrob Frank Craven. Travis owned and managed nineteen Arthur Murray dance studios, and lived with her husband Paul on their 840-acre ranch outside Norman, Oklahoma, where they raised quarter horses.

Doris was happy with her life. But things weren't as satisfying years earlier in her 50s, when, her husband said, "She kept moaning and groaning about not having a formal education. So I told her to either put up or shut up."

Doris decided to put up, enrolled in the University of Oklahoma, took several courses a year, and in 1992 became the school's oldest graduate, receiving a bachelor's degree in history and membership in the Phi Beta Kappa national honor society. Doris not only studied what happened in years gone by, she also demonstrated it. In a history class about America in the Roaring 20s, at the request of her professor, this still nimble ex-chorus girl taught her fellow students—all of them young enough to be her grandchildren—how to do the Charleston.

While the body visibly deteriorates with age, we're just beginning to appreciate that healthy, aging brains can remain remarkably vigorous if exercised regularly. Dr. John Morris, a neurologist at Washington University in St. Louis, suggested in a 1996 issue of the journal *Neurology* that "there may be a pool of people who not only have no important cognitive declines, but no brain changes of consequence for mental function, even into their 80s and 90s."

Washington super-lawyer Clark Clifford demonstrated this idea just weeks away from his 85th birthday, when he testified before the House Banking Committee for more than six hours. Clifford recalled facts and figures going back for years, referred to Committee members by name, and never hesitated once during a testimony that would have been a daunting experience for far younger colleagues.

The Indomitable Leibowitz

It's not easy to think of an intellectual in his 90s whose powerful mind and personality has an entire nation in an uproar, yet such is the case with Israel's Professor Yeshayahu Leibowitz of Hebrew University in Jerusalem. Leibowitz earned a formidable reputation as a biochemist, neurologist, philosopher, theologian, social critic, and editor of the *Encyclopedia Hebraica*, and was even nominated for the Israel Prize—his country's most prestigious award. Yet Leibowitz was such a controversial figure that Israel's prime minister vowed that if Leibowitz were awarded the honor, he would boycott the award ceremony.

According to one newspaper story, Leibowitz pumped out opinions like rounds from a machine gun. Leibowitz, for example, has said that Israeli soldiers risk becoming "Judeo-Nazis" when they serve in the occupied Arab territories. He's also said that Israel herself is so fiercely nationalistic that it is in danger of becoming a fascist state, "possibly with concentration camps for Jews like me."

No matter how you feel about Leibowitz—and most Israelis either love or hate him—you can't help admiring someone of his age who's still capable of raising so much intellectual hell that he has a whole nation up in arms.

"What's on Your Mind?"

Although the brain does shrink in size as we age, and some large nerve cells in the brain do wither, there is scientific evidence that older people are just as capable of growing new connections between their brain cells as young people. "Increasingly," says Dr. Gene Cohen, former deputy director at the National Institute on Aging (NIA), "changes that were said to be aging are now thought to be due to illness."

The secret of remaining mentally sharp is dramatized by the "use it or lose it" hypothesis that's now being confirmed experimentally through animal studies. Animals forced to negotiate a maze to survive grow more connections between their brain cells than those placed in unchallenging surroundings. "You can't lose by keeping your brain active," says the NIA's Dr. Stanley Rapoport.

All this is highlighted in an NIA publication called "*What's on Your Mind?*: *A Quiz on Aging and the Brain*," which asks a series of questions about how the mind works. These answers are among the most interesting:

1. Older adults can and do learn new skills relatively easily. In fact, in properly designed programs, training can benefit older individuals as much as, and some-times more than, younger people.

2. *Experience-based intelligence remains stable or improves slightly well into late adulthood.* In many jobs, the exper-tise of older workers allows them to be among the safest and most productive employees. The speed and effi-ciency of processing information can decline, however, with increasing age. But recent scientific experiments

show that, with practice, older adults can reverse some of these effects.

3. *Nerve cell loss begins by about age 2 and progresses throughout life.* But normal nerve cell loss is not believed to have a significant effect on overall performance because people continue to learn as they age. Excessive nerve cell loss associated with illness can cause problems.

4. *Memory loss in older people can have many causes, and often can be treated.* While Alzheimer's disease or other dementia disorders can cause memory loss, other factors can include depression, reactions to some drugs, and head injury.

5. *While scientists have not proven that "mental gymnastics" keep an aging human brain healthy, they have found that there might be some benefit to "exercising" the brain.* Laboratory research shows that animals in challenging environments can release chemicals in their brains, stimulating brain cells to produce new extensions which may help improve communication among cells.

6. *A dread of death is not typical for healthy older adults.* When it occurs in older people, it is usually related to depression or a struggle with terminal illness. In healthy adults, a fear of death is actually more common in middle age.

7. *Worry is not a problem for the vast majority of adults.* One recent study of people in their 90s found over 70 percent report that they are in good spirits, never lonely, and free from worry.

8. *Emotional state plays a greater role than normal aging changes in causing sexual problems in older adults.* Depression, which can significantly interfere with sexual interest, motivation, and fantasy life in later years, is one of the most common causes of impotence in older men—and is treatable.

Dr. Richard Restak, associate professor of neurology at Georgetown University Medical School in Washington, D.C., is the author of seven books on the brain. Restak says that while older people may not be able to retrieve information as fast as the young, they often have a wealth of experience stored in their memory. This experience has been built up over years of high-level problem-solving in intellectually demanding disciplines such as medicine, diplomacy, science, and law.

Marketing strategists Jack Trout and Al Ries understand this reality, and in an *Advertising Age* article said, "In law firms, high-priced senior partners try cases and work out strategies, while junior partners do the research. So it should be in advertising agencies. Solving today's tough marketing problems requires experience. The thinking should be done by seniors, not juniors."

Well said!

Going Strong

Four-time Pulitzer Prize-winning poet Robert Frost was well into his 80s when President John F. Kennedy asked him to read at his inauguration. The ceremony was held on the East Portico of the Capitol on a bitterly cold day in January, with a wind so strong that it whipped around the pages of the poem

Award-winning writer Maya Angelou, 69, has been captivating readers for years with her poetry and autobiographical novels.

Frost held, making it impossible for him to read. Without missing a beat, the white-haired poet recited another one of his works from memory.

President Bill Clinton was the next to invite a poet to speak at his inauguration, and he chose 64-year-old black writer Maya Angelou, who composed a new work celebrating the colorful diversity of the American people. Maya Angelou, now 69, holds some fifty honorary degrees, has written innumerable books (including her best-known *I Know Why the Caged Bird Sings*), and every year makes around eighty appearances on the lecture circuit, earning $15,000 per talk.

Classic studies of older people who do great things, such as Harvey Lehman's *Age and Achievement* or W. Dennis' later article in the *Journal of Gerontology*, contain fascinating insights into the age at which individuals are most productive. Lehman and Dennis agree that older people are far more productive in many disciplines than their younger colleagues. However,

Dennis's work corrects several omissions critics see in Lehman's findings, and puts the peak performance at an even more advanced age than Lehman.

Let's be conservative, however, and go with Lehman, who found that the best work in mathematics, physics, genetics, entomology, bacteriology, psychology, anatomy, electronics, and other scientific disciplines is done at age 35, while in astronomy it's between 40 and 45.

Outstanding work by older people is much more common in philosophy, literature, music, and the arts. The Italian High Renaissance master Titian's *Martyrdom of Saint Lawrence*, and the unfinished church pietà he was at work on when he died in his late 80s, are among the world's artistic treasures.

Concert pianist Arthur Rubinstein at 89 suffered from a serious eye condition that prevented him from reading a note of music or seeing the piano keys beneath his fingers. Yet relying completely on memory, he gave a recital habitués of New York City's Carnegie Hall still treasure.

Handel composed the *Messiah* at age 56, and Verdi his *Falstaff* in his 70s. Michelangelo designed the Church of Santa Maria degli Angeli at age 88; Sophocles wrote *Oedipus Coloneus* at 89; Picasso kept painting into his 90s; and Grandma Moses was turning out delightful canvasses such as *Catching the Thanksgiving Turkey* up until her death at 101.

Advancing age, surprisingly enough, doesn't seem to be a handicap in mind games, such as bridge and chess, which demand strategic virtuosity and a top-flight memory. World champion chess players Emanual Lasker and Vassily Smyslov continued to thrust and parry at that exalted level into their 60s, and Waldemar von Zedtwitz won the World Mixed Pairs Bridge Championship (with Barbara Brier) at age 74.

The one calling where men and women in the homestretch of their lives are most in command is leadership. The age of

U.S. presidential candidates, for example, peaks between 55 and 66. (In the 1992 presidential race two of the three candidates—George Bush and Ross Perot—were in their 60s.) Outstanding world leaders are often well-seasoned, to say the least. India's four-time Prime Minister Indira Gandhi was 66 when she was gunned down by two members of her personal security guard. Golda Meir became premier of Israel at age 71. Ronald Reagan was still president of the United States at 77, Winston Churchill was prime minister of Great Britain at 80, and Conrad Adenauer was chancellor of West Germany at 87.

So if your hair is silver and you want to keep on going—or even begin something entirely new—you've got plenty of role models who have done it with grace and style.

The Amazing Mr. Bell

Particularly intriguing are inventors such as Alexander Graham Bell or Thomas Alva Edison who do memorable work when young, and remain productive well into their harvest years and beyond. Bell started tinkering with the telephone at age 25, and made it work a year later when his assistant sitting in another room heard Bell say, "Mr. Watson, come here, I need you." Bell immediately founded the American Bell Telephone Company, and then settled down to an illustrious career, including taking over the presidency of the National Geographic Society in 1898 at age 51 following the death of his father-in-law, the founder.

Bell continued to be captivated by the power of science. He erected an 80-foot-tall, three-legged viewing stand in 1907 to demonstrate the strength of the tetrahedron (the entire structure weighed less than 10,000 pounds). He led the group which

Telephone pioneer Alexander Graham Bell, also renowned as a teacher of the deaf, with his most famous pupil, Helen Keller, in 1908. Though deaf and blind, Helen Keller led a life of extraordinary accomplishment.

created the Aerial Experiment Association, whose bi-winged Silver Dart flew for half a mile in 1909 just five years after the historic flight of the Wright brothers. He designed a five-ton torpedo-shaped hydrofoil that set a speed record of 70.86 miles per hour in 1919—a record which remained unbroken for ten years.

Bell did not think of himself as an inventor at all, but rather as a teacher of the deaf. His first student was his young wife, who was left totally deaf from a severe attack of scarlet fever. But Helen Keller, who was born blind, deaf, and unable to speak, was his most famous pupil. Bell helped to direct her education, and years later she dedicated her autobiography to him, professing that she did not dream her first meeting with him "would be the door through which I would pass from darkness into light, from isolation to friendship, companionship, knowledge, and love."

A debilitating fever had robbed Helen Keller of both her sight and hearing when she was 18 months old. All she could remember from infancy was seeing the shadows of leaves on her bedroom wall. Yet this courageous woman grew up to inspire a nation with her incredible accomplishments, right up until her death at 84. She learned to speak, graduated cum laude from Radcliff College, enjoyed dancing and horseback riding, and even mastered German and Greek, which she loved.

Raw Courage at Work

There's certainly no law against putting your feet up and letting the workaday world pass you by. It's a free country. But there is another option, and it's surprising how many old-sters these days are grabbing at it and remaining part of America's booming economy.

A hallmark of quite a few older achievers is their re-markable ability to remain intellectually productive throughout their lives, even though burdened with terrible handicaps and suffering. Sigmund Freud, the father of psychoanalysis, had excruciatingly painful cancer of the jaw, innumerable opera-tions (including one in which metal appliances were used to replace bone removed from his jaw), but he kept writing books and articles, and seeing patients until his death at 83, refusing all the while to take any form of pain killers which would dull his mind.

Helen Hooven Santmeyer suffered from typhoid fever, hep-atitis, undulant fever, a serious spinal column injury, and emphysema, which made it difficult to breathe and confined her to a wheelchair. Yet this didn't stop her from writing her bestselling, 1,344-page novel …And Ladies of the Club, pub-lished when she was 88—and immediately chosen as the Book-of-the-Month Club's main selection.

We use such a small part of the brain throughout our lives. Whether you're young or old, you have about 100 billion nerve cells in your brain, each one of which has thousands of connections to other parts of your mind, a continually changing collection of feelings, thoughts, and memories. Equally fascinating is the fact that since the brain is a physical organ, the more you exercise it, the more it develops. Not only that, but you can intentionally alter the way your brain is organized, that is, the way it makes its connections. You do this by developing new abilities such as learning a foreign language, how to play a musical instrument, or simply by mentally exploring something new, even though you can never be sure where it will lead. 3M researcher Art Fry was trying to come up with a better bookmark for his hymnal when he stumbled upon the hugely successful stick-on Post-it note.

Conventional wisdom is that young minds can master new disciplines quicker than older ones and that is undoubtedly true. Creativity and lightning-fast data retrieval are usually associated with youth, just as wisdom, judgment, and a rich database are considered to be attributes of age. But while a quick creative mind is a gift from God, nothing can replace years of hands-on knowledge gained from, say, representing thousands of clients before the bar, or treating an equal number of ill or injured patients.

I had a fascinating discussion about this subject with Frank Debernardis, president of a medical technology firm in Princeton, New Jersey. At the time, he was also managing the nearby American College of Physician Inventors, which helps promote and place medical devices developed by doctors.

Many of the most important advances in medicine were invented by workaday physicians such as Willem Kolff, who developed the world's first artificial kidney, or John Gibbon, who invented the heart-lung machine to temporarily maintain cardiopulmonary function during surgery. Doctors are still hard at work inventing new medical devices, and according to Frank Debernardis, many of them are well past their 50th birthday.

Charles Klieman, M.D., for example, is a Los Angeles surgeon who's invented more than a dozen medical devices over the last two decades when he wasn't in the hospital operating on patients suffering from thoracic or cardiovascular problems. "It's a great feeling," says Dr. Klieman, "to know you are contributing something that will help make people's lives better."

This feeling is shared by other older doctors, including Herb Durdik, M.D., chief of general vascular surgery at the Englewood Hospital in Englewood, New Jersey, who invented the umbilical vein graft. This graft allows doctors to revascularize a patient's arm or leg with an obstructed blood flow. Dr. Durdik told *American Medical News* that inventing provides "the same kind of thrill as operating on a patient and making that person well. It gets back to the whole reason for getting into medicine in the first place."

Keeping Your Mind Trim

Once they retire, far too many older people slowly begin to withdraw from the complexities of today's rapidly-changing world. They are like prisoners of war or political hostages placed in solitary confinement who allow themselves to rot mentally rather than to constantly test their minds and exercise their evaluative powers. One study describes how an imprisoned soldier kept his brain in shape by constantly reviewing the battles of the Civil War right down to the number, type, and equipment of troops in various engagements.

Technology has also come to the rescue of old and young alike who want quick access to information important to their work. Dr. John Capps, an internist in Gastonia, N.C., was written up in *Physicians and Computers* magazine for a simple, inexpensive system he used to organize his most vital information. Once set up, the system allowed him to search through hundreds of records instantly—and update them just as quickly. He could also put anything into the system's memory, such as a list of patients to contact when a new medicine was released, or a daily reminder to himself of patients who should have a mammogram or a cholesterol-level check.

Until fairly recently, experts on cognition, which deals with our awareness of the world around us, made little effort to study older people as a separate and distinct group (just like the experts on marketing discussed in Chapter 6). Gerontology, the scientific study of aging, had barely entered the language, and developmental psychology concerned with how we mature was virtually synonymous with child psychology. One result of all this was the widespread assumption that our cognitive abilities, from perception and learning, to intelligence and memory, regress as we age.

We now know better, although the study of people as they age is still in its infancy. Scholarly works on aging such as *The Elderly as Modern Pioneers* (Indiana University Press, 1988), are beginning to set the record straight by pointing out that while young adults may be better at some things like academic intelligence, their elders probably have the edge in others such as social and practical forms of intelligence.

Whatever we achieve in life involves the fitness of our memory, but here again the experts differ about what happens to our memory as we pile on the years. Many believe we have three distinct types of memory: primary, secondary, and tertiary, depending on (to outrageously simplify things) how much information we remember, how recently we acquired it, and how long it will be retained.

Some experts believe older people, to mention just one example, have weak secondary memories used in acquiring and processing new information, which is then retained in permanent storage. But other experts say our secondary memory is as good as (and sometimes better than) younger people's if the information we're dealing with is familiar and/or interesting.

The one certainty in all this is that the human brain is a "use it or lose it" organ.

In recent months, a new piece of technology called Magnetic Source Imaging or MSI has begun allowing doctors to actually scan the precise workings of various parts of the brain. Dr. Rodolfo Llinas of the New York University Medical Center says he "can imagine the day when people will come in once a year to see how their brain is doing, just like they go to the dentist to get their teeth checked."

In the meantime, there are steps we can take to improve our memory even as we move into our late 70s and 80s. Psychologists who have studied memory recommend the following strategies for keeping our memory sharp as we age:

➤ Relax. Tension works against remembering.

➤ Pay attention. Focus on what you want to remember.

➤ Jot down important lists and appointments.

➤ Take your time; don't rush.

➤ Get organized. Designate a special place for things you can't afford to forget.

➤ Mention names of new acquaintances several times in conversation.

In Search of Wisdom

L ifelong learning has become a desirable option for many older people, who are obviously more at ease than the young with the idea of education for the sake of the joy of increasing their knowledge, rather than a financial payoff.

This interest in learning can be seen in the educational program enjoyed by fifteen mainly octogenarian residents of the Kimball Farms retirement community in Lennox, Massachusetts. Robert Scott, 83, who taught American history to undergraduates at nearby Williams College for 44 years, gives a seminar on "The Burden of Southern History: Slavery and Racism 1800-1900." Other courses are given by residents of the community, including a class in English handbell ringing by a retired music teacher from Louisiana, and another on microbiology by a retired Smith College professor. The educational program is cherished by residents of the 63-acre compound, particularly by those for whom it represents the first opportunity in more than half a century to pursue academic study.

There's another payoff from late stage learning described by Warner Schaie, professor of human development and psychology at Penn State University, who says, "Getting new experiences, reading new books, following current events—those are the best predictors about who is going to do well. Individuals who are at greatest risk," he adds, "are those who retire and decide they don't have to think anymore."

Well-heeled seniors who graduated from alumni-cherishing institutions such as Duke, Stanford, Yale, or the University of Pennsylvania can enjoy academic adventures offered by these schools, including $6,000 cruises through Europe. The University of Illinois recently offered a trip to its alumni that,

Eighty-nine-year-old Mary Fasano rejoices with classmates during Harvard University's spring commencement.

for $17,000, took them via nuclear ice-breaker, helicopter, and small skiff to the North Pole.

There is no shortage of learning alternatives for seniors. The American Association of Retired Persons' *Directory of Learning Opportunities for Older Persons* lists as many as 334 educational programs sponsored by community colleges, four-year colleges, universities, businesses, and religious organizations.

Perhaps the best-known of the adult education programs is Elderhostel, founded in 1975 to encourage seniors to regularly massage their brains. Today there are some 1800 Elderhostel facilities throughout the world where more than 300,000 students a year get a campus dorm room, cafeteria meals, three college-level courses, and extracurricular activities for just $350 a week.

Older Americans have a feast of learning opportunities awaiting them, from college and university credit courses leading to bachelor or graduate degrees, or the alternative of simply auditing them for their own pleasure. A growing number of these institutions now offer seniors free or reduced tuition for special programs such as the Center for Creative Retirement at the University of North Carolina at Asheville, Greater New Orleans Consortium for Educational Opportunities for Older Adults, and American University's Institute for Learning in Retirement in Washington, D.C., boasting a potpourri of courses including Great Opera Singers, Whither Cuba & Fidel, History of India, and China Today.

The satisfaction and pride we can gain from enriching our minds and keeping them active is immeasurable—and ageless. Just ask Mary Fasano, who in June 1997 graduated with a liberal arts degree from Harvard University at 89—the oldest person to earn a degree in Harvard's 361-year history.

2

LET THE GOOD TIMES ROLL

*Tomorrow will be the first time in my life I don't have
anything to do.*

—Bob Dole, 73, the day after his defeat in the
1996 presidential elections

*As I now move, graciously, I hope, toward the door
marked Exit, it occurs to me that the only thing I ever
really liked to do was go to the movies.*

—Gore Vidal

*Those of us who are old can afford to live dangerously.
We have less to lose.*

—Maggie Kuhn

Outside magazine, which doesn't write much about senior citizens, thought enough of 88-year-old Norman Vaughn to devote five pages to him, describing him—possibly with younger readers in mind—as "an old-fashioned, almost obsolete phenomenon: an inspirational figure."

Adventure had been Vaughn's life since he was 22, when he helped Admiral Richard E. Byrd lay the groundwork for the world's first flight over the South Pole. Byrd and three

companions completed the flight in a Ford trimotor at 8:55
A.M. on November 29, 1929. Vaughn has written about this historic moment in his book *With Byrd at the Bottom of the World.*

Life for Norman Vaughn has been one spirited, non-stop
adventure after another, including four marriages (the most
recent to a woman 37 years his junior), despite a right knee
made of plastic and metal as the result of bad spills on the ice,
living in a log cabin deep in the Alaskan back country, and
competing more than a dozen times in the famed 1,150-mile
Iditarod dogsled race.

Vaughn is the kind of man who thought nothing of slipping
into a climbing harness and having himself lowered by winch
268 feet down a 42-inch-wide hole cut into millions of tons of
ice in Greenland. He was after parts of five P-38 fighter planes
which ended up there with a pair of B-17 bombers as they were
being flown to England during World War II.

Then, not too long ago, a stooped and bearded Norman
Vaughn hitched up his dogsled, mushed 1,200 miles to Mount
Vaughn (which Admiral Richard E. Byrd named after him in
1942), and climbed to its 10,302-foot, ice-covered peak.

"I want to tell all senior citizens," said Vaughn, "that the
digits 65 are a terrible mistake, that this fictitious age is not a
mandatory moment for retirement. So throw away your arm-
chairs, get a hobby, and live longer younger."

A Fashionable Maturity

The new reality of aging in America today is that millions of
us don't want to put our feet up when we hit the Big
Five-O or beyond. We're healthy, we've spent decades acquir-

ing and polishing valuable skills, we've raised our kids and sent them packing to start useful lives of their own, and we're damned if we're going to quit now. Most older people today— at least those lucky enough to live in the United States—are leading lives past generations couldn't imagine in their wildest dreams.

A living embodiment of this attitude is gerontologist Matilda Riley, a social scientist in her early 80s who works at the National Institute on Aging. Dr. Riley, who got her Ph.D. in sociology at age 61, tracks changes in the way older people live, work, and retire. Riley is a self-described revolutionary, fighting to change society's conviction that young people should *work, work, work,* while older people quietly stroll away from the workaday world forever.

The bottom line on this, Riley says, is a smattering of options for younger people whose lives might well be transformed by a sabbatical when they're, say, 35 or 40, and a shocking waste of hands-on experience when older people are put out to pasture toward the other end of life's continuum. Dr. Riley's ideas have been called hopelessly utopian. But of the millions of survivors of the baby boom generation, many undoubtedly share her philosophy. Taking a sabbatical looks like an idea whose time has come to a lot of young boomers, while many of those about to turn 65 have no intention of ending their productive years and hitting the shuffleboard court just because that's the way it's *supposed* to be.

You remember the old gag "Where does an 800-pound gorilla sit?" Answer: "Anywhere it wants to." That's the baby boom generation. And since so many boomers in their 50s are now in Washington running the country, we are beginning to look at the passage of time in an entirely new way. Maturity, believe it or not, is well on its way to becoming fashionable.

American seniors, hold your hats.

Suddenly on the Outside Looking In

Adventure enthusiast Vaughn is right. Far too many people of retirement age have found themselves entirely unprepared for life after the gold watch and no place to go on Monday morning. Traditional housewives may be more fortunate, since their daily round goes on with one glaring exception—the husband who used to be at work is now underfoot, being swept from room to room. You can only clean the garage, mow the lawn, and go to the supermarket so many times before you realize to your horror that you're on the outside looking in. The 7:18 A.M. train has left the station, your old commuter pals are still on it reading the paper, drinking coffee, playing a few hands of cards, and getting ready for the day ahead. But not you. You're no longer Atwood of IBM, TRW, or Electric Boat, but just plain old *you*.

Particularly if you're not ready for such a change, like so many seniors these days who find themselves deeply involved with the suddenly important business of reading the newspaper, walking the dog, getting a haircut, curling up with the latest Elmore Leonard thriller, getting to the Moonlight Grille between 5:00 and 7:00 P.M. for the $5.95 Early Bird Special, and then rushing home to watch "Jeopardy."

But it doesn't have to be that way—and isn't, for millions of seniors who planned for their harvest years long before they finally arrived. For them, there aren't enough hours in the day to do all the things that keep them productive, fulfilled, and happy.

I know. I'm one of them.

Retirement's Surprising Delights

T here are some older folks who simply want to take it easy and do nothing at all after they retire, and that's their prerogative. Singer Dean Martin, who died within a week of New Year's Day 1996 at age 78, was an entertainment superstar: he was comedian Jerry Lewis's sidekick, a member of Frank Sinatra's famed Rat Pack, and a top draw in Las Vegas. Yet in his later years, according to Nick Tosches in his book *Dino: Living High in the Dirty Business of Dreams*, all he did was sit around in his mansion in the Bel Air section of Los Angeles watching old cowboy movies. Tosches wanted desperately to interview Martin but was refused. The writer went ahead anyway, talking with dozens of the star's old friends—many of whom didn't realize he was still alive!

But many seniors can't wait to retire so they can begin doing what really turns them on. And that's spending serious time pursuing their favorite hobbies, which come in literally hundreds of wild and wonderful varieties, including antique collecting, astronomy, baseball cards, insects, ceramics, magic, photography, prints, railroad maps, stamps, sea shells, and travel.

The recently-opened American Visionary Art Museum on the edge of Baltimore's Inner Harbor celebrates the work of artists who are entirely self-taught, including one who built a model of the old luxury liner Lusitania out of 192,000 toothpicks. But what dazzles your eye as you approach the place is a huge, colorful "whirligig" of spinning ice-cream scoops, milkshake canisters, air filter cups and other stuff created by an elderly North Carolina mechanic. Talk about recycling!

Gardening, enjoyed by nearly 80 percent of all U.S. house-holds, is the nation's number one hobby. One person's hobby, of course, can be another person's rebirth. Just look at award-winning plant geneticist Jerry Twomey, who blazed into promi-nence in his 70s, rather than his 30s, when most genetic scientists are at the height of their powers and notoriety. Twomey, an amateur gardener from a small town just north of San Diego, California, won the prestigious All-American Rose Selection Award in 1991 for his exciting new rose "Sheer Elegance"—and then won it again in 1992 for another new variety called "All That Jazz."

Twomey began his plant magic as a youngster in his native Canada, started breeding gladioli at age 15, and won $10,000 at the 1939 New York World's Fair for creating the "World's Most Beautiful Glad" which he named the "Margaret Beaton" after his grandmother. Twomey went on to graduate from the University of Manitoba where he studied plant genetics, and was enlisted by the Canadian government to develop vegetable seed for the Allies during World War II.

Well-heeled plant breeders working at century-old family nurseries in this country and abroad would give their eyeteeth to achieve in a lifetime what Twomey has single-handedly accomplished twice, more than a decade after he retired from his 9-to-5 job.

Twomey's avocation has blossomed into a second career and an expanding business. He's developed disease-resistant hybridized roses home gardeners can grow without spraying, and holds patents on all the new breeds he's developed, which he sells through nurseries across the country at a growing profit.

Whatever ideas Jerry Twomey and his wife Joan may have had about taking life easy and putting their feet up are today nothing more than distant memories. This vintage couple is having too much fun, and giving far to much pleasure to other flower fanciers, to even *think* of retiring. As Thomas Jefferson once said, "although an old man, I am but a young gardener."

Bird watching, our nation's second-favorite hobby, is avidly pursued by an estimated 20 million Americans for whom glimpsing a whiskered tern or spot-billed duck is the ultimate turn-on. Dedicated birders who get news of a rare sighting over the North American Rare Bird Alert hotline, or subscribe to the BirdChat computer network, think nothing of jumping on a jet and flying across the country in the hopes of glimpsing a new species among the 850 or so varieties believed to be native to North America out of some 8,700 worldwide. The handful of birders who say they've seen 800 or more species, and whose names are enshrined in the American Birdwatching Association's publication *Winging It,* are the undisputed superstars of the birdwatching world. Their names are as familiar to birders as Joe Lewis, Red Grange, or Babe Ruth are to sports fanatics.

Hobbyists are into everything: rescuing and refurbishing old farm machinery, saving rare creatures threatened with extinction such as Indian elephants, Australian parakeets, and Canadian finches—you name it.

One collector of old radios, including the familiar cathedral-style set with its ornate cabinet (the centerpiece in many living rooms before the coming of television), has rigged up his 1930s set so he can listen to recordings of old radio shows. "It's fun," he says. "At night you can draw the curtains, turn the living room lights down low, and by the glow from the radio's dial listen again to Jack Benny, Mary Livingston, and Rochester. It's a time warp."

Collecting art has transformed the lives of two ordinary New Yorkers of modest means who recently pledged some 2,000 of their contemporary American paintings, drawings, and sculptures to the prestigious National Gallery of Art in Washington, D.C. Herbert Vogel was a postal clerk and his wife

Rip-roaring "Banana" George Blair (known for his signature neon-yellow wet-suit) shows his stuff—water skiing on one bare foot.

Dorothy was a librarian back in the 60s when they decided to live on her salary and use his to buy art. The childless couple began by purchasing inexpensive pieces focusing on minimalist and conceptual art. It wasn't too long before every inch of their small one-bedroom Manhattan apartment was covered with paintings. The Vogels soon became well-known and respected figures in New York City's fashionable art world as their collection grew to contain thousands of first-rate works of more than 200 top artists. And once they retired, they kept on collecting with more gusto than ever.

While strength and agility inevitably decline as we pile on the years, joie de vivre and raw courage do not. Seniors can do just about anything youngsters can do, although it may take a bit longer, and in some instances even open us up to ridicule as when Truman Capote said of fellow writer Katherine Anne Porter, "She must be about 60, but oh how she can do the hootchy-cootchy."

While sniggering can devastate self-conscious 16-year-olds, seniors know who they are and do wild and crazy things without a second thought. Californian Elliot Bolter, who learned to skate when Calvin Coolidge was President, regularly dons bright fluorescent protective knee and wrist gear, laces up his Rollerblades, and skates right along with the teenyboppers.

And let's not forget "Banana" George Blair, 82, who regularly performs his specialty in the U.S. and abroad: water skiing barefoot at up to 40 miles an hour. At age 71, he became the only person ever to barefoot water ski on all seven continents, earning him a place in the *Guinness Book of World Records*. Banana George has appeared in numerous television commercials, wowed audiences on shows such as *Late Night with David Letterman* and *Oprah*, and in 1991, he received the highest possible honor as a water skier: induction into the Water Ski Hall of Fame.

"People say I should slow down," says Banana George, "but I'm just getting warmed up."

The Kitty Litter King Whoops It Up

E d Lowe of Cassopolis, Michigan, who looked like white-bearded country singer Kenny Rogers, is a prime example of someone who lived at full throttle during his harvest years. Ed invented Kitty Litter back in 1947, built it into an $85 million business, sold it a while back for a small fortune, and let the good times roll until his death at age 75.

Ed's wealth enabled him to gratify some of his most eccentric whims. One morning Ed and his wife Darlene left their spacious home (a converted old barn on a 2,300-acre spread) and drove down the highway, where they spotted a mountain of used pickle barrels. Ed slammed on the brakes, bought 200 barrels, and had them trucked back to his place, where he used some to build an 18-hole golf course. From then on, Ed held a Pickle Barrel Golf Classic for some 150 guests each year—if you didn't score a "pickle-in-one" on each hole, you were out.

Ed Lowe got to thinking one day that there might be some folks in the United States who needed a hometown, so he bought Jones, Michigan, with its grocery store, bank, sawmill, and tavern—the works. Anyone who wanted to claim Jones as their hometown could register in the town hall, Ed said, adding that "after a while we decided to close it down, so we sold it at auction for $500,000."

"I grew up tough during the Depression," Ed said. "We didn't have any money and I remember burning corn cobs for heat, going without a warm jacket, and always having cold feet because I had to use paper to cover up the holes in my shoes. So today I collect jackets, shoes and hats—I've got hundreds of 'em.

"My wealth wasn't sudden," Ed told me, "it kind of crept up on me. This probably explains why Darlene and I still enjoy the

Ed Lowe, who invented Kitty Litter, made a fortune and had the time of his life during his harvest years.

simple pleasures of life, like going into some of the grungiest taverns you've ever seen and drinking beer and eating ham sandwiches, or telling each other when we go to bed at night about the highlights of our day. It's usually seeing a little kid sitting on a stoop, or getting a nice smile from a waitress rather than some big deal. So we enjoy life. We have a good time."

In the Name of Art

If there's ever a time when you can be wild and crazy, and do whatever floats your boat, it's when the kids are grown, the mortgage is paid, your closet is bulging with more clothes than you'll ever wear again, and you begin to think about what you're going to do with the rest of your life.

One of my patron saints in this regard is Bulgarian-born artist Christo Javacheff, who's in his 60s, and years ago began doing something completely off-the-wall. He's still at it, only it's bigger, better, and nuttier than ever. Christo creates monumental, and outrageous works of public art which frequently take years to plan, cost millions of dollars, and are hardly set up before they're knocked down. His works can turn up anywhere on the planet, from a 24-mile-long fabric curtain called "Running Fence" which briefly embellished northern California in 1976, to a simultaneous display of 3,100 gargantuan blue and yellow umbrellas which dotted California and Japan in 1991.

But what's really made Christo an international celebrity is his penchant for wrapping things. Big things like a group of islands off Miami, Florida, which he surrounded with pink polypropylene fabric back in 1963.

Christo's greatest masterpiece, which he worked on for more than 20 years, is called *Wrapped Reichstag*. For two weeks in 1993 he covered Berlin's sprawling, 102-year-old parliament building with a million square feet of silver-colored fabric. The cost: about $7 million.

Christo isn't the only one doing wacky things in the name of art. Sixty-two-year-old John VanBarringer lives in Big Rock, Illinois (about an hour's drive from Chicago), which is flatland country, far from the soaring western mountains he loves. So he's spent $10,000 or so—along with countless hours a week for the past 40 years—building a mountain on the sweeping plains. VanBarringer is a tall, powerfully-built man with a white mustache who's already trucked about forty tractor-trailer loads of rock, sand, and gravel onto his 32-acre spread. The mountain currently stands about 15 feet tall, covers as much land as a baseball diamond, and will eventually rise to 50 feet—topped by a 25-foot steel cactus. VanBarringer says his mountain is for his neighbors who never had the chance to travel out West, along with his own ideas of what artistic freedom is all about.

Trouble is that local country officials don't agree, and have ordered him to tear it down. Apparently his mountain is built on a flood plain, which is against the law. VanBarringer, however, is not easily intimidated. "I'll sit in jail if it comes to that," he says—and his neighbors believe him.

On the Road Again

F ew experiences in life give older people more satisfaction than traveling, now that they've got the time and money.

One of my greatest pleasures since becoming a bona fide senior citizen is gallivanting around the world, sampling its many and often unexpected offerings. I had worked abroad for years as a foreign correspondent for *The Wall Street Journal* in constant pursuit of information about whether the British Exchequer was about to raise or lower the bank rate, or how the leaders of a newly democratic West Germany were planning to revive their country's war-ravaged economy.

That was all very interesting stuff, to be sure, but it is a far cry from the often uproarious and completely unplanned adventures I'm enjoying today. Like the children in a small French village, who upon seeing all 6 feet 6 inches of me walking down the street, announced "The giant is coming! The giant is coming!" They acted as if they'd been expecting me for years, and rushed over to feel my legs to see if I was walking on stilts.

Older Americans are undoubtedly the world's greatest travelers, which is why we're so aggressively courted by organizations catering to seniors, including those offering to help up find delightful companions to explore the Grand Canyon, the bistros of Paris, or perhaps each other (see Chapter 4 for more on the latter).

The Travel Companion Exchange newsletter of Amityville, New York, for example, lists 500 people eager to meet others. Partners-in-Travel in Los Angeles provides its members with a list of tour operators who regularly work with singles, a publication filled with guidelines and advice, and a directory featuring fifty-word profiles of members (identified only by their first names and phone numbers or mailing addresses) seeking traveling companions. A note of caution, however: these and similar organizations cannot control their membership, and one should proceed with caution because of confidence artists looking for vulnerable seniors—particularly women.

The American Hotel and Motel Association estimates that travelers 60 and older account for nearly one-third of all room nights sold within the lodging industry, and this percentage is certain to increase as the number of vigorous, affluent older folks with plenty of time to enjoy life continues to shoot skyward: between 2010 and 2030, the over-65 crowd is expected to grow eight times faster than the U.S. population as a whole.

Two new developments within the travel and tourist industry are of particular interest to seniors. One is "ecotourism" in out-of-the-way nature preserves such as the Galapagos Islands, some 650 miles west of Ecuador. And the other might be called "meditourism," enjoyed by health-conscious seniors who check into places like the Texas Medical Center in Houston for individually-tailored health programs designed to keep them in peak physical condition.

Those eager to escape the intrusion of the high-tech during their holidays, incidentally, can check into Lawrence Rockefeller's Caneel Bay resort on St. John in the U.S. Virgin

Islands, which bans tabletop phones and televisions from its 171 luxurious rooms and cottages. Talk about getting away from it all!

"To Serve, Not to be Served"

I f you had to pick the one activity which attracts more older people than any other, it would undoubtedly be helping others. As William Penn said, "I expect to pass through life but once. If, therefore, there be any kindness I can show, or any good thing I can do to any fellow being, let me do it now and not defer or neglect it, as I shall not pass this way again."

The motto of the giant American Association of Retired Persons (AARP) is "To serve, not to be served," and it's but one of countless nonprofit groups through which millions of older people regularly volunteer their time. It is a priceless national resource, giving untold pleasure to all those who help and are helped.

The AARP, which puts the dollar value of volunteer work by Americans of all ages at well over $110 billion a year, says its volunteers include "retired accountants who counsel older taxpayers in filling out their returns, homemakers and retired educators teaching health maintenance and good driving skills, retired legislators and lawyers representing older consumers' interests on national boards, and men and women of all backgrounds helping shape laws to fit the needs of older citizens."

Quite a few oldsters these days are burning up the track as environmental activists with the help of programs such as the Environmental Alliance for Senior Involvement (EASI). The program recruits older people, along with their children and grandchildren, to help preserve and restore America's natural environment for future generations.

Among EASI's most successful projects is one designed to protect groundwater supplies in El Paso, Texas, and Elkhart, Indiana, by having its volunteers educate the public about the danger of dumping automobile oil and other pollutants on the ground or down sewers. The volunteers also monitor the area for some 2,000 other sources of groundwater pollution.

An unsurprising fact discovered by those running the EASI is that "the public is much more cooperative with a smiling elderly person than with a government investigator." In Orange County, California, for instance, senior volunteers "proved to be more effective than the Public Utilities Department in collecting information needed for the [oil] wellhead project because they were more readily welcomed by local businesses and the community."

One volunteer effort that's been getting a lot of attention lately is its Criminal Justice Services program, which helps police departments throughout the country make use of older folks' time, energy and know-how. For instance:

➤ In West Virginia, police and seniors work through Operation Lifeline to help isolated elderly and disabled people with medical, food, and fuel services, along with daily telephone contact.

➤ In Oregon, police-trained seniors are helping older homeowners put identifying marks on their property in case it is stolen, and take steps to make their homes more secure.

➤ In California, older volunteers are translating crime statistics into code for processing by a municipal police department's computers.

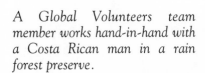

A Global Volunteers team member works hand-in-hand with a Costa Rican man in a rain forest preserve.

One of the newer programs for seniors is Global Volunteers of St. Paul, Minnesota, a nonprofit, nonsectarian group founded in 1984 which offers one to three weeks of volunteer work experience in primarily rural communities throughout the world. Hundreds of older folks leave their cozy homes each year and pay their own expenses to work alongside local people on human and economic development projects identified by the community as important to their long-term development.

Volunteers who want to work close to home have been able to serve in the Mississippi Delta building playground equipment, tutoring children, and repairing public utilities. Those interested in traveling further afield have flown to Tonga in the South Pacific to work on the construction of a community center for people living on the coast of its main island of Tongatapu. Global Volunteers plans to send more than 100

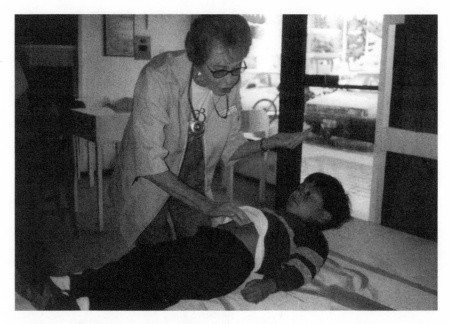

A Global Volunteers team member uses her medical skills to assess the needs of an Ecuadorian child.

teams of North Americans to project sites in fifteen countries worldwide.

Seventy-six-year-old Peggy Rabut of Westport, Connecticut spent several weeks in an economically depressed part of the Mississippi Delta painting, putting up wallboard, assembling street signs, and teaching crafts to children. "It's definitely not fancy living," she says, "but I just love it."

Donald Spratt was a 75-year-old semi-retired cattle and tobacco farmer from Weston, Missouri, when he spent eight days in a small Guatemalan village mixing cement and digging trenches for the foundations of eight new homes. 'We have so many things these people don't have," says Spratt, "dry warm homes, transportation, telephones, and contact with the outside world. But after a while," he adds, "you wonder are those advantages really worth what you give up? Because these villagers were happy. They had close-knit families, and they really looked out for each other."

Spratt got his chance to help out through Habitat for Humanity International in Americus, Georgia, an ecumenical Christian housing ministry working in partnership with people throughout the world who are in need of simple, decent housing that's sold to them at no profit through no-interest loans. Habitat is currently at work in 53 countries, and is approaching the completion of its 60,000th house.

As many as 93 million Americans donate some 20 billion hours of their time each year to helping others, including tons of seniors blessed with the time, talent, and eagerness to assist young people they see as their surrogate grandchildren. In late April 1997, President Clinton, along with former Presidents George Bush, Gerald Ford, and Jimmy Carter, plus thirty governors and dozens of corporate executives, gathered at Independence Hall in Philadelphia to kick off a three-day "Presidents' Summit for America's Future," praising and promoting volunteerism, especially to help the millions of "at-risk" young people in need of guidance and role models.

Who better for this job than senior citizens?

Signing Up with the Peace Corps

More than 130,000 no less adventuresome retirees, with skills ranging from library science to animal husbandry, have chosen a different career path for their harvest years: helping others under the auspices of the United States Peace Corps.

I spent a few eye-opening hours in Peace Corps headquarters in Washington talking with a number of its top officers. I

Peace Corps volunteers help children make tools in the tiny African republic of Togo.

have vivid impressions of the place, including the thought that it appears to be largely run by women. The Peace Corps is aggressively moving into new areas such as sending business experts to help energize the economies of the new states spun off from the old Soviet Union. In addition, the Peace Corps treasures its older volunteers—with good reason.

"Somewhere between 10 and 12 percent of our 8,000 volunteers and staff working in some 100 countries around the world are age 50 or more," the Peace Corps' Acting Director Barbara Zartman told me a month before Bill Clinton was sworn in as president of the United States. "We expect to have 10,000 volunteers in the field by 1996," she added, "of which well over 1,000 will be seniors. Today, for example, we've got an 83-year-old woman volunteer teaching English to magistrates in Poland, and we just sent a 79-year-old business development expert to the Russian Far East. Our older male volunteers, by the way, are particularly cherished in Eastern Europe and the former Soviet Union because these countries lost so many young men in World War II who would have been today's grandfathers.

"There are some special challenges that senior volunteers present in learning more difficult languages such as Hungarian or Polish, " Zartman continued, "so we make a special effort to place them in English-speaking countries. Quite a few seniors, on the other hand, leave our twelve weeks of intensive in-country immersion in a strange language and come out of it with what you might call a survival vocabulary of somewhere around 1,000 words.

"Health concerns are the other reality for senior volunteers. All of us accumulate a somewhat larger medical portfolio as we age and we're aware of this when sending seniors overseas. For example, we'll only send a senior who's had bypass heart surgery, to a country where there's a board-certified cardiologist."

When President John F. Kennedy announced the formation of the Peace Corps on March 1, 1961, older people were not eligible to serve. One of the first to be rejected was 65-year-old nutritionist Sue Sadow, who refused to take "no" for an answer and dispatched a telegram to Peace Corps Director Sergeant Shriver. The message read: "On my way to Washington, see you at 10 A.M. tomorrow to discuss my rejection for Sierra Leone." Shriver saw her, agreed to review her case, was impressed by what he saw, and before long Sadow was on her way to West Africa. Hundreds of other seniors followed in her wake.

There are literally thousands of examples of the good work Peace Corps volunteers have done in the more than three decades it's been in existence, from helping to restructure

Mongolia's banking system and upgrading agriculture in the Philippines to advising small-business people in Fiji.

My favorite story of the Peace Corps' accomplishments, however, was told to me by Barbara Zartman as I was leaving her office: "A Peace Corps volunteer in the Central African Republic visited a village where a little boy had been cast aside because he was thought to be retarded and not fit to attend school. The Peace Corps worker soon realized it wasn't that the boy couldn't *think*, but that he couldn't *see*, so arrangements were made for him to get a pair of glasses. The youngster was soon hard at work in school, and the volunteer returned home to the United States, only to learn 25 years later that the boy was now his country's Minister of Education."

Dangerous Men and Adventurous Women

O f course, you don't need to leave home to find something interesting to do. A thrilling leisure activity for millions of women—an estimated 30 percent of whom are 50 and older—is curling up with a romance novel like *Flirting With Trouble* or *The Rake and the Reformer*. The great majority of women who spend millions of dollars a year buying these paperback books are happily married, yet fantasize about intimate liaisons with the strong, virile, brooding, dangerous, and inarticulate men who haunt their pages.

In the anthology *Dangerous Men and Adventurous Women*, published by the University of Pennsylvania Press, nineteen female writers of best-selling romance novels attempt to explain why women are so turned on by these "bodice rippers," in which the hero has been variously described as "a devil, a demon, a tiger, a hawk, a pirate, a bandit, a potentate, a hunter, and a warrior."

What can women possibly see in what romance writer Susan Elizabeth Phillips describes as these "cynical men who have grown jaded with life and love, men of action who not only refuse to stand by the heroine's side from the beginning of the book, but frequently make life more difficult for her"? Claims Phillips, "The heroine isn't as big as he is; she isn't as strong, as old, as worldly; many times she isn't as well-educated. Yet despite all these limitations she confronts him—not with physical strength but with intelligence and courage. And what happens? She always wins! Guts and brains beat brawn every time."

Romance novels bring the fantasy of female empowerment to life since, in the end, to quote top romance writer (and editor of the anthology) Jane Ann Kretnz, the heroine not only captivates the hero, but has "taught the devil to love and to express that love *not only physically but also verbally*. 'Don't just show me, tell me,' is one of the prime messages that every romance hero must learn.... All his muscle, wealth, and authority are useless against her courage, intelligence, generosity, loyalty, and kindness."

It's estimated that from 35 to 40 percent of all mass market paperback books sold are romance novels. The genre's biggest publisher—Harlequin Enterprises—single-handedly sells more than 190 million books worldwide every year, more than 40 million of which are purchased by women 50 and older.

The fact that older people love to read should come as no surprise to anyone who ever visited a public library, spent time lounging around a condominium swimming pool, or strolled through a retirement home. *Reader's Digest* recently estimated that 44 percent of its 18 million American subscribers were 50 or older, which helps explain why the company was willing to pay an estimated $10 million to buy *New Choices: Living Even Better After 50* magazine, whose subscription-only circulation of some 600,000 copies per issue likely has no place to go but up.

Yet the media industry continues to shy away from wooing older people, even though we've got loads of time to read its newspapers and magazines, and lots of money to buy whatever they're selling—a mystery we explore, along with other money matters, in Chapter 6.

Senior Cybernauts

I t may happen to the best of us as the years pile up. Because we're not as limber as we used to be, don't want any part of unpredictable situations, or worry about what we'd do if we got sick or injured in an unfamiliar place, we stay closer to home. What to do? "Easy:" says *Forbes* magazine, "get wired." Become one of America's fast-growing family of "senior cybernauts."

One who did is 76-year-old Samuel Weissman. Although virtually confined to his small New York City apartment because of severe arthritis in his legs, every day he sits down at his computer, logs on to the nationwide Internet, and spends hours swapping electronic e-mail with pals in England and Australia, catching up with the latest news and gossip on the World Wide Web, and socializing with his contemporaries in the online Elders Group. "The network is better than [pain] medication," says Weissman. "I am absorbed for hours and completely forget myself."

Do the words "textual poachers," "emoticons," or "netiquette" mean anything to you? Probably not, unless you're a self-confessed data freak for whom an evening's fun is bellying

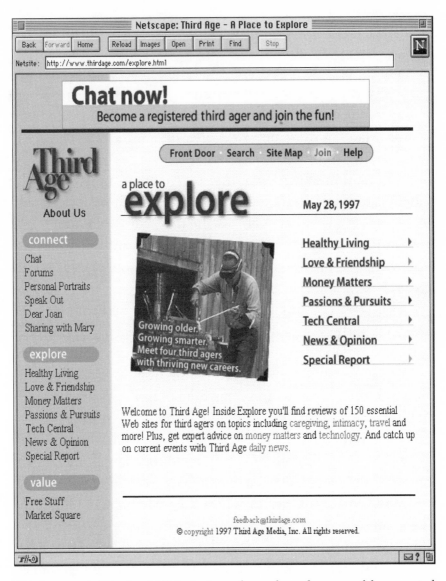

Thirdage.com's "Explore" Web site page shows the wide range of features and services that are only a click away.

up to your computer terminal, logging onto a service such as America Online (which has 8 million subscribers), and downloading up-to-the-minute information about every subject imaginable from thousands of sites on the World Wide Web.

Computer buffs are using a proliferating number of networks, including roughly 45,000 (frequently short-lived) mom-and-pop systems around the United States, regularly discuss anything of mutual interest from soap operas to self-aggrandizing messages posted on the systems' bulletin boards. Many of these networks offer discounts to students and senior citizens.

Information of particular interest to seniors ranges from the Goldenage Web site (which offers access to hundreds of subjects of importance such as health care providers and government services, travel and volunteer information, and hobby chat groups) to the culinary secrets of some of the world's great chefs.

Thirdage.com was designed to help its audience get the most out of the "'post-50' years, a time for creativity, continued learning, and exploration." It offers an interactive online community, in-depth articles on everything from love relationships to senior-related news, and a targeted consumer's marketplace. "Third Age," a translation of the French *Troisieme Age*, is a European term referring to the period of adult life when children are grown, work responsibilities have lessened, and one has the time and financial means to explore new (or old) passions.

Mary Furlong, CEO of Third Age Media and founder of the nonprofit organization SeniorNet, says that "Not only is thirdage.com the lens on the web for active older adults, but it is also a vibrant community where Third Agers can meet, make friends, discuss the topics of the day, and help each other make informed decisions on topics ranging from health care to caregiving to travel to purchasing a new car."

The Internet is a gold mine of information, and well-designed search programs make it easy to locate exactly the information you want.

An example of the Internet's diversity: some of the most popular culinary sites are The Electronic Gourmet Guide, The Internet Epicurean, Virtual Vineyards, and my personal favorite, Starchefs. Starchefs, which began attracting 500,000 "hits" or visits a week after going online in fall 1995, offers the latest news about restaurants and food festivals, and, best of all, features intimate profiles of great chefs and their food preparation secrets.

Then there's what a recent A&E television exposé called "Wired for Sex" described as the latest on the information superhighway: "electronic stimulators." Not surprisingly, it's all there, a feast for those craving to be "digitally humiliated," aroused by a little bondage-and-discipline action, or whatever suits their fancy. And, since you're doing it in cyberspace, it's guaranteed safe sex for old and young alike!

SeniorNet estimates that the 50-plus love affair with computers has been growing by 15 percent each year since 1990. A Nielsen/CommerceNet report issued in early 1997 counted 50.6 million North American Internet users—double the number of the previous year. Of these, 15 percent, or 7.6 million, are 50 and older. One newspaper poll found that 9 percent of people 65 or older now use personal computers at home, up 2 percentage points (nearly 600,000 people) from eighteen months earlier. "This is the first generation of Americans who have retired [after] using computers in business," says the vice president of marketing of one computer manufacturer. "They're much more familiar with them."

Today's seniors are using computers to send e-mail to their children and grandchildren, play video games, follow the stock market, do comparison shopping, handle their personal finances, research their family trees, interact with support groups, and write their wills. Computers are even helping those with Alzheimer's disease to organize their days and trigger their memories.

Alan Brightman, manager of Apple Computer's Worldwide Disability Solutions illustrates the tremendous advances in computers, which "...can anticipate your needs and alert you to what you should do next. 'Take the medication in the blue bottle. Call Billy and let him know you're okay.' The computer can even do it by voice."

Internet users with the right audio equipment can even talk to each other around the world for as little as $1 an hour. A good way to keep down those long-distance phone bills!

"Ask Me About My Grandkids"

Grandparents are usually goofy about their grandchildren, sporting "Ask Me About My Grandkids" stickers on their bumpers, and frequently visiting the little tikes, loaded with gifts.

Today's parents, especially given the unnerving rise in the number of American families in which both parents work or have been broken up by divorce, especially appreciate the fact that having Grandmom and Granddad around can add stability to today's hectic family life while giving children cuddly access to the family's history. Not to mention the premium put on Grandma or Granddad as built-in babysitters during the day, and often at night so hard-working parents can have an evening on the town.

A new twist on all this, cherished by parents fortunate enough to be on the receiving end, is for Grandma and Granddad to take the kids to a summer camp which sets aside a week or two just for them. Grandparents love it, since they can have little Mary or Billy all to themselves—without

Grandparents and their grandchildren pose for the traditional end-of-camp photograph following two weeks set aside just for them at the SAGAMORE Historic Great Camp in upstate New York.

parental overseeing—for an idyllic time filled with nature walks, berry picking, swimming, storytelling, marshmallow roasts, singalongs, and other bonding experiences.

University of Wisconsin-Parkside Professor Jeanne L. Thomas, in her article "The Grandparent Role: A Double Bind" in the *International Journal on Aging and Human Development*, notes that since so many of today's marriages end in divorce, it's vitally important for grandparents to understand what's expected of them in two-parent and single-parent families. Mothers in two-parent families said what they appreciated most about having grandparents around was the warmth they showed toward their grandchildren, their ability to strengthen bonds within the family, the sharing of their life's experience, and their knowledge of the family's heritage.

Mothers who were separated or divorced said the best thing about having grandparents in the family was the practical and moral support in child-rearing they provided on a day-to-day basis, particularly as "family watchdogs" ready to assume central roles in backstopping the family during times of crisis.

The availability of this kind of help is on the rise, since the number of parents over age 55 actually living with their children doubled to 4 percent from 1992 to 1996 alone, according to an analysis by the AARP. In a fast-growing number of American families, grandparents are not only more affluent hence self-sufficient than ever before, but are living enough extra years to create the heretofore unheard of four-generation family, embracing both grandparents and now great-grandparents.

One of the great givens of contemporary American society is that older folks know how to be good grandparents. After all, you don't need a Harvard Ph.D. to bounce grandchildren on your knee, take them on a shopping spree to Toys "R" Us, or read them *The Three Bears*.

Apparently, though, there's always room for improvement: researchers at Arizona State University devised a 12-week course called "Becoming a Better Grandparent," which was attended by more than 200 men and women age 50 to 80.

Among the more interesting findings to come out of this program, paid for by the Andrus Foundation (which funds gerontology research for the American Association of Retired Persons), was that grandmothers are much more actively involved with their grandchildren than grandfathers. Grand-dads are also less affectionate, and probably never once told their grandchildren "I love you."

Though the experts insist we grandfathers aren't as close to our grandchildren as we ought to be, I want to let my fellow granddads in on a little secret. Try to warm up to your grandchildren. It's a wonderful and all-too-fleeting experience, since, as we've heard time and time again, they grow up so fast. And who knows—you might actually learn something!

The other day I asked my 6-year-old grandson to name the most powerful creature on earth. "Is it the lion, the tiger, the elephant, or the polar bear?"

"It's not any of those, Pop Pop," he replied. "It's the germ."

I think I'm beginning to feel my age.

Reminiscing with Tolstoy's Granddaughter

A critical part of any investigation of how to get the most out of life when one is "old old" or "extreme old" is to talk with someone who's doing it, like my friend Vera Tolstoy, granddaughter of famed Russian novelist Leo Tolstoy, author of

The author with the vibrant Countess Vera Tolstoy, who is 94 and going strong.

epic masterpieces such as *War and Peace* and *Anna Karenina*. Vera used to sit on her grandfather's lap and sing him childrens' songs, and watch as he wrote his massive novels by hand (which her grandmother recopied over and over in pen and ink to reflect his torrent of editorial changes).

At 94, Vera is slim, ramrod straight, reads without glasses, swims at a nearby yacht club, cooks sumptuous Russian meals, and is one of the world's great raconteurs. She recently returned to her family's ancestral home in Russia for the first time since Lenin overthrew Tzar Nicholas II in 1917.

Over a three-course lunch she prepared (each with its own wine), Vera held me spellbound with stories of life on her grandfather's estate. She spoke of being forced to flee Russia at age 13 after Lenin and the Communists began murdering members of the nobility, including Tzar Nicholas, Tzarina Alexandra, their four daughters, and son Alexis, along with "priests, nuns, monks, and well-to-do peasants."

Vera spirited her mother and governess aboard various trains headed south to the Black Sea controlled by the White Russian Army loyal to the Czar. She was practically penniless when they crossed over into Yugoslavia in the crowded hold of a ship, took a desperately-needed job with a Turkish business-man more than twice her age who demanded she marry him, and had a son by him—and just as quickly had the marriage annulled.

Vera became a beautician and masseuse at a beauty salon in Prague, and later manager of a far grander one called the Barbara Gould Beauty Parlor on Avenue President Wilson in Paris. It was the 1930s, and Paris was filled with Vera's friends from the old Russian nobility. There was the Grand Duke Dimitri Pavlovich, and the even more renowned Prince Felix Yussoupov, who had been one of the richest man in Czarist Russia and, with the Grand Duke's help, had murdered the diabolical peasant Rasputin—the man who had wormed his way into the hearts of the Czar and Czarina by his mystical ability to relieve the suffering of their hemophiliac son Alexis. (Prince Yussoupov felt Rasputin's closeness to the royal couple was destroying the monarchy, so he poisoned him, shot him, and when that failed, finally drowned him.)

Vera then turned her life inside-out by taking a job singing in Russian, French, German, English, and Gypsy in a Paris café called the Blue Butterfly, and in other cities including the Knickerbocker Club in Monte Carlo, where she spent the evenings at the casino on the arm of the Grand Duke Dimitri. During World War II, Vera sang at the fashionable Sheherezade nightclub in Paris, whose clientele included the king of Sweden, Maurice Chevalier, and Marlene Dietrich, along with German officers who she says were served "champagne, caviar, and flaming shish kebab while we girls lived on rutabagas and gray bread."

Vera moved to New York City after the war, renting a room in the 57th Street apartment of Prince Kajar, whose family had ruled Persia from 1797 to 1924. She then talked Elizabeth Arden herself into giving her a job as a $35-a-week salesgirl, worked several years at Best & Co., became a naturalized U.S. citizen, and, until her retirement 25 years later in 1979, announced the news in classic Russian for the Voice of America in Washington, D.C.

Vera Tolstoy has led an extraordinary life, and she's still at it. She's active in the local Russian community, whose members address her as Countess, frequently visits with her son Serge Tolstoy in Washington, D.C., is constantly expanding and beautifying her home, and every two weeks sends packages filled with hard-to-get necessities (from soap to warm underwear) to needy friends in Russia.

What troubles Vera more than anything else—and it's common among the very old—is that nearly all her close friends and relatives have died or moved away, and she is increasingly alone in the world. The young can give the old no greater gift than to befriend them and make them part of their extended family. The rewards are many, and sometimes delight-fully surprising. Whenever my wife and I stop by after breakfast, Vera always greets us warmly with, "Good morning, children."

3

GOOD HEALTH:
THE ULTIMATE GIFT

Now that I have arrived at a great age, I might as well be 20.

—Pablo Picasso at 80

I don't want to fight old age, but I'm not about to invite it to live in, either. I want a nice symbiotic relationship with it, where we are totally unaware of each other.

—Betty White

My body's old, but it ain't impaired.
And I don't need your rockin' chair.

—George Jones, 65-year-old country singer

On a lonely back road in Florida, a youngster in a hot rod pulls up to an elderly man driving a 1981 Oldsmobile station wagon and laughs, "Hey Pop, wanna race?"

"OK," says the white-haired gentleman, who floors the gas pedal and goes from 0 to 60 miles per hour in 5.98 seconds, leaving the other car in a cloud of dust.

The old-timer that the kid had unwittingly challenged was my pal Harley Morse, a drag racer who has won more than 150 trophies in over 30 years of competition—the latest behind the

Ninety-year-old drag racer Harley Morse of Eustis, Florida, stands beside one of his souped-up '85 Monte Carlos.

wheel of his Olds station wagon, which hides under its hood a super-powerful 423 cubic-inch Chevy engine with a nitrous oxide injection system.

"I can hit the gas pedal or the brake as fast today as I could 30 years ago," Harley claims, and proceeds to demonstrate his lightning-fast reaction time by starting and stopping his Cronus stopwatch in an eighth of a second. "Your reaction time probably does slow down as you get older if you have to think about what you're going to do," he continues, "but hitting the brake or gas pedal is automatic, you don't have to think. If I lay a tool down and don't make a special effort to remember where I put it, I may have trouble finding it again. But I can drive a car as good today as I ever did. Maybe better."

These days, in his 90s and blessed with the ultimate gift of good health, Harley is still kicking up dust on the back roads of

Florida, having traded in his Olds for two 1985 Monte Carlos—each with a monster engine capable of going from 0 to 60 in less than 5 seconds. This unstoppable man, whose newest hobby is breeding racing pigeons, says "I'm an old man who never quits."

Aging is Not a Disease

One of the most delightful surprises life has to offer is how happy one can be at an age—such as 60 or 65—that young people (or even perhaps ourselves, years ago) consider to be bordering on decrepitude. "To young people, age is a thing to be *confronted*," says David B. Wolfe in *Serving the Ageless Market*, but "to the healthfully developing older person, age is a thing to be integrated into one's total reality. The stronger one's sense of life satisfaction, the younger one feels. In fact," concludes Wolfe, "substantial research indicates that as the mature person grows older, he or she gains an even richer sense of well-being, despite the inevitable increase in losses due to illness and death involving friends and family."

What we're beginning to recognize is that most older Americans feel pretty good, and the reason is that we're in surprisingly good physical and mental shape. That's the conclusion reached by the long-standing Baltimore Longitudinal Study of Aging, launched in 1958 and conducted in cooperation with the National Institute on Aging.

The study, which involved more than 1,000 men and women from their 20s to their 90s, reached two important conclusions: aging is not a disease, and there is no single, simple pattern of aging.

The study found that simpler functions of the human body deteriorate less than the more complex ones. For example, the speed at which nerves send their messages throughout the body decreases only mildly with age, while maximum breathing capacity declines steadily in most people as they grow older.

It was also revealed that while older people are more susceptible to a variety of diseases, *none are brought on automatically by the passage of time.* Aging, in other words, does not lead to a general weakening of all physical and psychological functions.

Some abilities do decline, while others remain stable, or actually improve. The study concludes, "The individual body, mind, and spirit show great capacity for variability and adaptability." While age 70 seems to be the point at which many abilities begin to visibly decline, a 70- or even an 80-year-old can still be in far greater physical condition than someone much younger. All of which leads the authors of the study to conclude the following:

➤ Vision, stamina, and the ability to concentrate may be altered only mildly over the years, while some capacities such as vocabulary may actually improve.

➤ Cardiac output of older hearts that are free of disease is comparable to that of younger hearts.

➤ Height tends to shrink due partly to the change in bone structure, which is more severe in women than men.

➤ Oxygen consumption declines because of the loss of muscle tissue.

➤ Older bodies contain less water than younger ones, and since drugs are distributed throughout the body by being dissolved in water, we need lower concentrations of medications as we age.

➤ Personality remains remarkably stable throughout life. People who are cheerful and optimistic when young usually remain so throughout life, as do those who are grouchy and mean-spirited.

➤ The nervous system changes little with age. Older and younger people are nearly equal in their ability to walk a straight line, stand on one leg, walk on their heels, gaze upward, or feel sensation in their hands.

➤ Kidney function decreases with age. But many individuals maintain adequate kidney function as they age, and for a minority kidney function actually increases in later years.

➤ Smell and taste decline, as does hearing, especially at higher frequencies.

➤ Sexual activity becomes less frenetic, although those who were more sexually vigorous in their youth usually remain so after age 40. Aging seems to have little effect on the quality of sexual pleasure in healthy women, although sexual desire and frequency of orgasm may decrease. (See Chapter 4 for more details on sexuality).

➤ A person's ability to respond to infrequent and unpredictable stimuli—the study calls it "vigilance"—declines sharply after 70 in many people, as does the reaction time required to respond to the stimuli.

➤ Mental performance, on the whole, remains strong at least to age 70, after which it declines, although not uniformly. An interesting footnote here is that men in their 70s who are still good at problem-solving tend to live longer than those whose mental abilities have slipped. Thus, mental activity may be as important a determinant of longevity as physical activity.

The National Institute's study of seniors is already dated, and future findings will no doubt continue to change our understanding of aging. Which reminds the study's authors of the familiar bumper sticker: "I don't want to grow old, I want to grow older."

Confessions of a Dancin' Granny

To the thousands of retired people who have run their race and are now ready for round-the-clock relaxation, Sun Lakes, Arizona, is paradise. Sun Lakes has it all, from golf and tennis to swimming and art classes—set among a breathtaking landscape of green lawns giving way to serene desert and snow-capped mountains.

Nestled in the midst of all this easy living was a fat, out-of-shape woman named Beverly Gemigniani who, at 48, felt that life had passed her by. "My arms were flabby," she says, "my tummy hung out, and you couldn't tell my waist from my hips because everything just kind of mushed together like a soft ice cream cone." She was ready to make peace with her flab when an inner voice told her to do something she hadn't done in years: exercise and eat intelligently.

Before long, Beverly was spending hours a week working out at her health club and ending her love affair with burgers and fries. She also began teaching other women how to shape up—as her own shape evaporated from a fulsome 16 to a fabulous 4. Of course, Beverly could have stopped there and declared victory. But instead, she's done something that has

Beverly Gemigniani of Sun City, Arizona (center row, right), with five of her Dancin' Grannies, ranging in age from 58 to 72.

made her—and other Sun Lakes women—national celebrities.

She dreamed up the Dancin' Grannies, a group of marvelously fit women aged 58 to 72 who regularly perform aerobic routines at events such as the Macy's Thanksgiving Day Parade

and the President's Great American Workout, held on the
White House lawn, sharing top billing with big-name athletes
such as tennis star Chris Evert and the Harlem Globetrotters.

The Dancin' Grannies are now a growth business producing
everything from a Dancin' Grannies Health and Fitness
Calendar to four exercise videotapes that have sold some one
million copies so far.

Beverly Gemigniani says her success began with her decision to take better care of her body: Exercise is critical, and so
is her healthy new diet, loaded with things which are actually
good for her. We can learn a lot from her energetic example:

➤ Breakfast is usually a glass of hot water flavored with
the juice of half a lemon, followed by three different
natural cereals combined with banana, strawberries, or
a peach in low-fat milk.

➤ Lunch is raw vegetables and fruit, along with corn tor-
tillas made with low-fat cheese, or occasionally a tuna
sandwich on nine-grain bread with shredded romaine
lettuce.

➤ Dinner is vegetables again, either stir-fried or steamed
with homemade spaghetti sauce or small amounts of
chicken, fish sautéed with garlic and basmati rice, or a
huge baked potato stuffed with diced onions, fresh
tomatoes and low-fat cheese. Salad dressing is made
from olive oil, fresh-squeezed lemon juice, unpasteur-
ized vinegar, and herbs. Adding a little jicama, red
peppers, or parsley will give salads a change of flavor
and texture, she says, as will boiled fresh beets kept in
the refrigerator until needed.

The message to seniors everywhere is that physical fitness
feels great, and there's no better time than today to get started.

Turning On to an Energetic Diet

D iet is certainly big in the longevity sweepstakes. It's the rare doctor these days who doesn't have a list of do's and don'ts for patients to take along the next time they shop at their local supermarket.

Dr. William P. Castelli, Medical Director of the Framingham, Massachusetts, Heart Study, National Heart, Lung and Blood Institute, is an expert on healthy cooking with particular emphasis on low-cholesterol cuisine that tastes good and is easy on the heart. A vegetarian diet is tops, he says, but you can still have a heart-wise diet by holding your intake of saturated fat to 22 grams or less per day. Castelli says you could have select-grade beef hamburgers containing only 4 grams of saturated fat for breakfast, lunch, and dinner and still be well within your daily allowance.

Guidelines for Low-Cholesterol, Low-Triglyceride Diets, is a list of eating suggestions distributed to doctors' offices by Warner-Lambert (a health care company). Foods to avoid include marbled beef, whole milk, potato chips, candy, jams and jellies, coconuts, and butter. Foods to eat are whole-grain breads and dried beans, along with plenty of fresh fruits and vegetables daily. People who eat a diet rich in fruits and vegetables significantly reduce the risk of cancers of the lung, larynx, mouth, esophagus, stomach, colon, rectum, bladder, pancreas, cervix, ovary, and endometrium, according to at least 156 studies of this subject reviewed in *The Journal of Nutrition and Cancer*.

Although the medical community is still divided as to their efficacy, vitamin supplements are coming back into vogue. A cover story in *Medical World News* headlined "Mighty

Vitamins" begins by noting, "Report after report suggest that vitamins A, C, E, and beta carotene may reduce the incidence of heart disease and cancer, and even blunt aging-associated damage like cataract formation and arthritis." However, a few paragraphs later we read that the value of vitamin supplements is not proven in scientifically-controlled clinical trials. The claims about the benefits of beta carotene, for example, were put to rest in early 1996 by Dr. Richard Klausner, Director of the National Cancer Institute, after spending years monitoring its effect on over 40,000 volunteers—including 22,071 doctors. "With clearly no benefit and even a hint of possible harm," said Dr. Klausner, "I can see no reason that an individual should take beta carotene." Still, according to a Louis Harris poll, "41 percent of Americans take vitamin supplements, mostly in the form of multivitamin pills."

Experts are also still arguing about whether it's better to be thin or a bit tubby as we age. A study in the *Journal of the American Medical Association* found that the lowest death rate among 11,703 Harvard and Stanford university graduates was among those who held their weight to within just over two pounds of what they weighed as students. Those who gained or lost more than 11 pounds, on the other hand, had higher death rates from all causes except cancer. After noting that more than 25 percent of American adults are overweight, the article stressed how important it is "for overweight individuals to lose excess body fat and then to maintain stable weight at a more desirable level."

An estimated 60 million overweight American adults pay a staggering $100 billion a year for food they wish they didn't eat, diet and weight-loss programs to help take off the resulting pounds, and medical costs for obesity-related health problems. This is all very serious business, since obesity is a significant health risk, particularly among females.

The Food and Drug Administration has some important new drugs under review to help in the battle against obesity. The drugs reduce both the desire to eat and the absorption of much of the fat in whatever food is consumed, and support the current belief that obesity is a chronic illness that must be treated long-term, rather than a simple lack of willpower.

Getting and staying in shape is one of life's most rewarding accomplishments, and provides a feeling of mental as well as physical power. It's well worth doing whatever it takes.

How Ronald Reagan Stayed in Shape

If Dancin' Granny Beverly Gemigniani ever wanted to compare notes with another aging fitness enthusiast, she could look at Ronald Reagan's health regimen while in office, described in a book I co-authored with his personal physician T. Burton Smith, M.D. In *White House Doctor* (Madison Books, 1992), Dr. Smith describes how Ronald Reagan "...would usually bring home a stack of work, take it into his study, and then change his clothes and join his wife Nancy in the mini-gym in their quarters equipped with a stationary bicycle, treadmill, and weights which they used religiously. 'You've got to do it,' the President would say, 'because it's very easy to put off. You can always find an excuse. So just do it.'

"When the President was at his 688-acre Rancho del Cielo ("Ranch In the Sky") high up in the Santa Ynez mountains...he'd keep in shape by clearing brush, chopping wood, and riding his horse El Alamain given to him by the former Mexican President Jose Lopez-Portillo.

"The President also had a good diet," wrote Dr. Smith. "Breakfast was usually orange juice, whole wheat toast, cereal, decaffeinated coffee, and sometimes fruit in season. He ate few eggs, and used margarine instead of butter. For lunch he'd have cottage cheese, a salad, soup and fruit which he ate at his desk in the Oval Office. The evening meal in the White House was usually fish or chicken with red meat perhaps once a week. President Reagan would occasionally sip a little wine with his dinner, but never smoked. His diet satisfied me. You can't beat it."

While it may not be breaking news, the importance of a healthy lifestyle, of taking as much control as possible over one's own physical well-being, really can't be overemphasized.

As I was writing this book, William McGowan, the hard-driving man who built MCI into the nation's second biggest telephone company, died of a heart attack. I knew McGowan from some work we'd done together back in 1983: We'd started early on a Saturday morning, and I was bowled over by this man's non-stop cigarette smoking, coffee drinking, obvious lack of exercise, lousy diet, and—perhaps worst of all—the fifteen hours a day, seven days a week he spent building MCI into a $10 billion communications galaxy.

McGowan had a massive heart attack in 1986, followed by a heart transplant in 1987, after which he started living a healthier life. But it was too late. He died while participating in a regular exercise program for heart patients at Georgetown University Hospital. Bill McGowan was 64.

How tragic. Here was a genuine American business legend who had taken on mighty AT&T and walked away with a big piece of its hide. He had done what he set out to do some 25 years earlier, including ending a lifetime as a bachelor by marrying an attractive and successful businesswoman, building his dream house in the exclusive Georgetown section of Washington, and giving $3 million to endow the William McGowan School of Business at his alma mater, King's College in Pennsylvania. Life should have been sweet for Bill

McGowan, and a wonderful 10 to 15 years—at least—longer. But he had destroyed his health, and it was payback time.

The Greatest Exercise on Earth

Rotund and jovial British actor Robert Morley, who was so out of shape he was able to play an over-the-hill King Louis XVI at 30, detested physical fitness right up until the day he died from a stroke at age 84. "My only exercise was winding my watch," he once told a reporter, "but that proved too exhausting, so now I have one that's self-winding."

Robert Morley must have been lucky—or a closet fitness addict—because in the United States alone about 250,000

Just a few brief walks each day can help you get in shape.

deaths each year are attributed to inactivity. It's a given in the longevity business that some form of regular exercise is essential to a healthy life. For example, women who rarely exercised as young girls may be prime candidates for bone-weakening osteoporosis when they reach middle age. And by 74, one-third of all males and two-thirds of all females are unable to lift a 10-pound object—the equivalent of a gallon of milk.

The American Heart Association has just elevated lack of exercise to a position close to high cholesterol, high blood pressure, and smoking as risk factors for heart disease. It has been estimated that a mere 10 percent of Americans exercise regularly and are fit (i.e. they exercise moderately for thirty or forty minutes at least three times a week). This means there are roughly thirty to fifty million mostly sedentary Americans who could begin getting in shape by simply taking five two-minute—or only two five-minute—walks each day.

I'm a serious walker, striding at least a mile a day to get the morning paper at my local convenience store. Walking is easily the greatest exercise on earth, and the only "special equipment" a walker needs is a sensible pair of shoes that are comfortable, provide solid support, and don't cause blisters or calluses. Walkers are also in good company. Ralph Waldo Emerson and Henry David Thoreau were great walkers, as were Thomas Jefferson, Abraham Lincoln, and Harry Truman. So if you're still jumping in the car to buy an item or two in a store only a few blocks away, try walking. Your cardiorespiratory system will love you for it.

While walking is the easiest form of exercise to get into, the American Heart Association also recommends hiking, stair-climbing, aerobics, jogging, running, bicycling, swimming, tennis, basketball, and other sports. The American Medical Association adds to the list gardening, shuffleboard, and—get

Both champion weight lifters, Joe Yanovitch, 63, watches 71-year-old Bill Sweeney bench press 225 pounds.

ready for this—even housework, which should come as no surprise to anyone who has ever done it.

Exercise is preventive medicine. Harvard University researchers have found that vigorous exercise such as a brisk thirty-minute walk can reduce the risk of late-onset diabetes by 23 percent if done once a week, by 38 percent if done twice, and by 42 percent if done five times or more. According to an article in *Medical World News*, these findings are important because "exercise may be the only practical way of preventing diabetes. While obesity is a dominant risk factor for the disease, it is notoriously difficult to control."

The truth of that statement was brought home to opera star Luciano Pavarotti—who at age 57 tipped the scales at nearly 300 pounds—when his doctors told him to cancel all his concert engagements for two months and begin a crash weight-loss program. The world-renowned tenor was forced to withdraw from commitments at the Metropolitan Opera and the Opera Company of Philadelphia. But when your health and perhaps your life are in danger, you do what you have to do, beginning with eating less and exercising more.

Case in point: I've taken physical activity seriously for years, and conscientiously work out three days a week at Bailey's Powerhouse Gym with youngsters a third of my age. I figured I was in great shape for a senior citizen until I met 63-year-old, 242-pound Joe Yanovitch, the 1995 World Drug Free Power Lifting Association bench press champion in his age and weight division. "I don't live to lift," states Yanovitch plainly, "I lift to live. As long as I can lift 450 pounds from a squatting position, I'll be able to get out of my chair."

A Good Night's Sleep

> Methought I heard a voice cry "Sleep no more!
> Macbeth does murder sleep," the innocent sleep,
> Sleep that knits up the ravell'd sleave of care,
> The death of each day's life, sore labour's bath,
> Balm of hurt minds, great nature's second course,
> Chief nourisher in life's feast.
> —Macbeth, Act II, Scene ii

These lines, surely some of Shakespeare's most memorable, are spoken by the conscience-stricken Macbeth, who has just murdered the King of Scotland in his sleep. Macbeth confesses to his wife, who has egged him on to do the deed, that he is fearful he may never get another night's rest.

Macbeth has every right to worry: sleep acts like a healing potion to erase the tensions and stresses of each day, and a good night's sleep is essential to preserving a healthy body and mind. The actual number of hours we need varies widely. The average person can get along on seven or eight hours sleep a night, while one in a hundred requires as few as five hours, or as many as ten. Although most of us have little trouble dropping off the moment our head hits the pillow, roughly 100 million Americans have sleeping problems. One-third of this number suffer from at least occasional bouts of chronic insomnia, and one out of six need a sleeping pill to get through the night.

The American Sleep Disorders Association recognizes three types of insomnia: "transient," which lasts just a few days and is often caused by illness, stress, or worry; "short-term," which continues for about three weeks; and "chronic," which goes on for more than a month, and sometimes for years.

Until quite recently, there were few rigorous comparisons between drug and non-drug approaches to helping chronic insomniacs, who often spend more than half an hour falling asleep at least three nights a week, or wake up unable to get back to sleep for more than half an hour in the middle of the night. But research done at the Sleep Disorders Center and financed by the National Institute of Mental Health indicates that behavioral methods combined with sleeping pills work better than total reliance on drugs.

It's the rare person who doesn't have trouble sleeping now and then, and if you're one of them, here are four simple rules worth considering before resorting to medication:

1. Go to bed only when you're drowsy. If you haven't fallen asleep within fifteen minutes or so, get up and read, or do some needlework (or anything else that's relaxing) and then try again. Keep this up until you

finally doze off—and try to avoid watching television, which acts as a stimulant.

2. Use your bed for sleep and sex. Anything else, from watching television to eating a late night snack— unless it's something easy to digest like milk and cookies—will only get in the way of why you're really there.

3. Stop any bad habits which keep you awake when you should be sleeping, such as taking naps late in the after- noon, or drinking coffee or alcohol during or after dinner. Don't exercise too close to bedtime, and avoid smoking at bedtime or (if you awaken) during the middle of the night.

4. Try to go to sleep and get up at the same time even on weekends, when you could sleep late—even if you've tossed and turned all night.

If you've followed these rules and still have difficulty get- ting to sleep, you might try taking an over-the-counter antihistamine such as Benadryl which tends to cause drowsi- ness and is non-addictive. If this doesn't work, the experts recommend using sleeping pills on a carefully controlled basis. Here are some sleeping pill guidelines:

➤ It's perfectly all right to take a sleeping pill to get through those rare times when you have trouble dozing off, let's say before an important speech or trip, or on an overnight flight from New York to Paris. You might try something like Halcion, which acts fairly quickly and disappears from your system in six hours or so. You may need to experiment a little to find a dosage that won't leave you drowsy in the morning; some people find that just half a pill does the trick.

➤ If your insomnia lasts for about a month, you might try taking sleeping pills every night for two or three weeks. At the same time, look carefully into exactly what's causing the problem—once you recognize the cause, you can work to put it behind you.

➤ If you're a chronic insomniac who is dependent on sleeping pills, it is best to consult a doctor or professional therapist, who will examine the sleep-preventing aspects of your life and help you to determine what can be done about them.

Aging will never be trouble-free—Julia Child has said, "If you pretend old age is not going to happen, it will fall right on you"—but part of the joy of maturity is the wisdom and self-knowledge that enables us to truly look after our own interests, and listen to our body's needs.

Decompressing Stress

One of the things so many successful older people have to deal with is stress, which may have less to do with job pressure than the tensions generated by getting your income tax return in the mail by April 15th, or suddenly having your daughter, son-in-law, and their three children descend upon you for the Thanksgiving holidays.

The word "stress" as we use it today was coined more than 50 years ago by Dr. Hans Selye, a Canadian physiologist, who found that it sped up the aging process. World-renowned authority Dr. Paul J. Roach, President of the American Institute of Stress and Clinical Professor of Medicine and Psychiatry at New York Medical College, noted in a brief article in the *Medical Tribune* that when Selye "subjected experimental animals to chronic stress, they developed accelerated atherosclerosis, gray hair, wrinkled skin, cataracts and microscopic pigment, degenerative and atrophic hallmarks of aging. They died much sooner than their litter mates." The good news is that we are able to locate and alleviate sources of stress in our lives.

Medical experts in the United States and abroad offer the following tips to cut down stress in our lives:

➤ The two major factors which produce stress are a lack of personal control over your life, and an excess or lack of something you want, such as work, responsibility, information, or attention.

➤ Individuals frequently react to stress by excessive eating, drinking, smoking, drug-taking and sex, which, instead of alleviating the stress, exacerbate it.

➤ It's important to distinguish the annoying, but essentially harmless, hassles involved in everyday living from chronic, ongoing, uncontrollable stress. The latter can trigger serious health problems, the most common of which are probably heart attacks.

➤ Be aware of the stress in your life and do everything you can to reduce it, from improving conditions at work to practicing relaxation techniques such as exercise and meditation. Such resources are available in most communities.

Since so many of us older people are already up to our ears in the negatives of aging (real or imagined), anything we can do to detect and reduce stress in our lives is probably for the good. Stress can never be totally conquered, of course; if it could, we'd all be in something close to a vegetative state. We do need some stress in our lives, if only to keep us on our toes. The challenge? To keep our stress level within bounds.

Cosmetic Surgery to the Rescue?

In an effort to remain attractive, quite a few women and a growing number of men are turning to skin "solutions." They're spending $1 billion a year on moisturizers, according to *Consumer Reports*, and another $3 to $4 billion on cosmetic surgery procedures (mainly facial operations), which have soared 69 percent since 1981, says the American Society of Plastic and Reconstructive Surgeons.

"There's hardly a square inch of body surface—or a body part—that can' t be accentuated or minimized," adds *American Health*. "A brief tour of what plastic surgery patients both young and old are eager to buy," says the magazine, "would include hair transplants to fill in bald spots; face lifts, nose jobs, and artificial dimples; breast lifts and tummy tucks; sculpted buttocks and implants that contour calves."

Countless operations are performed daily on those who are no longer young, but want to keep the physical ravages of age at bay for a few more years at least. These are a major source of revenue for plastic surgeons, who charge $1,500 for dermabrasions and chemical peels which remove top layers of aging skin to reveal the smoothness underneath, $2,000 or more to get rid of a pot belly, and $7,000 to tighten sagging jowls. Surgeons charge $40,000 or more to remove hairs from the back of a balding man's neck and transplant them to the top, where they're in shorter supply.

It wasn't too long ago that people who wanted to get rid of age spots, birthmarks, spider veins and other benign skin blemishes had to run the risk of leaving a disfiguring scar behind by cutting, burning, bleaching, or freezing them off. This frequently created unsightly scars or the permanent loss of skin pigmentation, and as a result many skin doctors suggested masking them with makeup and letting it go at that.

Today, all that's history thanks to the invention of the skin laser, which uses a sharply focused beam of light to vaporize these blemishes, which are then absorbed in the bloodstream. These laser treatments can be done in a doctor's office without anesthesia, and take anywhere from one visit to etch away age spots, to several for large birthmarks or tattoos.

An article in *Health* magazine titled "Face Lift City," advises that wealthy women living in Palm Springs, California, should begin seeing plastic surgeons for liposuction, breast augmentation, collagen injections, buttock lifts and the like in their 40s because, says one local socialite, "there's no way they can get you back together after 65."

Local massage therapist Gary Remes is quoted saying he's seen the best and the worst of cosmetic surgery done on his clients, and the worst can get pretty bad. "A woman came in for a massage the other day, and when I got her on the table I saw she had had what's called a full coronal—which involves cutting from the top of the head down to the ears so they can pull the whole scalp up. She had double breast lifts and silicone implants. And she also had her nipples relocated and a tummy tuck and a fanny lift. All at once. All she needed was two bolts

in her neck and I could get her a husband with a flat head."
(*Viva* Frankenstein!)

A physician with hands-on knowledge of cosmetic surgery, a procedure increasingly being used by older people, is Dr. Mark Gorney, a San Francisco plastic surgeon and Senior Examiner for the American Board of Plastic Surgery. "Fully half of my patients are 50 or older," says Gorney, "and what they ask for most are face lifts and getting the bags under their eyes removed.

"Unfortunately, and I say this advisedly, there's a pathologically excessive emphasis on youth, beauty, and sexuality in America. Age may be revered in China, but in America it's a signal that you're ready for the junk pile."

Gorney is right. While cosmetic surgery is certainly a personal decision, it *is* about time we took it upon ourselves to reverse the worn-out stereotypes of aging.

Triumphing over Age-Related Diseases

Throughout history, medical science has brought under control many killers and cripplers of older people, including pneumonia, chicken pox, measles, and scarlet fever. The medical community is now turning its attention to the modern scourges which are destroying millions of older lives every year. Foremost among them are heart disease (the leading cause of death among older people, claiming close to 600,000 lives a year), stroke, cancer, mind-robbing Alzheimer's disease, Parkinson's disease, amyotropic lateral sclerosis (familiarly known as Lou Gehrig's disease), and now human immunodeficiency virus (HIV) that causes AIDS (Acquired Immune Deficiency Syndrome).

While exercise, diet, and drugs are the Three Musketeers in the battle against aging, alternative medicine is getting more attention these days (see Chapter 7), and technology is also doing its part with developments such as artificial joints and cardiac pacemakers—and now ear implants that will dramatically restore the hearing of 90 percent to 95 percent of those who are deaf, says Dr. Robert A. Schindler, professor and chairman of otolaryngology at the University of California's School of Medicine.

"This is the most successful sensory prosthetic device ever made," said Dr. Schindler, who has devoted more than two decades to the project and believes its principles will eventually be applied to the reanimation of body parts in recovering stroke patients and quadriplegics. The implant is being developed collaboratively by UCSF, the Research Triangle Institute of North Carolina, and its manufacturer MiniMed Technologies of Sylmar, California, and will cost about $14,000 when it's eventually sold to the public. MiniMed is also one of two companies developing implantable insulin-delivery pumps for diabetics. Its in-the-body pump, which must be refilled every three months, can provide more precise delivery of insulin than the usual needle in a vein, and should be on the market in several years.

In 1991 a man in critical condition in the intensive care unit at the Texas Heart Institute at St. Luke's Episcopal Hospital in Houston was given the first implant device to assist a failing heart until a heart donor could be found. The implant, placed in his abdominal cavity just below his diaphragm, powered by a compact battery pack slung over the shoulder, took over for the ailing heart's left ventricle, which pumps oxygenated blood to the body. Soon after the surgery was finished, the man was able to walk about without being tethered to a cumbersome external power console. Surgeons see this as a major step toward the day when patients will routinely receive totally implantable artificial hearts.

The death rate from cancer—the number two killer in the United States after heart disease—continues to fall. The November 15, 1996, issue of the journal *Cancer* reported that overall cancer death rates, adjusted for age, declined for the first time since 1900, having fallen each year from 1990 to 1995. The total drop of 3.1 percent was largely attributed to a continuing reduction in cigarette smoking among men.

Twelve patients with advanced melanoma, and no other treatment options standing between them and death, recently became the first to have antigen-producing genes injected directly into their tumors, which, it is hoped, will stimulate their immune systems to destroy the cancer. If the treatment works, it will mark the breakthrough beginning of the use of genes as a drug to fight heretofore intractable ills such as cancer and heart disease in adults, and inherited diseases including cystic fibrosis, dwarfism, and hemophilia in children.

Scientists around the world are continuing their efforts to improve the well-being of people of all ages by pushing back the frontiers of curative medicine. Dr. Lisa Schnell and Dr. Martin E. Schwab of the Institute for Brain Research at the University of Zurich in Switzerland, for example, have used a genetically engineered protein to encourage the fusing of nerves in the severed spinal cords of rats. The significance of this procedure, according to Dr. Fred Plum, head of neurology at New York Hospital–Cornell Medical Center, is that it "represents the first giant step towards promoting nerve regeneration in disorders such as paraplegia from accidents, paralysis from stroke, and weakness and poor coordination due to nerve degeneration from diseases such as Parkinson's, Alzheimer's and Lou Gehrig's disease."

Alzheimer's disease, whose best known patient is former president Ronald Reagan, is an irreversible, degenerative disease of the nerve cells of the brain for which there is now no cure, although some promising research is underway. Alzheimer's usually appears in the seventh, eighth, or ninth decades of life when it increasingly steals its victims' memory and in later stages their identity. A 78-year-old woman suffering from Alzheimer's, for example, turned to her son and asked, "Who is that man in the house?" It was her husband, to whom she had been married for almost six decades. More than four million Americans have Alzheimer's disease, and that number, according to the Mayo Clinic, is expected to triple in the next 20 years as more people live into their 80s and 90s.

The fact that there is currently no cure for Alzheimer's discourages people from finding out if they have it. When the New York City chapter of the Alzheimer's Association asked its members if they would want to know years or decades in advance if they had as much as a 90 percent chance of getting the disease, only 63 percent of the respondents said "yes." New findings about Alzheimer's devastating impact on the brain, however, may eventually make it possible to diagnose the disease years before it leads to senility, allowing victims to plan for the future while they are still alert enough to do so.

Solid progress is being made in combating Parkinson's disease, the second most common neurodegenerative disease after Alzheimer's. Parkinson's disease occurs when brain cells that produce dopamine, a key chemical messenger, start dying in large numbers. This disorder of the nervous system, which first causes uncontrollable trembling and eventually attacks muscle activity throughout the body, is suffered by about 1 percent of the population over 50 years old, including the Reverend Billy Graham and Muhammad Ali. Parkinson's disease can't yet be cured, but there have been some encouraging advances using both surgery and drugs.

Investigators are also testing the first drug to slow the course of Lou Gehrig's disease, which affects some 30,000 people in this country.

Gay men represent the majority of the 56,000 AIDS cases diagnosed in people over 50, a number that has been growing steadily throughout the epidemic, accounting for 11 percent of all new cases in 1995. According to a study released by the University of California at San Francisco, a main reason those over 50 are at such a disproportionate risk from this killer disease is that they are only one-sixth as likely as those in their 20s to use condoms, and to be tested for infection.

The National Institute on Aging claims that older people are especially vulnerable to the AIDS virus because of the age-related decline in their disease-fighting immune systems, and because they receive the highest rate of blood transfusions during routine medical care.

An astonishing amount of research is being done in the search for new drugs that can extend the life of AIDS patients. These drugs are unquestionably prolonging the lives of those fortunate enough to afford them, although AIDS kills frail older men in their 60s and above a lot faster than it kills those in their 30s or 40s. Costs can easily hit $20,000 a year or more. By far, the most important of the new drugs are called protease inhibitors, and have already reduced HIV infections to undetectable levels among thousands of patients, including basketball legend Magic Johnson.

The Food and Drug Administration approved protease inhibitors on March 1, 1996, and an FDA advisory panel also recommended a third anti-AIDS drug which is expected to receive fast approval. Protease inhibitors show their best results when used in combination with AIDS drugs, and appear to reduce the amount of AIDS-causing HIV in the blood by 90 percent or more while increasing the number of disease-fighting cells in the body's immune system.

Thanks to these and other drugs in the pipeline, being diagnosed with an HIV infection in America today signifies illness, but no longer certain death. In early 1997, for example, a small midwestern insurance company started offering life insurance policies of up to $250,000 to some people who are HIV positive. Its rationale is that their ailment should now be seen as a treatable chronic disease, rather than a terminal illness, since HIV patients today can expect to live 10 or more years after being diagnosed.

Researchers at Duke University's Center for Demographic Studies has just released a report indicating that, because of medical advances, a smaller pecentage of American seniors suffer from serious disabilities today than fifteen years ago. If this trend continues, Duke researchers say, the number of seriously disabled people 65 and older will decline significantly in the years ahead.

Killers and cripplers of every description are under attack as never before, dramatically enhancing the lives of us all.

Exciting Advances in Prescription Drugs

People 65 and over represent only 12 percent of the U.S. population, yet account for 35 percent of all the money spent on prescription drugs. Far too many of us rely on drugs for every little ache and pain—real or imagined—stocking our bathroom medicine chests and bedside tables with almost every elixir known to modern pharmacology. This makes us vulnerable to adverse drug reactions such as delirium, gastrointestinal bleeding, serious falls, and even chronic schizophrenia, which rises from 10 percent for people taking just one drug to 27 percent for those juggling six drugs.

Drug-taking by older people is often a hit-or-miss affair. Overdoses and underdoses—or no dose at all—are more common than generally realized.

Doctors who prescribe drugs for their therapeutic value offer the following advice to older people taking drugs (which have increased in price by 152 percent—or three times the rate of inflation—since 1980):

1. Keep a written record of all your prescription and over-the-counter medications.

2. Know how and when to take medications and how you should—and shouldn't—feel when you take them. Don't dismiss a new feeling as just a sign of old age.

3. Ask your pharmacist for assistance in understanding the medicine label on both prescription and nonprescription medicines. Be sure to tell your pharmacist about any chronic health problems you may have.

4. Organize your medicine schedule at home, possibly by using some of the special medicine bottle tops or sectioned containers available for this purpose.

New drugs are constantly coming onto the market, and what's exciting about so many of them today is that they're precisely calibrated to get their healing power into your system with fewer adverse side effects. Recent developments include long-duration transdermal patches, once-a-day pills, pumps, and time-released pulses.

You're probably familiar with the recently developed nicotine patch which helps people quit smoking by continually releasing tiny doses of nicotine into their bloodstreams, or with the contraceptive patch which protects women against pregnancy using the very same controlled-release transdermal technology. Now this method is being used to inject other drugs into patient's bodies exactly where they're needed and at a constant rate.

The popular anti-angina drug Procardia, which patients had to take three times daily to control the life-threatening lack of blood to the heart muscle caused by coronary disease, has been replaced by a once-a-day controlled-release version called Procardia XL. This pill has a pump-like construction which pushes the drug through a microscopic hole directly into the body's fluids.

Another version of this pill has already been approved for high blood pressure, and in a few years, an even more advanced form is expected to treat hypertension, which often leads to heart attacks in the morning, when blood pressure puts great stress on the heart.

Today's hypertensive drugs are taken before bedtime and have lost their punch by morning, when most needed. The new pill will have a layered construction, allowing it to hold off releasing the drug until an hour or two before sunrise—precisely when it can do the most good.

When taken under our doctor's care, rather than some pill-popping regimen we've dreamed up on our own, today's prescription drugs are a godsend for us seniors.

A New Breed

Archie: *Edith, if you're gonna have a change of life, you gotta do it right now. I'm gonna give you just 30 seconds. Now, come on, CHANGE!*

Edith: *Can I finish my soup first?*
— All in the Family, *1972*

Today's older person is a totally different breed from those who grew to maturity as recently as a generation or two ago. By aggressively looking after ourselves physically and mentally, and by taking advantage of new medical breakthroughs as they become available, the last third of our lives can be especially rewarding.

This certainly applies to the 40 million or so women from roughly age 40 to 56 who are currently going through menopause, and to the 60 million who will be in or past "the change" by the year 2020.

These are the years of hot flashes (lasting from fifteen minutes to an hour), night sweats, short-term memory loss, mood changes, migraine headaches, and reduced desire for sex—all of which can be helped by estrogen hormone replacement, which successfully treats 90 to 95 percent of these symptoms.

So far, fewer than one in five women replace lost estrogen hormones, which the ovaries stop producing in abundance at about age 35. Reasons for this run the gamut from not being able to afford estrogen therapy to fear it will trigger breast cancer, from feeling good and not even thinking about it to a reluctance to begin any treatment which may have to continue for years.

Yet because estrogen can be so beneficial, and is so easy to take in the form of pills or a transparent patch worn on the abdomen or buttocks, it is being used by more and more women to combat the discomfort and risk of infections and irritation.

Quite lyrically, the distinguished anthropologist Margaret Mead often referred to this era in a woman's life as "postmenopausal zest," an opportunity for the flowering of fresh delights from new, and perhaps daring, interpersonal relationships, and a chance to pursue with increased vigor dreams too long deferred (see "The Golden Girls" in Chapter 4 for more about newly-empowered women).

A National Agenda for Research on Aging

The Institute of Medicine of the National Academy of Sciences is hard at work researching ways to keep us all alive and well a bit longer, based on suggestions made by a committee of eighteen national health care leaders, assisted by sixty-three outstanding scientists. Their report emphasized "that for every $100 spent on caring for sick and disabled elderly patients, only about thirty cents went to research on the conditions that affect persons in the later years of life. This observation is all the more telling," said the report, "in the light of recent advances in the study of aging, in fields ranging from molecular biology to behavioral studies, that offer the promise of discoveries to improve health and functioning markedly for those 65 and older.

"Despite recent advances," the report continued, "research and health care have fallen short of the needs of the older generation. For example, at the present time the United States requires almost 10,000 physicians with special competence in geriatrics to manage the complex clinical problems of those 75 years of age and older. Yet there are apparently far fewer physicians available to meet this need which has nowhere to go but up. More medical school faculty members—as many as 6,000 by the year 2000—will be needed to train these and other health care professionals (principally in the behavioral and social studies and in health care delivery), and to support the development of an adequate cadre of scientific investigators in age-related studies."

The team of experts then went on to assign a high priority to the following nine areas of research it considers critical, and into which millions of dollars of federal money is already beginning to flow:

1. Improving our understanding of the basic mechanisms of aging.

2. Studying problems of disability and functional impairment in older persons, placing emphasis on prevention.

3. Increasing our understanding of the interaction between disease and aging, as well as age-related diseases.

4. Investigating how to reduce morbidity and mortality rates among older people.

5. Focusing on research results which can be put to work improving the lives of older people with all deliberate speed.

6. Coming up with new ways of reducing the cost of health care.

7. Advancing our knowledge of the behavioral and social factors involved in health and disease to help older people maintain their social and biological health.

8. Upgrading the pharmacological treatment of older patients.

9. Looking into the relatively neglected ways to helping older people to enjoy better health.

"The time is ripe," concluded the Institute of Medicine report, "to narrow the gap between the needs of an aging society and the scientific knowledge base." As we shall see, this increase in overall longevity among American men and women has profound implications for the future.

Good Health in Print

There's no shortage of publications devoted to helping us lead fulfilling lives while aging, such as the sharply focused newsletter *Health After 50*, written by doctors at the Johns Hopkins Medical Institution (see Appendix for subscription information). The newsletter contains such tips as:

➤ Take an aspirin every other day if you're over 50, because it may cut your risk of a first heart attack by nearly half.

➤ Look into dental implants, which are fixed into the underlying bone as an alternative to dentures.

➤ Don't take minoxidil for baldness, because it may produce serious side effects (especially if you have any cardiovascular disease), and generates only a limited growth of new hair, mostly for men under 30 who have been balding for less than five years.

The National Institute on Aging, as we've seen, is opening up some new vistas into the aging process. One NIH report, called *Bound for Good Health*, offers current scientific information from authorities nationwide about staying healthy as we age. Among the report's innumerable down-to-earth observations are:

➤ Regular household light bulbs are better for older eyes than tubular fluorescent lights.

➤ Salt should be used with caution. Overuse is associated with high blood pressure, which increases as we age, and should be controlled if outside normal readings.

➤ Regular cancer checkups are a must beginning at middle age, as is a basic knowledge of the symptoms of this killer disease, which almost always strikes without the usual early warning sign of pain.

➤ Experts agree that older people too often become overly concerned with having a daily bowel movement and that constipation is frequently an overemphasized ailment. Many seniors are also heavy users of laxatives which is usually unnecessary, often becomes habit-forming, and can lead to the loss of normal bowel function.

➤ Hearing loss is common as people grow older, and those who have difficulty with words or other sounds from music to approaching traffic should have their hearing checked by physician.

Golfing legend Arnold Palmer, 67, was back on the fairway in early 1997, six weeks after successful cancer surgery. One youngster looking on just to see how the old-timer swings his driver was today's golfing sensation, Tiger Woods.

➤ The human body is less able to adjust to long exposure to hot or cold weather as it ages, so older people should be on guard. A drop in internal body temperature during cold weather could prove fatal if not detected and treated. Hot, humid weather can also trigger other serious illnesses, such as heat stroke.

➤ The U.S. Public Health Service strongly urges older people to be immunized against influenza, pneumococcal diseases (especially pneumonia), diphtheria, and tetanus.

Additional resources for health-related information are offered in the Appendix, and should be readily available in your community through health care organizations and libraries—and even on the Internet.

A Dud at 70, A Stud at 80

W hen hard-working comedian George Burns turned 96, a reporter asked him if he still chased girls, drank four or five martinis a day, and smoked fifteen to twenty cigars a week. "Yes," said Burns. "But what does your doctor say?" asked the incredulous reporter. "My doctor's dead," said Burns.

They always say laughter is the best medicine, and some of us may chuckle ourselves healthily into a ripe old age, like George Burns. But the rest of us may need to look a bit more sensibly at aging—and recognize that taking an active role can make all the difference. While there is no way to stop the degeneration of the human body as we age, the process can be slowed down—and in some cases even reversed—through the judicious use of exercise, along with a quality diet, hormones, some incredible biogenetic breakthroughs (discussed in Chapter 7), and—yes—even cosmetics or cosmetic surgery.

While visiting the National Institutes of Health, my eye was caught by studies of the advances being made in slowing or actually reversing the aging process in hundreds of laboratories around the world. Richard Cutler, a research chemist at the National Institutes of Health's Gerontology Research Center in Baltimore, has been quoted as saying that "aging is unnatural. There are no such things as 'programs' that age us for our own good, or for the good of the species. Aging really results from random changes in the normal processes that maintain us and keep us alive."

Recent studies have proven that 90-year-old nursing home residents can become stronger, steadier, and less prone to fall after a modest weight-training program. Even the heart and kidneys of a person over 65, if free of disease, can function as well as a young person's, says Dr. T. Franklin Williams, former Director of the National Institute on Aging.

The reason so many Americans of all ages are out of shape, says Dr. Walter M. Bortz II, professor of medicine at Stanford University, is that unlike our hunting and gathering ancestors, "we no longer have to move to eat."

The result? The human heart has withered to the smallest size of any animal in proportion to body weight.

"What's the biggest killer in America?" asks Dr. Bortz. "Coronary artery disease. And why are our arteries killing us? Because we are like zoo animals, tended to as if somebody were regularly throwing food into our cages."

Dr. Bortz, a trim Californian in his late 60s who has run the Boston Marathon, says that when he and other medical researchers examined the arteries of a dozen middle-aged males who had completed a grueling 100-mile endurance race, "we saw...that they were immense. Who cares what your cholesterol level is if your arteries are an inch-and-a-half across?"

The doctor concludes, "I can write a prescription for good rest, good nutrition, good exercise. That's it. The biological data are absolutely compelling." And the key is to get older people to say to all who will listen that "I am in charge of myself. I am empowered. I am taking care of myself. I am not being taken care of by my family, my company or my government."

This will come as no surprise to Ernie MacDonald, a 70-year-old neighbor of mine. Ernie is reed thin, yet is constantly exercising. I paid no attention to him until one day he suddenly stopped jogging and broke into a 100-yard dash in what looked to me like Olympic time. Then he stopped, caught his breath, and was off again flying like the wind for the pure joy of doing it. When I asked him his secret, he said, "Twenty years ago, I was diagnosed as having congestive heart failure, and told I could die at any minute. So I started running and haven't stopped. Besides, there are fellows out there 75 and 80 who beat me every time we race, so I've got to keep trying to go faster."

If Ernie should ever need a little inspiration, he can find it in the life of toolmaker Noel Johnson, who was in such bad shape his doctor had given him no more than six months to live. Johnson had been warned that even mowing the lawn could kill him, so, figuring he had nothing to lose, he started walking, then jogging, then winning just about every race around for older runners—including the 26.2-mile New York City Marathon at age 84, and again at 88. Johnson's achievements got his picture on Wheaties boxes at age 77, led to his writing a book called *A Dud at 70, a Stud at 80*, and kept him going strong right up until he died at age 96.

4

THE JOY OF VINTAGE LOVE, ROMANCE, AND SEX

The best recipe for a long, healthy life is to eat half of what you do now...exercise regularly...and make love every day.
> —Gerontologist, Rockefeller University

An orgasm a day keeps the doctor away.
> —Mae West

Older women make the best lovers because they think they're doing it for the last time.
> —From the soap opera *Santa Barbara*

A 63-year-old California woman and her 57-year-old husband recently became the proud parents of a healthy baby girl, making her the oldest known woman in history to bear a child. The birth was made possible by the donation of an egg from a much younger woman—certainly a kind of miracle!

Having babies automatically bestows a youthful aura on couples of all ages venturesome enough to try it, and reminds us all of the ageless fascination with love and romance, not to mention more carnal delights.

Even 71-year-old Hugh Hefner, founder and editor of *Playboy* magazine, says he's never been happier. "Hef" is married to Kimberley Conrad, a former "Playmate of the Year" less than half his age who has already given him two sons. All of which speaks well for actor Tony Randall, who married a 25-year-old actress when he was 75, became a father for the first time at age 77, and recently exclaimed that "the best thing that ever happened to me happened after age 70."

Relighting the Fires of Romance

People over the age of 50 are generally "empty nesters" freed from the expense of raising children, paying college tuition, and finding the cash to make monthly mortgage payments. We don't see ourselves as Mom and Dad anymore, but almost as newlyweds ready to relight the fires of romance—or at least put a little gasoline on the embers.

Study after study has found that the best years of a couple's life frequently begin after the children have left home and started lives of their own. In their book *'Til Death Do Us Part: How Couples Stay Together*, social scientists Jeanette and Robert Lauer write that the hundreds of couples they interviewed who were married for fifteen years or more "typically viewed the 'empty nest' as a positive factor...allowing the couple to recapture some of the freedom and fun of the early days of the marriage." The grown children, needless to say, remained an integral part of the family, even though at a distance.

New York lawyer and former National Organization for Women president Karen DeCrow is on the record as saying her sex life is wonderful. "When a 20-year-old woman has sex with a man she worries about how she looks. Does she do it right?

Should she look messy? Should she look neat? By the time you're 50, you're more relaxed. I would definitely say sex is better. Everything in life is better."

The entertainment industry isn't quite ready to celebrate vintage romance, but it occasionally gives it a whirl, often with unabashed critical acclaim. One little gem is Turner Network Television's "Foreign Affairs," starring Joanne Woodward as a prim New England college teacher and hulking Brian Dennehy as an Oklahoma sewage engineer. The pair fall deliciously in love while exploring England—and later each other.

When Robert Butler, M.D. and Myrna Lewis appeared on the *Today Show* in 1976 to discuss their new book *Love and Sex after 60*, host Barbara Walters told parents they might want to remove any children from the room while this obviously hot topic was being discussed. What was so explosive was the author's suggestion that "Perhaps only in the later years can life with its various possibilities have the chance to shape itself into something approximating a human work of art. And perhaps only in later life, when personality reaches its final stages of development, can love-making and sex achieve the fullest possible growth.

"Sex does not merely exist after 60," the authors insist, but "it holds the possibility of becoming greater than it ever was. It can be joyful and creative, healthy and health-giving. It unites human beings in an affirmation of love and is therefore also morally right and virtuous." Perhaps because Butler and Lewis, who are married, are willing to deflate common myths of sexuality in old age, *Love and Sex After 60* has gone through several editions and remains popular in bookstores.

While the sex drive is not the boiling cauldron we experienced in our youth, the desire for intimacy is, if anything, greater than ever. Yale University psychologist Robert Sternberg says the single most important element in the success of a romantic relationship is not mad, passionate lovemaking, but rather the sharing of ideas and interests with one's lover, the sense of growing personally through the relationship, taking pleasure in doing things for the other person, giving and getting emotional support, and simply being happy when in the other's company.

A Garden of Delights

Romantic delights, so precious to us Big Band era romantics, are coming under scrutiny from the likes of Helen F. Fisher, a research associate at the American Museum of Natural History's Department of Anthropology.

In her new book, *Anatomy of Love: The Natural History of Monogamy, Adultery, and Divorce*, Fisher says we get "high" when we fall madly in love because our brains produce a chemical called phenylethylamine, a natural amphetamine or central nervous system stimulant. This feeling of infatuation eventually wears off, not because that initial thrill is gone, but because the brain gets used to phenylethylamine, and endorphins eventually begin to act as a kind of light sedative.

Yet we humans are sexual creatures, no doubt about it, and the garden of delights available to lovers of all ages is illustrated by frequent surveys involving hundreds of men and women about how they would like to spend a romantic day and evening together. Among their favorites: a candlelight dinner for two, watching an oceanside sunset, and being snowbound together in a woodsy cabin.

There is no shortage of older people who are as romantically involved in their harvest years as they were when the corn was green. This is often the case where money and notoriety

The joys of a sumptuous picnic-for-two are ageless.

have replaced flawless faces and drop-dead-gorgeous bodies. Charlie Chaplin, Loretta Young, and Nelson Rockefeller immediately spring to mind, as do Sam Goldwyn and Barbara Hutton—and let's not forget George Bernard Shaw, who lived contentedly in a marriage for more than twenty years without sex (by mutual consent) before starting at age 65 a red-hot, ten-year love affair with a beautiful 24-year-old American woman.

You'd think Elizabeth Taylor would begin slowing down at age 65 after being married to hotel heir Nicky Hilton, British film star Michael Wilding, impresario Mike Todd, singer Eddie Fisher, Hollywood legend Richard Burton (twice), United States senator John Warner, and most recently construction worker Larry Fortensky—and these are only the men she *married*. Liz Taylor is still turning heads, and firing up imaginations from youngsters worrying about their complexions to oldsters pricing cemetery plots.

Leading Double Lives

T remendous recent advances in health care are permitting
untold numbers of grandparents and even great grandparents to lead double lives these days. They're still close to their
families, but because of death or divorce, are also single again
and dating. Up to now, there has been little but anecdotal evidence about the dating habits of such older people. But a
fascinating study called "The Nature and Functions of Dating
in Later Life," published in *Research on Aging: A Quarterly of
Social Gerontology and Adult Development*, has thrown some
surprising new light on the subject.

The study, carried out by Western Washington University
professors Richard and Kris Bulcroft, began by noting that the
subject of dating after 60 has largely been ignored. One reason
is "the perception that dating among the elderly is so infrequent that extensive studies are not warranted. Another is that
the low rate of remarriage among older people implies that relatively few of them date."

What the Bulcrofts and others have found is very different
from this stereotype. To begin with, older people are romantic
creatures who still get turned on by the opposite sex, and thrill
to each other's company. But what they're after is totally different from hot-blooded teenagers who've just discovered sex, or
the 20s and 30s crowd who are into marriage and starting a
family.

More than anything else, older people crave a "long-lasting,
gratifying, and intimate personal relationship," say the
Bulcrofts, "that will serve as a sexual outlet and a hedge against
loneliness." In other words, they want to "go steady" again.

The Plain Facts—and the Good News

The place of sex in older lives has been surveyed time and time again, and the results are fairly close from one study to the next.

➤ Well over one-third of men and women in their mid-70s, for example, say they are sexually active.

➤ The vast majority of older lovers say companionship is what they want most. About one in twenty give sex top priority.

➤ While the joys of a loving relationship, from simple companionship to the security of having a life partner, are paramount in older couples, physical intimacy is also important and enjoyed several times a month by those 65 and considerably older.

It's well known that older people must cope with physical and emotional problems unknown to the young, not to mention several powerful societal taboos. What an older man or woman wants in a partner, according to the Bulcroft study, is someone who's healthy, mobile, likes to dance, and drives a car. Someone who has these attributes, and the means to make them known to a potential companion, should have little difficulty finding someone with whom to not only "go steady," but to have sex (approximately 90 percent of the older daters the Bulcrofts studied "were sexually active with their dating partners").

Sexual activity in older people can mean anything from a hug and peck on the cheek after an evening of watching TV to intense physical intimacy right out of the Kama Sutra. All men may long to be nonstop lovers able to perform on demand, but as the years roll by, anywhere from 10 million to 25 million are dogged by some degree of impotence. And when they hit 60, an estimated one-third of these men have what a panel of experts organized by the National Institutes of Health called "erectile dysfunction."

This unhappy state of affairs is caused by a variety of physical and psychological ills including diabetes, vascular disease, high blood pressure, and neurological disease, along with the taking of either prescription or illicit recreational drugs (which alone account for about 25 percent of male impotence).

The good news from the NIH panel of experts in urology, geriatrics, nursing, psychology, and other specialties is that impotence can be treated with "a multidisciplinary approach." This treatment begins with counseling and psychotherapy, continues through injections with drugs or vacuum devices that increase blood flow to the penis, and may include the insertion of silicone erectile implants or vascular surgery.

Medical science is even energizing the sex drive, muscle strength, and mental acuity of older men with the help of skin patches containing the male sex hormone testosterone. Experiments done at Oregon Health Sciences University and St. Louis University with men between 60 and 89 show that testosterone patches made by the ALZA Corporation, applied at home and worn for sixteen hours a day, also have the potential to improve or even reverse frailty in older men.

To the Rescue!

It's well known that for a great many older women unable to find a suitable romantic partner, masturbation has come to the rescue. Noted sex authority and feminist Betty Dodson says "Sex for one is an erotic concept whose time has come. It can be a form of sexual self-help. It is safe sex. And it provides sexual satisfaction for people who are without partners."

Dodson's philosophy is embraced by a tall, blonde, attractive, twice-married 56-year-old woman I know who has endured years of semi-celibacy with the help of a battery-driven vibrator she calls "Rambo." When I mentioned this to another gorgeous blonde of about the same age, she said, "Tell me about it. My back yard is filled with dead batteries."

A slightly more adventuresome woman who was married for 26 years without experiencing an orgasm and had gone completely without sex for 5 years following her husband's death, met a man and decided to celebrate her 62nd birthday by going to bed with him. She arrived at his home with a glamorous new nightie, two pillows from her bed at home, two scouring pads (she felt his kitchen was untidy), a small magnetic stick-on plastic replica of a vanilla soda with a red cherry on top that she affixed to his refrigerator door, three whole wheat muffins, a cardboard heart decorated with rhinestones, and a vibrator (which she used immediately following her date's valiant, but apparently unsuccessful efforts at lovemaking).

Two days later, he received a handwritten letter from her thanking him for a delightful sleepover—and suggesting that his refrigerator needed defrosting.

Love's Unending Song

Older lovers engaging in high-speed sex can rejoice in a report in Harvard University's *Heart Letter* which says that "sex puts less strain on the heart than either mowing the lawn or making the bed, and poses little danger to heart patients returning home from the hospital." It then goes on to caution couples that, "Of the very few deaths associated with sexual activity, 78 percent involved extramarital sex." (Something to keep in mind!)

The delights of sex for those no longer young were recently spelled out by Georgia Witkin, Ph.D., an assistant clinical professor of psychiatry at the Mount Sinai School of Medicine. What she had to say must have boggled the minds of curious teenagers, while getting nods of recognition from those of us who knew it all along.

"Great sex," says Dr. Witkin, whose latest book is appropriately titled *Passions*, "is not defined by fantasies that come from nowhere to distract you, nor by instant physical arousal; nor by sudden spasms. There's another, gentler side to sex, which is more sensual and, therefore, more satisfying—

Late-in-life lovers can achieve intimacy and satisfaction unknown to the young.

and, thanks to the infinite wisdom of Mother Nature and Father Time, it gets better as we mature." This should lift the spirits of all of us in the homestretch of our lives.

A living example is the Hebrew Home for the Aged's 1,200-bed nursing home and Alzheimer's research center in the Bronx, New York. The Home gives its elderly residents permission to enjoy intimate relationships, and will even ensure their privacy. A nurse at the Home says when she first learned about this attitude "I was shocked. You don't think of your grandparents having sex."

But they do.

Here's what we have to look forward to romantically as the years roll by:

► **50s:** Many women find their sex drive intensifying, often including multiple orgasms, while men have more difficulty achieving erections and less pleasure in their ejaculations.

► **60s:** Men may have even more trouble getting an erection, and women in attaining adequate vaginal lubrication, which may lead to a decline in lovemaking. But extended foreplay and loveplay, which build intimacy, can be just as satisfying.

► **70s:** It can now take more than half an hour of physical and mental arousal before a man gets an erection. But the joys of lovemaking continue, since by now, couples are virtuosos at turning each other on, and sex is less "goal" oriented.

► **80s:** Lovemaking has now reached a level of physical and intellectual coming-together unknown to the young, growing out of years of loving companionship and the knowledge that their earthly journey together is drawing to a close.

The Flourishing Dating Industry

B ack in the days when we were hot-blooded youngsters, opportunities for girls and boys to meet, fall in love, get married and thus ensure the continuation of the species were arranged by families and friends, or simply occurred through chance encounters at clubs, fraternal organizations, school dances, church socials, and the like.

Today's megamatchmaker? The U.S. free enterprise system.

Singles bars used to dominate the romance industry, but no more. Now it's the video dating biz, along with professional matchmaking firms, which began by bringing straight white men and women together, but now specialize in doing this for members of all races, ethnicities, and sexual orientations, for the disabled, and even the May-September crowd (she's 55, he's 38). And we seniors are targets of opportunity—although admittedly a fair piece from the bull's eye—for this flourishing romance industry, where revenues can top millions a year.

Hundreds of video dating services with names like Great Expectations and the Romantics Development Corporation have blossomed throughout the United States. These firms act as high-tech Cupids, bringing clients of all ages together via video profiles in the hope that sparks will fly and wedding bells chime.

The romance industry's old guard consists of firms like The Patricia Moore Group, Inc., which says it's been

"California's Premier Introduction Service Since 1984." The Patricia Moore Group, which has offices throughout the state, arranges introductions between its upscale clients who pay an advance fee of some $4,000, even though only 25 percent end up stroll-ing down the aisle toward (hopefully) a lifetime of wedded bliss.

The idea of a flourishing, multimillion dollar, no-nonsense romance industry is absolutely mind-boggling (at least to an old hearts-and-flowers type like me), and to get a first-hand run-down on how it works, I asked Patricia Moore's sexy young marketing director Trish McDermott to join me for an early morning cappuccino at an intimate San Francisco coffee bar a block from her office.

The first thing I asked Trish was whether older people use her services. "Absolutely," she said. "Dating services aren't just for young people anymore. You can be looking for someone to round out your life at 25 or 65, although I admit older people are very surprised we deal with them. A lady will call us, and the first thing she'll say is, 'I have to tell you something, I'm 61.' And I'll say, 'That's fine, many of our clients are your age and older.' And she'll say incredulously, 'They are?'"

"It's easier to match seniors," says Trish, "because they're more relaxed, more willing to compromise than younger people who are goal-oriented, have a long shopping list of precisely what they want, and won't settle for anything less. It's almost like they're buying a car. Younger men look first for physical beauty, while younger women want men to be tall, and eco-nomically, socially, or politically powerful. And if they don't meet exactly the right person, they're eager to move on to the next introduction.

"If I tell an older man I have a woman for him who has everything he's looking for except she's short instead of tall, he'll probably say 'OK, I'd like to meet her' because seniors look for companionship. If they both enjoy golf, or love the fine arts, they'll delight in just being friends. Younger people believe it's a waiting game, and that if we introduce them to enough people, Mr. or Ms. Right is bound to turn up.

"A great many single people in their 30s and 40s have young children and from the get-go it's 'You like me, you like my kids.' Older people's children are usually grown and family is no longer their primary focus. With them, it's more about 'You and me. Can we enjoy each other?'

"Older people who've been married for a long time and are suddenly single often feel the entire dating world has passed them by. 'I was 21 the last time I dated,' they'll tell us, 'and now I'm 62 and have forgotten how to date.' So we'll give them some pointers. We'll tell them there's a lot of research documenting the fact that a man and woman form a lasting impression of each other in the first eight to ten seconds or so after they meet (which is just about enough time to say 'Hello' or 'Nice to meet you'). So we tell our clients to put their best foot forward. Stand up straight, dress your best, and for goodness' sake don't do what so many seniors do and talk about your last relationship. You know: 'My wife divorced me after 45 years of marriage.' That's a no-no.

"One thing we have noticed is the number of men between 55 and 65 who want to meet women in their 30s capable of bearing children. That's a very difficult search for us because it's nearly impossible to find a 30-year-old woman willing to date a 60-year-old man. We've done it, and we've gotten some married off, but it's tough going.

"We also get women who tell us, "I'm 55 and want to meet somebody younger because all the 55-year-old men I know are out of shape, have pot bellies, and I want a guy who's still active. I like to dance, play tennis, swim, do all of those things, and I'd really like to date someone younger." But it's even more difficult finding younger men willing to date older women, than younger women who'll go out with older men."

"Youth, youth, there is nothing but youth," exclaimed the ever-quotable Oscar Wilde in his classic novel *The Picture of Dorian Gray*, in which a painting of Dorian ages grotesquely while he remains forever young. Youth-entranced older men have long wooed and won much younger women, but only recently have women decided what's good for the gander is also wildly exciting for the goose. Nineteen-ninety census figures suggest that quite a few women are now married or living with much younger men and having the time of their lives doing it.

"Older men seem so authoritarian, so patriarchal, while younger men are kind of like happy puppies, pleasant to be around, look good, and if you like a sexual life you'll have a sexual life," says Phyllis Sidney, a 60-ish businesswoman who runs Los Angeles' December/May Club to help nonsmoking older women meet nonsmoking younger men.

A creative variation on dating services is "It's Just Lunch," which was started by Andrea McGinty, ex-marketing manager of a jewelry firm, whose fiancé walked out on her five weeks before their wedding. McGinty charges $650 for arranging eight "dutch treat" lunch dates for her young, upwardly mobile, intelligent clients (90 percent have undergraduate degrees and 80 percent have graduate degrees). These clients enjoy substantial incomes, but work long hours and "need help with their social lives."

McGinty's clients call in after each date to report on what they liked or didn't like about their luncheon companions, and the feedback is then used in arranging their next date. And how is McGinty's own love life progressing? Well, a little while back, a Chicago lawyer who had just signed up for her service asked McGinty out for a date. After giving it some thought she returned his fee and joined him for dinner. Not long after, they were married.

Capitalizing on the Hunger for Love

Dating companies that earn their livings bringing people together have been getting competition from businesses using romance to lure customers. These services run from friendship to fetish. A few examples:

Sandro's Italian Restaurant in New York has an oversized oak table called *il tavolo-degli amid* ("table of friends") for customers who don't want to eat alone and—who knows—might meet the amici of their dreams.

Laundromats are getting into the romance business by setting aside one night a week for singles. A female habitué of a New York laundromat likes to peek inside men's dryers to see what's tumbling. "If a man has matched towels it's a good sign," she says, "but a better one is Gold Toe socks."

Well-known and respected newspapers and magazines such as the *Chicago Tribune* and *Albuquerque Journal*, alternative weeklies in most major U.S. cities, newsletters for attorneys, teachers, and physicians, and college alumni magazines have been running personal ads for years and are cleaning up. And why not. "It's a cost-effective way to meet people," says one newspaper's classified ad manager.

This seems to be the case, indeed. I once talked with a 52-year-old Pennsylvania woman who divorced her alcoholic first husband after eighteen years of marriage (and six children), said goodbye to her impotent second husband after close to 3 years of a never-consummated marriage, and immediately started searching for hubby number three by advertising in the Personals section of *The New York Review of Books*. The ad cost about $50, and she received more than 200 replies from the U.S. and abroad. Talk about return on an investment!

There's a seamier side to the personals, of course:

Flesh-peddling publications such as the old *Police Gazette* and *Playboy* have been joined by a raft of nudie magazines showcasing luscious babes with their phone numbers. Among the newest of this genre are those celebrating vintage gals such as *Older Women Make Better Lovers* magazine, which features "Personality Profiles" of nude delectables, including 53-year-old superstar Delia Dawn.

Specialized publications such as the no-holds-barred *Washington City Paper* in the nation's capital are replete with hundreds of lovers-wanted ads such as "Sinful, imaginative, extremely sensuous, sexy, and beautiful dominant commands all true subservients to explore their submissive nature and experience exotic encounters with a powerful mistress.... Discretion assured."

None of this would come as a surprise to Germany's Beate Uhse, now 76, who was the first woman allowed to fly fighter planes in Hitler's Luftwaffe during World War II, and in early 1996 opened in Berlin what well may be the world's largest museum devoted exclusively to erotica. The museum, filled with an extraordinary array of pornography, sex toys, and lingerie, was financed with profits from Uhse's 50-year-old sex paraphernalia business, which racks up sales of more than $80 million a year.

Three Million Aging Gays and Lesbians

It's probably not an overstatement to say that until the generation which came of age during World War II, romance, love, and sex were thought of as something that went on exclusively between males and females. Gay and lesbian sex—Oscar Wilde called it "The love that dare not speak its name"—was safely confined to the closet, only to explode into the national consciousness almost overnight.

A weekly shopper in my part of the country is probably typical: its "Personals" column has been expanded to include "Women Seeking Men," "Men Seeking Women," "Women Seeking Women," "Men Seeking Men" and "Friends Seeking Friends." It seems it's suddenly OK to be straight or gay, with bisexuality coming on strong (comedian Woody Allen helped out by noting that bisexuality doubles your chance of getting a date on Saturday night). The American Psychiatric Association finally got around to declassifying homosexuality as an illness in 1973, and by 1997, *Time* magazine was celebrating homosexuality by putting TV actress Ellen De Generes on its cover under the headline, "Yep, I'm Gay."

The American Society On Aging recently hosted the first national conference of its kind on homosexual romance among the elderly. Called "Diversity With a Difference: Serving 3 Million Aging Gays and Lesbians," the event was attended by a larger-than-expected crowd of 250 people at San Francisco's Nikko Hotel.

Del Martin, 70-something coauthor of *Lesbian/Women*, described how gays and lesbians of her generation had to struggle to survive McCarthyism, purges of homosexuals from the

U.S. State Department and the armed services, and police raids on gay bars and private parties.

"Those of us who have reached old age in or out of the closet," said Martin, "are survivors in a society that still doesn't look as kindly toward old same-sex lovers as it does toward younger ones."

Martin stressed that despite many victories, society still discriminates against older homosexuals. She said, for example, that while bequeathing property to a spouse is taken for granted among straight married couples, she had to produce no fewer than eight documents when updating her will to name her lesbian partner as her beneficiary.

Martin cited figures gathered by the Older Women's League showing that women make up 85 percent of all surviving spouses over 65, and 80 percent of the elderly who live alone. "If our society were not so lesbophobic," she said, "lonely old widows might find satisfaction in a woman-to-woman relationship."

American society these days seems to reflect a kinder, gentler attitude toward gays: more than a dozen states have rejected prohibitions against same-sex-marriages, although Utah, South Dakota, Idaho, Kansas, and Georgia have enacted bans against them.

Discrimination against homosexuals of all ages should continue to evaporate, despite the 1996 outlawing of same-sex marriages by the Congress in a bill President Clinton signed in September 1996. Another bill outlawing job discrimination against gays was turned down by a hair, even though polls indicate that more than 80 percent of the public believe gays should be protected from employment discrimination. But the politicians' current rejection of equal rights for all under the

law is being attacked, and its days may well be numbered. You
can see this in ways both large and small, for example:

➤ On July 10, 1997, Hawaii began extending to gay couples the benefits enjoyed by married people. The new
law, the first in this country, gives any two adults who
cannot legally marry the right to share medical insurance, state pensions, joint property ownership, inheri-
tance rights, and the right to sue for wrongful death.

➤ Barney Frank is an openly gay member of the U.S.
Congress whose partner and lover since 1987 has been
Herb Moses, who works for the Federal National
Mortgage Association. The Clintons have had Barney
and Herb as their guests in the White House along
with married couples.

➤ The University of Chicago and Stanford University
now give gay and lesbian partners the same employee
benefits as married couples, as does the City of Denver,
and more than 300 U.S. corporations including
Eastman Kodak, Walt Disney, Xerox, Microsoft, and
IBM.

➤ Chelsea House Printers is bringing out a series of forty
books on gay topics for teenagers under the direction of
Dr. Martin Duberman, Distinguished Professor of
History at the City University of New York. Thirty of
the books will be biographies of well-known gays
including Noël Coward, Elton John, Gertrude Stein,
and Liberace, with the remaining ten books devoted to
health, social, and cultural issues.

➤ Nearly two decades after gay liberation first hit the
headlines in a major way, the transgender community
of men who prefer to be women and vice-versa is

beginning to fight for its place in the sun. Several thousand Americans have undergone sex-change surgery; perhaps as many as 60,000 more are considering it based on what psychiatrists call "gender identity dysphoria."

➤ June has been designated Gay Pride month, and most major U.S. cities hold annual festivals, parades, and marches to celebrate lesbian, gay, bisexual, transsexual, and transvestite lifestyles.

The Approach of AIDS

Claiming that we're in the midst of a "second sexual revolution" that has spanned the last 45 years or so, Drs. Samuel and Cynthia Adams have compiled the results of interviews with some 7,000 men and women about their sexual proclivities. These findings are published in the Adams' new book, *The Janus Report on Sexual Behavior*.

"The first sexual revolution was about 1948, after World War II, and was marked by the pill," explained Dr. Samuel Adams on NBC's *Today Show*. "People suddenly didn't have to worry about women getting pregnant. Then came women's lib. Then came gay lib. Then afterward, if you'll remember, came the Woodstock Generation where anything goes: the Pepsi Generation, and AIDS which frightened everyone.

"People started predicting the demise of American sex. We didn't believe that, and it turned out we were right. But people are a lot more prudent than before. If a man used one condom, he may now use two, while some women will use a diaphragm and jelly."

An event which was to strike terror into lovers of all ages, particularly in the gay community, occurred on October 2, 1985, with the news that 59-year-old movie star Rock Hudson had died of something called AIDS. Young people by the thousands were getting this deadly disease from the contaminated needles they used to shoot heroin and other drugs into their veins, and from sexual encounters unprotected by condoms.

The death of famed Russian-born ballet dancer Rudolf Nureyev from AIDS on January 6, 1993, provides an agonizing insight into the progress of this disease. Nureyev, a homosexual, apparently contracted HIV 13 or 14 years before his death in Paris at age 51, according to an interview with his doctor in the French newspaper *Le Figaro*.

Nureyev discovered he had HIV in 1984, but his doctor believes he contracted it 4 or 5 years earlier. Nureyev kept his deadly illness a secret, fearing that the United States, where he frequently performed, would not let him back in if it were discovered he was HIV-positive. Nureyev continued his career until the summer of 1991 when he began to visibly deteriorate, entering what his doctors called the "final phase" in the spring of 1992, when he was admitted to a hospital for an operation for pericarditis, an inflammation of the membranous sac around the heart.

Though desperately ill with only months to live, the great dancer found the strength to fly to New York to fulfill an engagement to conduct Prokofiev's Romeo and Juliet at an American Ballet Theater benefit on May 6, 1992, at the Metropolitan Opera House, where he received a thunderous ovation. He returned to Paris in July, experienced renewed symptoms of pericarditis, but refused treatment, deciding instead to rest at his home in the Caribbean. September found him hard at work choreographing a new production of "La Bayadere" for the Paris Opera Ballet, but illness forced him home once again, and back to the hospital, where he stayed until his death the following January.

An estimated 10 to 15 percent of Americans with HIV or AIDS are in the over-50 age group, and a quarter of those are age 60 or older. The primary means of transmission is through unprotected sexual contact. The National Association on HIV Over 50 was founded in 1995 to assume a leadership role in alerting often isolated and ignored seniors to the dangers of the disease, and can be reached through the Good Samaritan Project in Kansas City, Missouri. Arming ourselves with thorough information can make all the difference in prevention and treatment.

As discussed in detail in Chapter 3, recent progress in combating the AIDS virus is encouraging, to say the least. Doctors are predicting that the once-terminal virus may be largely eradicated by the turn of the century, thanks to new combinations of powerful drugs, which are finally bringing it under control.

An Honorable Pact with Solitude

Loneliness has been called a national epidemic by leading sociologists and psychologists, and the latest Census Bureau figures back them up. One-person households, says the Bureau, have risen from 9.3 percent of all households in 1950 to 23.9 percent today, and those most likely to live alone are people over age 65. Almost 44 percent of older homeowners live by themselves, and more than half of these are widows.

A great many Americans are obsessed by loneliness, as illustrated by the response to a recent *New York Times* editorial on the joys of Valentine's Day. No sooner had it appeared than Pete Beckwith of Lafayette, California fired off a letter reminding the paper that "There are legions of lonely people who, for one reason or another, are virtually always without love. There is no holiday devoted to them, their fears, their anguish and the strength they muster to meet each day which they know will be no happier than the last." He then went on to "propose that we establish a 'No Valentine's Day' holiday and extend a brief touch of understanding to those without love, who are much greater in number than you think."

Television is the "significant other" in the lives of most lonely older people, who undoubtedly feel much closer to the late Lawrence Welk (still going strong on TV reruns) than they do to the warm-blooded types they run into when they leave the house.

Older people are particularly prone to loneliness. One in ten Americans suffer from it, according to a study done at Northwestern University in Evanston, Illinois. Loneliness often results in depression, or alcohol or drug abuse, inevitably leading to poor health.

Michael E. Roloff, Ph.D., professor of communication studies in the School of Speech at Northwestern, says a major reason for pervasive loneliness in adults is the absence of a romantic relationship. "Because they find dating to be a highly anxious experience, they are then hesitant to attend social functions and ask for introductions to someone they are attracted to." Dr. Roloff believes these people can help themselves, however, by following a two-step solution. "Communicate your availability, and present yourself as a desirable commodity."

An unnerving "answer" to loneliness has blossomed in Japan: make-believe families you can rent by the hour. A company hires attractive men, women, and children, who go through two years of rigorous training in the basics of getting along with old folks—such as how to laugh at their jokes. After being thoroughly briefed on the backgrounds of their elderly clients, whom they lovingly address as "Mom" and "Dad," they are rented out at the equivalent of $1,100 for three hours. The company has a long and growing waiting list of oldsters eager to pay for several hours with an ersatz family, and is having difficulty keeping up with demand. This demand could increase dramatically, since one out of every four Japanese people will be over 65 by the year 2025.

To come back down to earth, one might heed the words of the great Spanish writer Gabriel García Marquez, from his book *One Hundred Years of Solitude*: "...the secret of a good old age is simply an honorable pact with solitude."

In his book *Feeling Good: The New Mood Therapy*, Dr. David Burns emphasizes that it's actually better being alone than with an unsuitable mate because:

> ➤ It gives you a chance to try new things that might not be possible with a spouse.

> ➤ It forces you to take responsibility for yourself.

> ➤ It helps you develop your personal strengths.

> ➤ It provides the opportunity to explore what you really think, feel, and know.

This is certainly true: solitude can be a growing experience, and needn't be synonymous with loneliness. Says writer Alice Koller, "Being solitary is being alone well: being alone luxuriously immersed in doings of your own choice, aware of the fullness of your own presence rather than the absence of others. Because solitude is an achievement."

One may enjoy solitude after having experienced a lifetime of love—just as a long period of solitude may not mean that love has passed one by for the last time. My wife had been single for some twenty years, and I for half that, when we met, fell in love, and have been reveling in couplehood ever since. Who would have thought that age can hold so many surprises!

Finding New Freedom

"For many women who grew up in the 1950s, the time after their children leave home has become their first chance to exercise a variety of options," say psychotherapist Diana Cort-Van Arsdale and psychologist Phyllis Newman in their new book *Transitions: A Woman's Guide To Successful Retirement.* "They can now concentrate on their own needs, pursue new careers, and focus on their relationships with their husbands in a different manner. Without their children, many women greet their future with relief as a time to find new freedoms."

One of these new freedoms, made possible by the fast-growing number of divorced older women with successful careers, is the decision not to remarry. "Our parents' generation stayed together to the bitter end." say Cort-Van Arsdale and Newman. "We have the option to begin anew." Another way to begin anew is to simply live together without benefit of clergy, which more and more older couples seem to be doing.

Many older women who have successful careers, a pleasant home, and friends with whom they can share intimacies, prefer to live alone. Their idea of a dreamboat is an elegant gent who will take them out to dinner and dancing on Saturday night, maybe sleep over, and then disappear the next morning after coffee and croissants until Saturday night rolls around again.

The Golden Girls

A long the same lines, widows who are past age 50 and have been on their own for an average of 12 years are as satisfied and optimistic about their lives as contemporary married women, according to a study conducted by Ohio State University and funded by the AARP Andrus Foundation. These widows learned new skills, became involved in new activities, and made new friends, all of which helped compensate for the loss of their husbands.

There are those post-menopausal women—Germaine Greer, author of *The Change: Women, Aging and the Menopause* (as well as *Daddy, We Hardly Knew You* [Knopf] and other works), is a marvelous example—who see the last third of their

Renowned feminist writer Germaine Greer, now in her late 50s, celebrates the options available to older women when they "... gaze outward, find the beautiful, and feed upon it."

lives as a heaven-sent opportunity to say "Goodbye and good riddance to men (all those weak, clinging gents who are drawn to beautiful women like moths to a flame).

"It came to me as a great surprise," Greer said in a *Newsweek* cover story on the joy of menopause, "that on the other side of all that turmoil, there is the most wonderful moment in one's whole life—really, the most golden, the most extraordinary, luminous instant that will last forever." She then goes on to insist it's men who are really the most upset by menopause.

"It was the men who decided that women who didn't want them anymore must be dead. Women didn't say that. Women were getting on with business, reading, thinking, gardening, painting, whatever."

Men are profoundly uncomfortable with this notion, says Greer. "They say 'But what about us?' I say, 'I'm not thinking about you. I'm not interested in you, you bore me.' They say, 'But we're in pain and we're suffering.' I say, 'Someone else will take care of you. Go to Robert Bly [an expert on men and their relationships], please. Don't waste my time. I know it's sad to be rulers of the universe. But spare me. We spend our whole lives worrying about you, and the great thing about menopause is that we can at last say, "We don't worry about you anymore. You'll be fine. Bye-bye."'"

While Greer's feelings about male clinging vines are undoubtedly shared by numerous other post-menopausal women, the same article suggests there are enough aging swash-bucklers out there to keep countless older women happily enjoying life between the sheets.

June Reinisch, director of The Kinsey Institute for Research in Sex, Gender, and Reproduction at Indiana University, says their research has found that with each passing generation, the numbers of women who find post-menopausal life sexually invigorating keeps growing. This conclusion is supported by

University of Chicago psychologist Richard Carroll, who says 65 percent of women in their 70s are still sexually active.

If there's a problem—and there is—it's that there might not be enough older men out there to satisfy all those lusty older women. Cruise lines offer free passage to attractive older men willing to show unescorted ladies a good time by fraternizing with them short of the boudoir, and professional dating services are now doing the same thing by offering free "scholarships" to gents 60 and older who agree to go out with their mature fee-paying lady clients.

But older women shouldn't worry about the shortage of older men, says Ken Dychtwald, Ph.D., in his book *Age Wave: The Challenges and Opportunities of an Aging America*, because the problem can be solved through "share-a-man relationships."

"In some parts of today's man-short elderly society," says Dychtwald, "a form of polygamy is already proliferating. As I have visited hundreds of senior centers and retirement complexes across the country, I have discovered that this practice is much more common than outsiders would ever suspect. I have been repeatedly amazed by how often a single older man in one of these environments will divide his time among several 'girl-friends' with the situation acknowledged either openly or tacitly."

Dychtwald tells the story a trip to Miami, where he bumped into his former high school math teacher, Ed Phillips, aged 67. Phillips had just appeared on a radio show featuring interviews with eligible older bachelors and ended up getting dinner invitations from more than 60 local ladies. Phillips said he was stunned. "It was like I had become the pasha of Miami!" And did he end up sleeping with all these women? "Usually not," he said. "Mostly, these were pleasant, intelligent women who were hoping for some companionship, an evening of lively conversation, socializing, and some fun."

Oh, yes. There was one thing more. A lot of these women, said Phillips, "were terrific cooks and prepared wonderful meals."

Investing in Friendship

I n our longing for the excitement of love and romance, it's easy to forget the value of the sheer comfort and companionship of good friends. While we inherit our families, our friends, whom we make through our own efforts and interests, often become more important to us than blood relatives.

As writer Nancy Thayer put it, "...finding a true friend was in many ways like finding a lover, or rather, not just a lover, but a true love. Chemistry was involved: it often happened at once, out of your conscious control, your body went ahead and did it for you, you liked the person at once, that was it. You met your friend and could tell her everything, hear everything, help and be helped."

Friendship, which writer Annie Gottlieb calls "the sweetest form of love," comes easily to children, as anyone knows who's watched two inseparable 8-year-olds. Life for little Mitsy and Cassandra just wouldn't be the same if they couldn't spend hours together sharing secrets, and the best part of Mike and Eddie's day is when they're kicking a ball around. If you're a kid, you really need other kids to pal around with who understand where you're coming from. This same need for friendship is still there when we're older, only it's tougher to come by. Can you see yourself spotting another senior and saying "Hey, want to play?"

Yet having at least a few good friends as we enter the homestretch of our lives is no less important than it was when we were just starting out. Perhaps more so because this is the age when lifelong friends and family members begin to move away or pass away, leaving us feeling isolated and alone.

Studies by innumerable experts, from the American Medical Association to the Duke University Medical Center, agree that people with close friends are more likely to survive serious health problems such as heart attacks and major surgery, and less likely to develop cancer, respiratory infections, and other diseases than those who are essentially on their own. Duke researchers actually found that people without a spouse or close confidant were three times as likely to die within 5 years of diagnosis as were patients who were married or had a good buddy they could turn to for affection, advice, and outright assistance.

There's a growing interest among today's seniors in getting back in touch with friends they may not have seen or heard from in years. Many begin their search by talking with acquaintances who may know where they are, checking with the high school or college the person went to, or turning to the national telephone directories on CD-ROM disks which can be found in most large libraries, and include everyone in the United States in alphabetical order.

There are also services specializing in finding long-lost friends such as the Old Friends Information Services in Orinda, California, Infoquest in Sandpoint, Idaho, and Find People Fast in St. Louis, Missouri. These services usually charge under $100 to begin a search, and an additional $50 or so when the person is found. This compares with up to several thousand dollars charged by private detective agencies.

"It's so easy to lose touch with friends—not to mention close relatives—that it's well worth revving up your courage and calling old acquaintances you may not have spoken with in years. It's surprising, the number of people who don't keep in touch with old pals because they've nothing particular on their minds and don't want to intrude. One friend of mine solves this nicely by calling and saying, "I just wanted to hear the sound of your voice," and then brings me up to date on what he's doing and asks me what I've been up to. The whole thing takes only fifteen or twenty minutes, and we're back in touch.

Society, thank goodness, long ago recognized the importance of friends in older people's lives, and offers everything from senior centers and church groups to special outings and service organizations dedicated to helping others, such as the Red Cross, Salvation Army, Meals On Wheels, or Big Brothers/Big Sisters. These organizations, most of which probably have a branch office in the city closest to you, can be a godsend because they represent an opportunity to get out of the house, help others, and make new friends, including those who are considerably younger with Triple A life expectancies.

Perhaps the last word on the subject is best left to German poet Johann Wolfgang von Goethe: "The world is so empty if one thinks only of mountains, river and cities; but to know someone here and there who thinks and feels with us, and who, though distant, is close to us in spirit, this makes the earth for us an inhabited garden."

Lover, family member, or friend, the people whom we carry in our hearts are life's premier investment and greatest joy. Truly, the gift that keeps on giving.

5

A PASSION FOR WORK

Work, the loveliest of all four-letter words, surpassing even the importance of love—most times.

—Tennessee Williams

Find something you're passionate about and keep tremendously interested in it.

—Julia Child

I'm 80 years old. I want results now.

—Leon Hess, owner of the lackluster
New York Jets football team, explaining
why he had just fired the team's head coach

In his fascinating book *Anatomy of an Illness*, long-time *Saturday Review* editor and all-round Renaissance man Norman Cousins tells of visiting the home of Pablo Casals shortly before the renowned cellist's 90th birthday. When Casals shuffled into the living room on his wife's arm in the morning, says Cousins, he was badly stooped and had trouble breathing, yet would always begin the day by sitting down at the piano. Casals arranged himself with some difficulty on the piano bench, then with discernible effort raised his swollen and clenched fingers above the keyboard.

"I was not prepared for the miracle that was about to happen," says Cousins. "The fingers slowly unlocked and reached toward the keys like the buds of a plant toward the sunlight. His back straightened. He seemed to breathe more freely. Now his fingers settled on the keys. Then came the opening bars of Bach's Wobltemperierte Klavier played with great sensitivity and control.

"Then he plunged into a Brahms concerto and his fingers, now agile and powerful, raced across the keyboard with dazzling speed. His entire body seemed fused with the music; it was no longer stiff and shrunken but supple and graceful and completely freed of its arthritic coils."

When Casals finished playing the concerto, says Cousins, "he stood up by himself, far straighter and taller than when he had come into the room. He walked to the breakfast table with no trace of a shuffle, ate heartily, talked animatedly, finished the meal, then went for a walk on the beach."

From Casals' remarkable rejuvenation, Cousins draws the conclusion that there may be no greater powers available to us than a passionate devotion, a strong sense of direction, and a fierce will to live.

Secrets to a Long and Happy Life

If there's a secret to a long and happy life, in addition to the obvious good health and financial security, it's got to be an ongoing dedication to something you really love to do. It can be running, needlepoint, volunteering five days a week at the Well Baby Clinic, restoring old houses—anything.

But the most rewarding activity of all, to millions of seniors who want no part of retirement, is to continue competing in the dog-eat-dog workaday world.

One of the greatest pleasures in my life is having someone say upon meeting me for the first time, "Oh, you must be retired." "No," I reply with carefully repressed glee, "I'm not retired and have no plans to retire. I'm a writer who not only works at it seven days a week, but gets paid handsomely for hiking through Mexico's breathtaking Copper Canyon, finding myself alone inside Egypt's Great Pyramid of Cheops, gazing down at Lenin's mummified body in Moscow's Red Square—or eating Chicken Kiev in Kiev."

Perhaps the single most important insight I've had in writing this book is the fabulous number of older folks who are still getting up and going to work every morning—and loving every minute of it. Like Bill Monroe who was 84 when he celebrated his 56th anniversary with Nashville's Grand Ole Opry by joining the Blue Grass Boys and belting out "Mule-Skinner Blues." And Antonina Turnkovsky, who began dancing in Kiev shortly after the Russian revolution, and today, at age 90, teaches at the School of American Ballet in New York's Lincoln Center. And let's not overlook Strom Thurmond, 94, who recently marked his 41st year as a United States senator from South Carolina. The oldest person ever to serve in either body of Congress, Thurmond was voted into another six-year term in the last Congressional election. The senator has been around so long, said one Congressional colleague, that his body contains parts they don't make anymore.

Talented older workers who stay on the job are becoming a valuable commodity in American society. We can see just how great their contribution can be by looking at Pittsburgh Mayor Sophie Masloff who, in her mid-60s, called herself "an old

Jewish grandmother," yet was running that bustling city with undeniable aplomb despite the usual economic headaches common to every American metropolis.

Mayor Masloff, whose formal education stopped with high school, relied on aides to handle hardball questions fired at her during public meetings and press interviews, and occasionally got flummoxed—she once referred to sexy rock star Bruce Springsteen as Bruce Bedspring. But Pittsburgh voters loved their first female mayor, who was sworn in on May 6, 1988 following the death of the sitting mayor, and who was elected to a full four-year term in 1989.

Then there's 75-year-old Armand "Val" Feigenbaum and his kid brother Donald, 70, whose pragmatic management savvy routinely saves big bucks for the likes of Union Pacific, Cummins Engine, 3M, and Citibank. The bachelor brothers are principals of the General Systems Company of Pittsburg, Massachusetts, which generates revenues of $20 million a year by helping its clients get rid of waste, saving them a bundle on inspection, complaints, and product service while enhancing customer satisfaction. Union Pacific has used the Feigenbaums' advice, for example, to slash more than $700 million a year in "failure costs" since 1988 by getting its people involved in improving the railroad's scheduling, maintenance, and customer service.

A totally different kind of aging pioneer is white-bearded, 83-year-old McKinley Crews, who runs his own farm near Florida's Okefenokee Swamp. Crews lives with eight cows and nine cats, and has no plumbing, bathtub, refrigerator, telephone, radio, or electricity. This means he must take off his bib overalls and hop into bed every night before sundown with, perhaps understandably, no lady in his life.

Another farmer who's running his own operation is the legendary J.R. Simplot, who is now pushing 90. Simplot earned billions selling frozen Idaho French fries to McDonald's, and an additional fortune after age 84 by investing in computer memory-chip maker Micron Technology. Simplot never finished the eighth grade, yet tools around town in a Lincoln with a "MR SPUD" license plate, and keeps a firm hand on his businesses while investing additional millions in everything from luxury hotels to cattle ranches.

The whole idea of people reveling in their work until it's time to go was touchingly told in Richard Meeker's book, *Newspaperman*, which describes a meeting between two top officials of Syracuse University and the school's greatest benefactor, 84-year-old billionaire newspaper owner S.I. "Sam" Newhouse. The meeting took place in Sam and Mitzi Newhouse's sumptuous Park Avenue apartment, and it was soon evident to his guests that the man they had come to see was desperately ill, with only a few weeks to live.

Newhouse paid no attention to his distinguished guests, being far more interested in a jar of candy directly in front of him. In an effort to ease the tension, Mitzi brought out some photos of a place she and Sam had looked at recently in Florida, and were considering buying. Mitzi asked her guests what they thought of the place, and something in the question must have gotten through to Sam. "He sat bolt upright, and for a moment, as if distilled by the ravages of ill health and old age, his essence issued forth. 'Mitzi, don't,' he intoned, 'I'd rather buy another newspaper.'"

A Bright Man

One pal of mine who's still burning up the track is Douglas Leigh, who turned Times Square into "The Great White

Douglas Leigh, 90, whose spectacular advertisements turned New York's Times Square into "The Great White Way" (shown here, the top of Broadway), and who is still lighting up Manhattan from midtown to Wall Street.

Way" back in the 1930s with his spectacular illuminated billboards.

Leigh's love affair with electric light bulbs—millions of them by his own count—began on March 4, 1933, in the depths of the Great Depression, when newly inaugurated President Franklin Delano Roosevelt assured a worried nation that "the only thing we have to fear is fear itself."

It was on that day 22-year-old Doug Leigh entered the sign business with his first creations—a 25-foot-wide cup of A&P coffee perched atop a two-story Times Square building emitting endless billowing clouds of real steam; a box of Super Suds producing 3,000 huge soap bubbles every minute; a clown pitching monster quoits to form Ballentine Beer's famous three-ring trademark; and a 50-foot-wide waterfall advertising Pepsi-Cola.

In 1937, Doug introduced animated cartoons brought to life by a bank of photoelectric cells in signs high above the street. His billboards featured pictures from scampering rabbits to dancing silhouettes of Ray Bolger and Fred Astaire, along with advertised products such as cigarettes, whisky, and magazines.

Doug created his most memorable sign in 1941: a Camel smoker high above Times Square blowing colossal smoke rings. This advertisement was introduced into twenty-two other cities across the country and lasted until 1967.

Following World War II, Doug leased most of the U.S. Navy's fleet of surplus dirigibles, attached lighted advertising signs on their sides, and flew them over cities for clients such as Ford, MGM, and Mobil.

Doug Leigh is currently using his imagination to revolutionize other aspects of outdoor advertising, including lighting up many of New York's most famous landmarks, including the Empire State Building and Donald Trump's 40 Wall Street office complex, which will finish lighting during 1997, as he celebrates his 90th birthday—with no thought of retiring.

Vintage Achievers

A noteworthy study on aging and work, sponsored by the Social Security Administration and led by Dr. Eileen Crimmins of the University of Southern California, found that the number of seniors who feel unable to work has been declining sharply. Dr. Crimmins reported that only about 20 percent of men aged 67 to 69 in a representative sample of some 12,000 Americans said they were unable to work in 1992, down from 27 percent a decade earlier. The participation of those 55 to 64, particularly men, actually began rising in 1995 because of the

surge in jobs created by the vibrant U.S. economy. This determination of so many older people to remain in the workaday
world where the action is has opened the floodgates to vintage
achievement. Just a small number of examples:

Mona Van Duyn was named America's first woman Poet
Laureate at age 71 following publication of her book *Near
Changes*. Her book explores the qualities of love in old age and
she was awarded the 1991 Pulitzer Prize for poetry. And
recently, Polish poet Wislawa Szymborska, age 73, won the
1996 Nobel Prize for Literature and its biggest-ever prize of $1.2
million.

At 70, Argentina's Dr. Rene G. Favaloro recently completed a ten-story, $55 million heart clinic—one of the most
advanced medical facilities in all of Latin America —where he
routinely performs several coronary bypass operations a day
(adding to the 13,000-plus he's completed since pioneering this
life-saving procedure). And when Russian President Boris
Yeltsin needed life-saving heart surgery, America's 88-year-old
Dr. Michael DeBakey flew to Moscow to examine him, and a
few weeks later returned to monitor his surgery.

Pilot/photographer/author Anne Noggle was in her early
70s when she put the finishing touches on her book *A Dance
with Death: Personal Memoirs of Soviet Airwomen in WWII* following four reporting trips to Russia. "These women are my
heroes," Noggle says. "They flew combat and shot down
German planes and bombed and yet were mothers and grandmothers. They flew four-and-a-half years of combat, just
slogging it out, day in, day out, living in dugouts."

Perhaps the most exhaustive look at older achievement can
be found in The Long Careers Study of some 150 men and
women between the ages of 65 and 102, performed by Dr. Lydia
Bronte, Ph.D. in cooperation with New York City's Phelps

Stokes Institute. Dr. Bronte's study, which has been published as *The Longevity Factor* by HarperCollins, was designed to find the answers to four fundamental questions:

1. Why did these people continue to work, given the fact that during most of their lifetimes retirement at age 65 was held up as an ideal?

2. What factors enabled them to keep working?

3. How were their careers structured?

4. What can we learn from their experience in a society which is increasingly long-lived?

Dr. Bronte found that these nonstop career people had several characteristics in common, including a love of their work, a determination to stay active, generally good health (70 percent said they exercised regularly), and financial independence.

The careers of these older people fell into three groups, which Dr. Bronte has named the Homesteaders, who stayed in the same occupation all their lives; the Transformers, who made one major career change; and the Explorers, who changed careers repeatedly throughout their long lives.

The Homesteader group consists of creative people with an "intrinsic variety in their work which prevents them from becoming bored or burned out." Examples are actors Jessica Tandy and Hume Cronyn, authors like Will Barnet, scientists like Dr. Barbara McClintock, institution builders like J. Peter Grace of the chemical giant W.R. Grace, and "extremely people-oriented" individuals like Mother Clara Hale, founder of New York's Hale House, which takes care of infants suffering from AIDS or addiction to drugs.

The Transformer group is composed of people whose true careers blossomed at different times in their lives. Early

Transformers such as actor John Forsythe found their careers within several years after a false start. Mid-Life Transformers like Richard Bolles, author of the runaway bestseller *What Color Is Your Parachute*, labored through several mid-life career changes before finding their life's work. Late Transformers such as *Saturday Review* editor Norman Cousins, whom we met a moment ago, are presented with an unexpected opportunity which moves them from one successful career to an entirely new one. In Cousins' case, it was a life-threatening illness which he conquered himself with the help of laughter and megadoses of vitamins. He devoted the remainder of his life to teaching this same technique to others.

The Explorers are individuals who keep working at a job until they learn all they can about it, or get a more interesting offer. Some Explorers, such as John Gardner, change fields as well as jobs, moving from university professor to president of the Carnegie Foundation for the Advancement of Teaching to Secretary of Health Education and Welfare to chairman of the Urban Coalition and, later, Common Cause. Still others, like Dr. Jonas Salk, are professionally anchored in one field while making significant contributions in another. Salk's primary field is medicine (he created the famed vaccine against polio), and he is continuing to work aggressively to push back the frontiers of science through the Salk Institute for Biological Studies in La Jolla, California.

According to Dr. Bronte, two of the most intriguing end results of her study are that there does not seem to be any fixed age at which peaks of achievement are reached, and "there is virtually no age limit for doing new things or going into a different kind of work."

"The importance of these conclusions in today's long-lived society," she deduces, "is that a significant percentage of the over-65 population may wish to stay active. In the future, we may need both to revise our ideas about the pattern of adult life, and to restructure the rules governing retirement and age-based participation in organizations and institutions to make them more flexible."

Since running a moneymaking business demands brain-power and experience more than youthful vigor, top executives can keep at it as long as they're having fun. Some may be ready to take a time out when they reach their company's retirement age, as Lee Iacocca did after saving Chrysler, and some may keep going until they drop, like Wal-Mart's founder and number one stockholder Sam Walton.

"The day I stop working I won't be here," exclaimed Dr. Armand Hammer, when he was Chairman of Occidental Petroleum—as well as a physician, statesman, and philanthropist. Armand Hammer finally "stopped" at age 92.

Artists at Work

"I'm not interested in the past. I'm interested in the future," the late choreographer Martha Graham exclaimed when she was 94, while dance critics were still calling her work "dazzling" and "electrifying." There's a picture of Graham seated on a canvas chair with her arms flung outward, her ancient body completely wrapped in clothes save for her exquisitely expressive face, as she rehearses her young dancers for their new season at New York's City Center. "She is old and physically frail," said one critic, "but a great artist, perhaps America's greatest choreographer."

Electrifying choreographer and dancer Martha Graham with a sculpture by Isamu Noguchi in Judith. *Graham was 57 during this 1950 performance.*

Agnes De Mille, another towering maestro of the dance, wrote a prize-winning book about the life and work of Martha Graham in which she compared the influence of Graham's dance theater to the Diaghilev troupe in its heyday and the

Grand Kabuki of Japan. "Hers," said De Mille, "is the single greatest contribution in the history of the dance."

Erick Hawkins, a handsome choreographer who was once married to Martha Graham, has his own dance company, and is hailed by critics "as a master of hurtling, high-energy dance of the sort generally created by choreographers a quarter his age." One reviewer raved that his newest work *"Each Time You Carry Me This Way* [is]…a bold new dance piece that exuberantly celebrates the human body in the extreme." And in the midst of all this, Hawkins still finds time to regularly write about the dance. His latest collection of essays is called *The Body is a Clear Place.* Russian ballerina Maya Plisetskaya is still at it as well, having danced recently in *Isadora* at New York City Center surrounded by lissome little girls who could have easily have been her granddaughters.

It's not surprising that Maya Plisetskaya, Martha Graham, and Erick Hawkins, who have enjoyed great careers and been bathed in applause, if not adoration, would want to keep going until they drop. Can you imagine a Bob Hope, Katharine Hepburn, or Sammy Davis Jr. hanging it up while they've still got something to give, and there's an audience out there eager to see them perform? Not on your life.

Seventy-eight-year-old Ernest Borgnine, remembered for his starring television roles including "McHale's Navy," was wasting away at home when his wife, Tova, said, "You're too young to quit the business. Get a job!" So his agent let the industry know he was ready to return to work, and Borgnine was soon playing the friendly doorman and surrogate father in NBC's *The Single Guy.*

"I feel great," said Borgnine. "I have a whole new life. Instead of sitting around spinning old yarns, I have new ones to spin."

Entertaining Careers

If you've got cable television, you've undoubtedly been exposed to MTV, which features nonstop videos of the hottest rockers from Madonna to House of Pain. Explosive energy, gorgeous young bodies, sexual acrobatics, and the whole thing in living color—and controlled by a multibillionaire grandfather in his mid-70s named Sumner Redstone, who also owns Nickelodeon, the top-rated children's channel.

Redstone, who started out as a Boston-based movie theater magnate, is credited with fathering the multiplex theater with its dozen or so screens, and is now going global with his entertainment juggernaut. Redstone's Viacom International, the parent of MTV and Nickelodeon, has introduced music television to more than 200 million viewers in some seventy countries (with plans to do the same for Nickelodeon), and has launched still more youth-oriented amusements, such as the VH-1 music video channel aimed at baby boomers. Redstone got a call recently from fellow multibillionaire media colossus Rupert Murdoch, 66, suggesting they sit down and discuss what they might do together to generate even more excitement in the entertainment industry. Murdoch's upstart Fox Network, offering shows such as *The Simpsons*, is currently battling to push past faltering ABC and CBS to take on front-running NBC.

Stanley Durwood, 76, took the helm of his family's Kansas City-based AMC Entertainment Inc. in 1960, and shortly thereafter began building some of the first multiplex movie theaters with an average of ten screens apiece. Today, AMC owns more than 1,800 screens, making it the third largest theater chain after Carmike and United Artists. Now, according to

Forbes magazine, Durwood is introducing a new idea—the megaplex—with twenty or even thirty theaters that seat between 100 to 500 people. The new theaters will feature steeply pitched, stadium-size seats that are more comfortable than anything currently available, bigger screens, and state-of-the-art digital surround-sound systems. One problem? Their cost. A single 250-seat movie house can go for upwards of $1.5 million, putting AMC Entertainment's cost per theater at a hefty $30 million plus.

Peter Sealey was a middle-aged executive at Hollywood's Columbia Pictures (owned by his old employer Coca Cola) when the movie giant was bought by Japan's Sony Corporation, putting him out of a job. Sealey returned to school, launched two small companies, and was enjoying the good life when Coke asked him to get back into harness as its director of global marketing. "I had a beautiful place on the ocean, a hot tub, Chardonnay," Sealey told *Business Week*, adding that he "was blissing out listening to National Public Radio. I totally believed I would never return to Coke." But he has and is having the time of his life in his 50s.

While it's not all that surprising to see older people running businesses, it's inspiring to see arranger and composer Johnny Mandell, soon to be 70, still busy in the pop music industry dominated by youngsters. Mandell began his career in the big band era playing trombone with Buddy Rich and Count Basie, and moved on to compose dozens of film scores, win five Grammys, and arrange music for superstars young enough to be his children, including Michael Jackson, Barbara Streisand, and Nat King Cole's daughter Natalie (who, thanks to the magic of multitrack recording, produced a top-selling album singing duets with her long-gone father).

Broadway superstar Carol Channing, now in her mid-70s, starred in "Hello Dolly" nearly 5,000 times. In a recent article in *Variety* magazine, she is pictured wearing little more than a white feather boa covering her still-dynamite body. When asked why she drives herself so hard on stage nearly every night, Channing said "It's happiness. What am I supposed to save myself for? Something I don't do that well, like tennis? Sitting on the beach? This is my pleasure. I'm using every facility my brain and body can give me, to the hilt—everything I've got that is strong and healthy. Now, what on earth is better than that? That's magic."

To Retire, or Not to Retire

G ranted, this passion to keep working isn't everyone's bag. When retirement age rolls around, countless Americans are ready to grab the gold watch and run: While only about one in ten men between 55 and 64 was retired in 1960, by 1986 more than three out of ten had vanished from the labor force.

Recently, though, it appears that more seniors are deciding to keep at it. "The trend to retire at earlier and earlier ages has ended," says Martin Sicker, director of the American Association of Retired Persons Work Force Programs Department. The reasons for this turnabout range from couples putting off starting a family (which means they've still got children to educate when they reach early retirement age) to employers shifting more of the cost of health insurance to retirees, giving employees a powerful incentive to stay on the job. General Motors health care costs total a monstrous $3.6 billion a year, or $1,200 for every automobile it builds in the

United States. This is more than GM spends on steel for each car rolling off the assembly line, a fact which prompted the company to tell its retirees they'll have to begin bearing more of this burden themselves.

Another reason older people are reentering the labor force is that we're living longer, making work an attractive option for those who want to remain part of the youthful workaday world, or who fear their lives may outlast their incomes, since only three of ten retirees now receive a private pension. "I have obligations," said legendary method-acting teacher Stella Adler at age 86. "One of them is paying rent. So I think that would postpone any idea of retiring," which she refused to do right up until a year before she died at her home in Los Angeles at age 91.

Today there are nearly two million idle Americans 50 to 64 years old who are ready and able to work, according to a recently-completed survey commissioned by The Commonwealth Fund, a New York-based philanthropy institute. "The excitement of this study is that the pool of qualified older workers is so much larger than anyone knew, and with everyone worrying about the labor shortages forecast for early next century, that's very exciting," said the Fund's senior vice president.

The Commonwealth Fund's study of older workers at Days Inn of America, Traveler's Insurance, and a British chain of do-it-yourself stores provides what it calls "the first detailed economic evidence that older workers can be trained in new technologies, are flexible about work assignments and schedules, have lower turnover and absenteeism than their younger colleagues, and are often better salespeople."

Days Inn is the world's third largest hotel chain, consisting of over 1,100 properties linked by a nationwide computerized reservations system, and its experience with workers 50 and

older parallels the study's findings with the other two companies. Days Inn found that older workers:

> ➤ Can be trained to operate sophisticated computer soft-
>   ware in two weeks, or the same time as younger
>   workers. This includes today's factory production lines,
>   which, thanks to the computer, require more brains
>   than brawn.

> ➤ Stay on the job an average of three years, compared to
>   one year for younger people. This results in average
>   training and recruiting costs for older workers of $618
>   compared with $1,742 for their younger colleagues.

> ➤ Take longer to handle each call coming into the com-
>   puter center, but they generate more revenue for the
>   company because they book more reservations.

> ➤ Are willing to work all three shifts.

Businesses such as fast food restaurants, motels, and super-
markets which have traditionally depended on hiring hoards of
young people are turning to older workers as the supply of kids
dries up and the aging baby boom generation is followed by the
far smaller baby bust generation. The government expects the
number of workers aged 25 to 34 to contract by 13 percent over
the next ten years. McDonald's is already feeling this new reality and has established a special program to attract older people
at a time when, according to another Commonwealth Fund
study, "business leaders and popular commentators are becoming increasingly aware that emerging labor shortages may
constrain future economic growth."

The study points out that in recent years, the U.S. economy
has benefited substantially from two historic demographic
events. The first was the tremendous increase in births which

occurred from 1946 to 1964, flooding the workforce with millions of baby boomers, and the second was the huge expansion in the percentage of women in the labor force, rocketing from 37 percent in 1960 to coming within hailing distance of men in 1996.

Partly responsible for this remarkable transition is the fact that in the early 1980s, according to *BusinessWeek*, the number of women earning bachelor's degrees began exceeding men for the first time in history, and has been widening ever since. This change in the status quo is finally beginning to show up in the workplace. *Numbers News* reports that in 1995, about 23 percent of working women aged 25 to 34 "had bachelor's degrees, compared with just 20 percent of working men. What's more," says the magazine, "the National Center for Education Statistics expects women to earn 55 percent of all bachelor's degrees over the next decade. That's some 1.3 million more sheepskins than those expected to be earned by men."

Now that the explosion in new workers is about over, says the Commonwealth Fund study, "demographic factors will be a less favorable influence on the economy than they have been in the past." The rush of baby boomers into the labor force is now finished, and the far smaller baby bust generation starting work could trigger the beginning of a labor shortage—the first boomers began retiring in 1996. To make this demographic crunch even worse, the overall percentage of women in the labor force has started backing off from its peak hit a few years ago, and will likely decline still further.

We seniors are the beneficiaries of today's no-holds-barred demand for labor. Numerous companies face a fall-off in their business if they can't get help. Many employers, from convenience stores to upscale health clubs, are advertising for people to fill entry-level jobs of every description. A good many are offering seniors just about any working arrangement they choose, including free shuttle bus service to and from work, convenient hours, and freedom from heavy lifting.

It's also thought that retirees are returning to work not because they need the extra money, but because it gets them back into the camaraderie of the workaday world, where they know they are needed. This trend should be with us for years to come in today's roaring economy, where unemployment is approaching a quarter-century low.

Keeping Our Eyes Open

At the same time, cash-strapped corporations are out to slash costs wherever they can and retiree benefits, along with the high incomes of senior executives, are prime targets. Ford Motor, like General Motors, spends more on health care than on anything else except steel. And the Federal Equal Employment Opportunity Commission is aggressively bringing age-discrimination lawsuits against employers such as the Kidder, Peabody securities firm which dismissed seventeen older executives making $100,000 or more a year, and replaced them with younger workers being paid a fraction of that. The basis of the Commission's suits is the 30-year-old Age Discrimination in Employment Act, devised to protect those over 40 from age-based firing or refusal to hire.

If there are other negatives to senior achievement, it's in big corporations where there are fewer openings at the top as cost-conscious firms slash millions of management jobs, or as older executives with seniority cling to their jobs for dear life as aging baby boomers struggle for a chance to grab their place in the sun. Can you see Mike Wallace, who's 79, giving up his Sunday evening star turn on CBS's 60 Minutes? Or Japan's great movie director Akira Kurosawa stepping aside at 84 to make way for a younger cinematographer? Not on your life. They're too good, too vigorous, and want no part of hanging it up while they've still got lots to give.

To deal with senior management's unwillingness to step down, some leading companies such as Monsanto, General Electric, BellSouth, and Pacific Gas and Electric are telling valuable employees in their 30s or 40s that they may have to stay where they are for five or ten years, or even for the rest of their careers. Management calls this "plateauing." To soften the blow, the impacted employees are often given more responsibility, the chance to master other jobs, and more money than people in that position got in the past, plus the promise that one day they may be moved up the ladder toward the top.

This struggle between seniors and juniors eager to replace them is front-page news in academia, where the percentage of professors 55 and older is expected to climb from one-third to one-half of the faculty by around the turn of the century. "Generational tensions abound in higher education today," says W. Andrew Achenbaum, Professor of History and deputy director of the Institute of Gerontology at the University of Michigan in its *LSA Magazine.*

Achenbaum tells the story of fellow professor Sidney Fine, "a living U.M. legend." Since joining the faculty in 1948, Fine has inspired more than 20,000 undergraduates with his passion for twentieth-century history, along with a score of well-known professionals who have emerged from his graduate seminars. Fine, a prize-winning author with a dozen books to his credit, is usually found in the school's Bentley Library when he's not lecturing, holding office hours, or listening to opera. Achenbaum says Fine is "enthusiastic as ever about teaching, as still vigorous and productive."

But it looked like he'd have to retire—until Michigan Govenor John Engler signed a new law abolishing mandatory retirement for tenured faculty in the state's colleges and universities. U.M.'s president gave a celebratory dinner for Fine, as others talked of some elderly tenured professors as "stagnant," "worn-out" and "disengaged." Not everyone at U.M. was happy that Fine had been saved from enforced retirement. And even Professor Achenbaum wondered if the new law would "force colleges and universities to deny tenure to promising scholars in order to pay the salaries of 'deadwood.' Would scholars in their prime, eager to take on leadership responsibilities, begin to sympathize with Britain's Prince Charles?"

A recent cover story in *Forbes* magazine claimed that the key to successful retirement is actually a flexible, set-your-own-hours second career. Journalist Carolyn T. Geer went so far as to say that "Despite all the age discrimination laws, employers are often motivated to get rid of older workers. They'll buy you out, they'll push you out, they'll eliminate your division. Long before this happens, you've got to develop a second job opportunity. It doesn't have to be in your current line of work, but it should use the skills you have spent a lifetime acquiring."

A New Meaning for the Word "Homework"

One recent change in the American workplace is tele-commuting, a godsend to the surging number of people—including many seniors—who no longer need to endure the hassle of going back and forth to work.

Link Resources, a New York-based research firm, predicts that the number of people employed by companies which allow them to work at home will nearly double from 5.5 million in

1991 to more than 10 million by 1998. And the U.S. Department of Transportation predicts that by 2002, an impressive 15 percent of the nation's work force will be employed by companies which allow them to keep in touch via telephone, fax, e-mail, computer, and only occasional face-to-face meetings. Companies with telecommuting programs range from American Express, Apple, and AT&T to Prudential Insurance, Sears, and Xerox, and the number is expected to escalate. While telecommuting unquestionably isolates home-bound workers from the friendship and spontaneous interaction with other employees, it's generally believed they'll be more productive, since they're less likely to be interrupted or distracted.

In his book *The Road Ahead*, 41-year-old Bill Gates, founder of the Microsoft Corporation and the richest individual in the U.S (worth an estimated $41 billion and counting), predicts that high-speed networks will allow workers to leave urban areas and telecommute to work from virtually anywhere.

I remember people scoffing at futurist Alvin Toffler for predicting in his runaway 1970s bestseller *Future Shock* that in the years ahead very large numbers of people would work at home. Now, he says, it's happening.

Toffler says that a fast-growing number of today's young people want no part of a hyperactive lifestyle. Toffler believes that in the immediate future, life for many Americans will be more home-centered, and that extended families will reemerge. By using today's exciting new communications technology, Toffler concludes, "very large numbers of people will do some or all of their work at home."

I've worked at home for years, and can completely understand why so many people in our knowledge-based society are doing it, and why today's communications technology is making it easier and more efficient to telecommute than to spend hours each week driving back and forth to the office.

Being able to work at home is a blessing to older folks, and is enabling more and more of us to remain in the workaday world with a newfound sense of well-being.

Out of Retirement and into the White House

Distinguished urologist T. Burton Smith, M.D. (whom we met in Chapter 3) had just retired to his lush estate in the midst of an avocado grove in the exclusive Brentwood section of Los Angeles when Ronald Reagan asked him to drop everything and move to Washington to become his personal physician.

In the book *White House Doctor*, which I coauthored, Dr. Smith tells how he put the joy of retirement out of his mind and agreed to serve as Presidential physician to Ronald Reagan, who had been a patient of his since before he was elected governor of California in 1966. Smith also returned to his old stamping grounds at Los Angeles's St. John's Hospital "to get more of the kind of experience I might need in looking after the president of the United States. I also realized we'd be the oldest doctor-president team in U.S. history since I was 68 and he was 73.

"I worked in the hospital's cardiac care unit, intensive care unit, and recovery room. I hooked up heart patients to electrocardiogram machines, and then read the resulting EKGs. I inserted intravenous drips into the veins of a lot of patients so I'd be proficient even in the middle of the night, or out on the street. I answered all the hospital emergency codes calling for doctors to rush to the side of patients having heart attacks. I did all this for about six weeks, trying to become more of a whole doctor and not just a urologist.

T. Burton Smith, M.D. (second from left) came out of retirement to meet the challenge of being President Ronald Reagan's personal physician. Here, the Reagans depart Bethesda Naval Hospital seven days after Reagan had major abdominal surgery.

"When my wife Kit and I finally left for Washington," says Dr. Smith, "I felt confident I could handle any medical emergency involving the president. But the doctors and nurses already working in the White House weren't so sure about me—their new 68-year-old boss.

"So to be on the safe side, and help put their minds at ease, I went on to finish two, three-day intensive courses at a Washington military hospital in acute coronary life support and acute trauma life support. It was seventy-two hours of non-stop reading, instruction, and then drilling. I'd pretend, for example, that I was the head of a team which comes upon somebody 28 years old who's been in a motorcycle accident. He smells of alcohol, can't breathe, and needs immediate care. So *boom*, I'd start giving everybody orders. You do this, you do that, until the patient is out of danger and stabilized. By the time all this was over, I was confident I could handle any medical emergency which might hit the President—and so was my staff."

Spicing Up Your Life with a New Career

"Older Americans will have the option of post-retirement careers," says *BusinessWeek*, and you can see the proof everywhere you look.

Celebrated photographer Cornell Capa, now in his 60s, founded New York City's International Center of Photography at Fifth Avenue and 94th Street in 1977, and in 1989 opened a multilevel branch gallery with triple the space near Times Square. The Center is the nation's leading ongoing showcase for the best in American photography, with regular exhibits featuring the work of Barbara Kasten, Alexander Liberman, and James Nachtwey.

Golf pro Gary Player, who since turning 50 in 1985 has not only been one of the hottest players on the Senior Tour, festooned with other golfing legends such as Jack Nicklaus and Chi-Chi Rodriguez, but has written a bestseller called *Golf Begins at 50: Playing the Lifetime Game Better Than Ever*. It's interesting to note that golfers 60 and older, according to The National Golf Foundation, make up only 15 percent of those who love the game, but account for 35 percent of the total rounds played on U.S. golf courses.

Its important to keep doing what you love to do, or even try something different you haven't gotten to yet. Helen Johnson of Greendale, Wisconsin went back to school at age 57 and became a teacher, and at 77 learned to operate a 12-ton truck. Before long she was driving south of the border to El Salvador.

Another adventurous soul, Rose Hamburger, who was taken to her first horse race in 1909 by her father, from 1915 to 1988 witnessed every Preakness Stakes and every Triple Crown winner, and on her 105th birthday began handicapping horse races for the *New York Post*. When told she might make the cover of *Time* someday, she said, "I'd rather be on the cover of *Playboy*."

"It Ain't Over 'Till It's Over"

Well, as we heard from Yogi Berra, "It ain't over 'till it's over," and nobody understands this better than older entrepreneurs whose work helps keeps them forever young.

White-bearded, 70-something Walter Lappert retired to the westernmost Hawaiian island of Kauai with his second wife in 1981, and for a while spent much of his time strolling the beach in a flowered shirt, shorts, sandals, jaunty white cap, and cane, accompanied by his dog Maxi.

Life was sweet—with one exception. He didn't like the ice cream there. So, calling on fourteen years behind the counter of his own takeout shop in Sausalito, California, specializing in French crêpes and later fish and chips, he jumped into the ice cream business. Lappert told a reporter for *Nation's Business* that it cost him $110,000, or most of his life's savings, to build a small factory and store to turn out exotic "super premium" ice cream such as guava cheesecake, Kona blue espresso, mango, poha berry, and Kahai Pie (a mixture of Kona coffee ice cream, chunky macadamia nuts, coconut and chocolate fudge).

Lappert says he sold as much ice cream in three weeks as he thought he'd sell in six months, and since then he's boosted his sales of both ice cream and coffee to $15 million a year. Things are great—again, with one exception. Lappert can't enjoy his own ice cream. He had to give it up five years ago on doctor's orders. He could eat the fat-free and sugar-free flavors he's started selling, but can't bring himself to do it, claiming it would be "like driving a Ferrari with gloves on."

Starting a Business of Your Own

One thing about going into business for yourself: if your name is on the door, nobody can tell you you're through. Just ask Muriel Seibert, the first woman to become a member of the New York Stock Exchange. Now in her 60s, she runs her own discount brokerage firm.

In a ceremony in the White House Rose Garden on May 12, 1992, President Bush presented Amelia B. McCoy, a white-haired grandmother from Lamar, Oklahoma, with the National Small Business Person of the Year Award for building Handmade Rainbows and Halos by Amelia, Inc. from $7.78 worth of ribbons in 1978 to a $5 million business employing nearly 450 cottage-industry workers.

More than 25 percent of Americans age 65-plus are self-employed, versus 10 percent of all workers. Most are engaged in service businesses or agriculture. The national landscape is dotted with senior entrepreneurs who started moneymaking companies, are still actively running them, and glory in the fact that they can keep working. No retirement dinner and gold watch for them!

"You can slow down, but you can't stop," said Alvin Cherekin, now in his late 60s, who was a top advertising executive for three decades, retired, and then a year later (after busying himself with Japanese gardening and his home computer) launched a new advertising boutique with a 46-year-old colleague. They named the firm Fresh Carats, Inc. after spotting a "fresh carrots" sign in the luncheonette where they were plotting their new venture, and in no time were off and running creating ads for companies making perfume and bridal gowns.

Studies suggest that people who decide to become entrepreneurs later in life will have their best chance of success in the following businesses:

► **Retailing,** which can reflect their special interests, from dress shops and equipment leasing to auto-supply stores and pack-and-ship services.

► **Food purveying,** from restaurants and cafés to fresh bread shops and gourmet delis.

► **Handicrafts,** such as macramé or artificial flowers, which can be operated from home.

► **Consulting,** in marketing, benefits, public relations, and other specialties which retired executives can also run from an office at home.

► **Business backup,** such as secretarial and messenger services, graphic design, and high-speed copying.

► **Hospitality,** via hotels, motels, and bed and breakfast inns.

► **Franchising,** which is popular with seniors who own and operate Burger Kings, Avis car rental shops, and other well-known businesses under the guidance of professionals who own the concept and name, and charge a fee for their use.

It seems that nowadays I'm surrounded by contemporaries who are hard at work running successful businesses of their own. One is a petite, gray-haired lady who owns a small motel on the Atlantic Ocean surrounded by a giant Days Inn, Holiday Inn Resort, and Ramada Inn. Yet she keeps turning business away from her place, which is usually packed with families who love the homelike rooms with kitchenettes, outdoor grills, and tables, hopscotch and other games for the kids, chaises a few steps from the beach, and a conviviality which brings the guests together as if they're part of one big family looked after by a doting mother hen.

A few blocks away from the motel is a little store called Happy Farms, open seven days a week, and owned by an older gentleman in a wheelchair. You no sooner enter the store, and catch his eye than he begins rhapsodizing about his fruits and vegetables, which he personally selects and sells with near-theological devotion. It is impossible to leave the place without armfuls of produce you never knew you needed—in my case, bags of mangoes, pomegranates, and kiwi fruit. Now *that's* a successful business!

The Woman Who Wasn't Born Yesterday

Most aging entrepreneurs throw caution to the winds and give their new business idea all they've got. Like Frances Lear, who was married for thirty years to television mogul Norman Lear (*All In the Family*, etc.), and in 1988 took part of her reputed $100 million divorce settlement and launched *Lear's* magazine "For the woman who wasn't born yesterday."

In her autobiography *The Second Seduction* (Knopf), Lear luridly described her devastating encounters with incest,

Frances Lear, founder of Lear's magazine "For the woman who wasn't born yesterday."

alcoholism, manic-depression, and suicide. *Modern Maturity's* normally reserved reviewer labeled the book "a jaw-dropping shocker, even by the standards of the fearless and outspoken Lear. In fact, sensitive readers should be warned that they may take offense at sections of strong language and scenes of sexual candor." Such disclaimers are not needed for books by most women approaching 70th birthdays.

Before her death of breast cancer in late 1996, I had the good fortune to interview Frances Lear, whom I found to be a trim, elegantly dressed woman with huge glasses, volcanic energy, and a nonstop ego. She listed herself on the masthead of *Lear's* as founder, and her most visible contribution to the magazine during the years it was published was her monthly "Lunch" column in which she dined at a plush Manhattan eatery with well-known figures such as public opinion pollster Peter Hart. "Lunch" had a Q&A format orchestrated by Lear.

A typical exchange:

>   Lear: Peter, if you had your druthers, if you could redo
>   the world, what would you do?
>   Hart: What is this? Are you giving me a magic wand?
>   Lear: Yes. Wave it.

I was ushered up to Lear's sitting room office by her assistant, a robust young man whose desk was in a little alcove from which he could keep an eye on her. Lear began by saying she was exactly the person I'm writing about in this book devoted to people 50 and over who are having the time of their lives.

"I'm 69 years old," she said. "I have a career I love, I've had two face lifts, and I'm in the midst of a love affair (which, by the way, is wiser than marriage). I have a hundred million things that I didn't have before, but I also have pain. Physical pain, and mental pain. I may be suffering more now than I ever have before—at moments. But of course I'm happier now than I've ever been before.

"What I feel more than anything else about age," concluded Lear, "is that we should ignore it."

6

THE AGELESS DOLLAR

*Money is like a sixth sense, without which you cannot
make complete use of the other five.*
                    —W. Somerset Maugham

The most popular labor-saving device is still money.
                    —Phyllis George

I've been rich, and I've been poor—and rich is better.
                    —Mae West

I t was way back in 1946 that a struggling middle-aged New
York City pediatrician named Benjamin Spock published a
book called *Dr. Spock's Baby and Child Care*, which cost 25 cents.
The book has since sold more than 46 million copies, making it
the world's number two bestseller after the Holy Bible.

Dr. Spock, now 94, receives about $150,000 a year in royal-
ties from his book, which is scheduled to be revised for the
seventh time in 1998, and which, together with other income,
is enough to allow him and his second wife Mary (who was 2
years old when his famous book came out) to live royally.

Some 10 million Americans age 50-plus have enough
money so they'll never have to work again, and are free to
pursue just about any lifestyle which suits their fancy. Dr. Spock

Though he was once a struggling pediatrician, Benjamin Spock's book Dr. Spock's Baby and Child Care *now has sales second only to the Holy Bible.*

and his wife spend much of their time living aboard sailboats in Maine and the Virgin Islands.

Older Americans across the board are becoming more financially secure, according to figures released by the Census Bureau in late 1996, showing that the poverty rate for those 65 and older had dropped to the lowest level since 1952, when the Bureau began measuring oldster's poverty. Today's seniors have the lowest percentage of poor people of any other group in the nation, largely because of Social Security and private pensions. Census Bureau figures show that while 35.2 percent of the nation's elderly were considered poor in 1959, that figure had plummeted to 10.5 percent in 1995.

It's fascinating to look at how the increasing number of well-to-do seniors deploy their wealth—and attendant notoriety, from affairs with sex kittens (film great Charlie Chaplin was a virtuoso at this, finally marrying famed playwright Eugene O'Neill's daughter Oona when she was 18 and he was 54), to country boy Joseph A. Hardy, who founded the

84 Lumber Co. Several years ago, at age 69, Hardy started doing wild and crazy things, including shelling out $170,000 to buy the English title Lord of the Manor of Henley-In-Arden, plus another $10 million to snap up a mixed bag of modern art by Norman Rockwell, Andy Warhol, and Pablo Picasso, among others.

Money holds a special place in the lives of older people, since it puts raw financial power at our disposal at a time when our physical power, not to mention youthful good looks, are beginning to fade. And at no time have our financial options been greater than they are today. This is not to say that everyone who is financially secure, or even big rich, is happy. The authors of books on Bette Davis, Jackie Gleason, and Marilyn Monroe claim all three were dreadfully unhappy; Ms. Monroe killed herself with an overdose of sleeping pills at age 36. Oil king J. Paul Getty, called "the richest man in the world" when he died at age 83, was quoted by a biographer as saying "I never enjoyed making money, never intended to make a lot of it. Money doesn't necessarily have any connection with happiness. Maybe with unhappiness."

One older entrepreneur who got his big payday fairly late in life is 70-something Jerome H. Lemelson, who lives near Lake Tahoe, Nevada, and has been an independent inventor all of his adult life. Lemelson holds more U.S. patents than anyone else in history except Thomas H. Edison, and Edwin H. Land, known for inventing instant photography. Lemelson's five hundred-odd patents have earned him in excess of $200 million in worldwide royalties, which could eventually approach $1 billion as electronics and automobile companies which stole his inventions continue to pay up following his threats to sue.

The two biggest purloined patents? His automated manufacturing system integrating video images and computers to guide robots working on an assembly line, and the intermittent windshield wiper, which is now standard equipment on most of the world's cars.

"Where the Money Is"

W hen famed holdup man Willie Sutton was asked why he robbed banks, he replied, "Because that's where the money is." Here in the United States, the money is with older people, whose wealth is far greater than that controlled by their juniors.

The relative affluence of older Americans is laid out in an article in *American Demographics* by Wake Forest University Professor of Sociology and Public Health Sciences Charles F. Longino, Jr., and William H. Crown, director of policy studies at the Policy Center on Aging at Brandeis University's Florence Heller School of Social Welfare.

Longino and Crown found that elderly Americans control a substantial and increasing portion of the nation's wealth, which they base on Census Bureau figures showing that median household net worth begins at $57,500 for those 45 to 54, hits its stride at just over $80,000 for those 55 to 64, tops out at about $83,500 for those 65 to 69, declines slightly to $82,100 for those age 70 to 74, and then sharply decreases to $61,500 for those 75 and older. While these figures are several years old, the market value of all their assets minus all debts has undoubtedly increased while its distribution has likely remained the same.

One fascinating fact unearthed by Longino and Crown is that two percent of the wealthiest older people have family incomes that are actually near or below the poverty line. The reason is that they have valuable homes or land filled with

memories which they absolutely refuse to sell, making do with
Social Security, or whatever other money they have coming in.

A strategy these seniors can use to keep their homes until
the day they die, while simultaneously selling them for money
to improve their standard of living until that day arrives, is via
something called a reverse mortgage. Reverse mortgages are
becoming increasingly popular with older people who are richer
in real estate than in greenbacks.

A couple 62 or older can contact a reverse mortgage specialist such as the Capital Holding Corporation of Louisville,
Kentucky (the nation's largest), who will pay an initial fee of 10
percent on a $100,000 house. The homeowners can then opt to
receive either a monthly check based on their life expectancy,
or a check plus a cash reserve they can draw on in case of emergency. If the monthly payment received under a reverse
mortgage is simply too low to make a difference in the couple's
standard of living, they can always sell the house outright.

The poorest 20 percent of older American households have
an average net worth of about $3,400, and are heavily depen-
dent on government largess and charity, while the richest 20
percent are worth almost ninety times as much and are of lip-
smacking interest to purveyors of designer fashions, luxury
cruises, gourmet food and drink, and similar hallmarks of affluence.

Older people do not fare so well when their incomes, as
opposed to their accumulated wealth, are compared with those
a fraction of their age. But even here the situation is not as lop-
sided as it appears at first glance. While the median income of
households headed by people age 65 and older is only about 40
percent of those age 45 to 54, the older people have higher per
capita discretionary incomes since there are fewer of them per
household.

One powerful way they deploy this wealth is described by bestselling author Michael Lewis in his book *The Money Game*. Lewis notes that people over 65 "control 40 percent of the nation's stocks and mutual fund shares. Their tastes, preferences, beliefs and superstitions decide who has access to money and who does not. Old people might not move so well themselves," Lewis concludes, "but if they decide all at once they like a company, they can send its stock up like a shot through the roof."

The same phenomenon applies, by the way, to fabulously rich older people whose names are immortalized by their generous gifts to nonprofit institutions. Getty, Guggenheim, and Whitney spent millions building great art museums, Coca-Cola's Robert W. Woodruff gave a record-shattering $105 million to Atlanta's Emory University in 1979, and Inductotherm Industries' Henry W. Rowan and his wife Betty gave a runner-up $100 million to little Glassboro State College near their hometown in New Jersey. The college has since been renamed in the Rowan's honor.

Aging multimillionaires Herbert Simon and his brother Melvin could be blissfully retired in a chateau in the south of France surrounded by chorus girls and the world's greatest wine cellar. But instead they've just spent nearly five years building the new $625 million Mall of America ten miles from Minneapolis, which immediately entered the record books as the nation's largest shopping emporium.

Packed into space equivalent to fifty-two football fields on four floors are 400 specialty stores, dozens of restaurants, five nightclubs, a two-story 18-hole miniature golf course, a roller coaster, a waterfall, a log flume ride, a 14-screen movie house, plus twenty-four other attractions including a 300-foot long walk-through aquarium. With all this going for them, the

Simon brothers figure it should be a cinch to get 40 million people a year to stroll through their megamall, which is about as many as visit the world's number one tourist attraction—Walt Disney World in sunny Florida.

Staying Solvent after Retirement

Older people are eager to remain happily solvent after they've stopped working, and the best way to do that, according to an article in *The Wall Street Journal*, is to invest heavily in stocks which offer the best chance of beating inflation because they can generate significant capital gains over time.

This is certainly not the conservative advice usually offered to older folks, who are urged to invest in bonds and certificates of deposit because they produce a dependable monthly income without the daunting price fluctuations inherent in common stocks. The stock market dropped 29 percent in 1962, for example, after President John F. Kennedy attacked the steel companies for raising prices, lost nearly half its value in 1973-74 when the Arab oil embargo lit a fire under inflation, and slid 20 percent in 1990 after Iraqi invaded oil-rich Kuwait.

The trouble with fixed-income investments, says the *Journal* and the experts it quotes, is that the value of a retiree's fixed income investments gradually decline because of the money taken out each month to help meet living expenses, plus the inevitable erosion of the portfolio's value because of inflation.

A better approach is for retirees to pursue one of two alternative strategies:

Investment strategy number one calls for putting 54 percent of your money in stock funds, 36 percent in bond funds, and the remaining 10 percent in a money market fund on which you can write checks. You would also invest in short-term interest-bearing securities so you can ride out a bear market without cashing in any shares in your funds.

Investment strategy number two suggests older folks should forget about money market funds, which tend to offer modest returns, and invest only in stock and bond funds on a 50/50 basis (which may be varied depending on market conditions). Income and capital gains distributions from your funds should be reinvested in additional shares, and you can get any spending money you need each year by redeeming shares in your funds. If there's a market crash, sell shares in the fund that's held up the best—probably one of your bond funds. (See Appendix for resources of information about investments.)

While writing this book, I spent hours with one of Wall Street's aging high-rollers whose name is on and off *Forbes* magazine's list of the 400 richest Americans. This man made his vast and still-growing fortune by taking big risks and selling other wealthy individuals on doing the same through his company, which he likens to the private venture capital firms run by the Rockefellers, Whitneys, and other members of the old-money establishment. These super-rich families set up their own venture capital firms such as the Rockefellers' Venrock Associates to invest part of the family's fortune in high-risk companies whose shares stand a good chance of skyrocketing from, say, $10 to $100 when they're sold to the public, thereby keeping the family's coffers constantly replenished.

This game is far too rich for the average investor, particularly for older folks living on relatively fixed incomes. U.S. Savings Bonds, money market funds, or short term bond funds make more sense. But if you have a few thousand dollars to risk, and want to put a little sizzle in your life, you might consider investing in shares of something like a fund specializing in small and medium-sized growth companies—meaning relatively young outfits that are growing rapidly and profitably and are becoming leaders in their markets as a result of proprietary technology or know-how. There are quite a few aggressive, fast-growing stock funds out there to choose from, and it makes sense to consult your broker before placing your bets. (See Appendix for more about investment options.)

One irrefutable way to be financially secure in retirement is to significantly reduce your expenditures. An article in a 1996 issue of *Money,* "You Can Afford the Lifestyle You Want...," stated, "Forget the old myths. You can live just fine on less than 70 percent of your pre-retirement income—with a minimum of pain." The magazine quotes a recent *Money*/ABC Consumer Comfort Index which found that "...fully half of Americans aren't sure they will retire with enough income and assets to last for the rest of their lives." So what's the secret? Simply "...identify the central interests in your life and then sharply reduce expenditures for everything else."

Time Dollars

There's no shortage of ways seniors can make money with money. But another kind of "money" that's of growing interest to many older people these days is often called Time Dollars, which are already being put to work in many states under the auspices of senior centers, churches, community colleges, and similar neighborhood groups.

What's nice about Time Dollars is that they're immune to inflation, recession, taxation, and government budget cuts.

They're also invisible, because they're really service credits that provide people with a bookkeeping kind of purchasing power they receive in return for helping others.

Daisy Alexander, for example, who lives in a seniors' housing complex across the street from an elementary school, earned Time Dollars by tutoring kindergarten youngsters. She earns a Time Dollar for every hour she's with the youngsters, and deposits the "money" in an account run by a consortium of local volunteer organizations. Alexander, who needs a cane to get around, will often use Time Dollars she's earned to pay a friend to do her shopping. The friend can then turn around and spend the credits to get things she needs: anything from repairs to her home to looking after her pet dog or cat.

"Time Dollars," says the college professor who generated the idea, "are not used to buy commercial products, but instead reward what neighbors and families used to do for each other for free." They help people get things they might not otherwise be able to afford, affirm self-worth, and assist neighbors in forming a more tightly knit community.

As French actress Sara Bernhard put it, "Life begets life. Energy creates energy. It is by spending oneself that one becomes rich."

Funny Money

Aging comedian "Professor" Irwin Corey, who appears on stage with wildly disheveled hair, a frock coat down to his knees, a droopy black string tie, baggy pants, and dirty sneakers far too big for his feet, has a novel attitude towards money matters.

Comedian Prof. Irwin Corey, self-styled "world's foremost authority," ready to expound on his top-secret strategy for living a long and happy life.

On a trip to Bermuda, Corey walked into the restaurant of a posh hotel, picked up an old *Ladies Home Journal* laying on a coffee table, cradled it in his arm like a menu, stationed himself at the restaurant door, and began showing people to various tables after making sure to ask every guest arriving alone, "How many are you?"

One of Corey's funniest bits is his financial advice to his fellow seniors: "You shouldn't earn more than you can spend," he says, "but spend more than you earn and die in debt. Now, if you owe a lot of money you're going to live long; I mean the people you owe it to are going to make sure you live long. If you're 75 and owe $300,000, you're doing good. Because to pay off that loan at $30,000 a year with accrued interest would take you about 18 years, which means you'll actually live to be 93. So borrow, keep borrowing. Start with your friends. Borrow from them. And when they ain't got any more money make new friends. But keep borrowing."

All Older People Are Not Alike

Until fairly recently, businesses lumped older people together, while spending millions investigating how the consumption patterns of younger consumers differed from one year to the next. And they did this even though everyone knows, or should, that today's seniors are the wealthiest Americans in history. The median household wealth for homes headed by seniors is about $90,000, compared with less than $40,000 for Americans as a whole. Not only that, but those 65 and older, as we've seen, own most of the nation's financial assets (running into the trillions) which will be passed down to their children—the baby boomers—in the next 25 years or so.

While we 50-plus consumers have yet to get the attention of our offspring, we've at least been divided up into the following three groups, with another surprising group coming on strong:

Men and women age 50 to 65 are, for the most part, working and financially well-fixed. *Newsweek* magazine recently portrayed them as "intelligent, attractive, vital—and astonishingly enough, sexy and hip." Thank you, *Newsweek!*

People age 65 to 75 include what one analyst calls "self-compensators" who never got a chance to enjoy life when they were young, and feel it's finally time to kick up their heels. They represent an ideal market for extravagant, attention-getting products from sports cars to luxury cruises.

Those from 75 to 85 are beginning to slow down, and are top prospects for health care and leisure activities, and are major buyers of services they no longer want to provide for themselves, such as cleaning the house, mowing the lawn, or cooking meals.

The latest analysis of the 50-plus market focuses on consumers 85 and older, whose numbers are growing faster than any other segment of the population. Estimates are that their numbers increased from 123,000 in 1900 to more than three million today, and will quadruple to in excess of 12 million by 2040.

Most of these future elderly folks are today's baby boomers, who will begin arriving on Golden Pond between 2030 and 2035, when they'll reach 80 to 85. America, look out!

Wooing Affluent Oldsters

"Forget yuppies. Forget teeny-boppers. Tomorrow's most sought-after consumers will be well-off older people—woopies," headlines the *Economist*. "The over-50s," says the magazine, "already have as much discretionary income, money left over after necessities are taken care of, as all other age groups put together—around $150 billion in America, or half the country's total. As it expands, the worldwide woopie market will be measured in trillions of dollars."

Business has finally awakened to the fact that millions of older people are loaded, though this sector of the population is all too often overlooked. A recent study done by New York's Fordham University showed that 50 to 64-year-olds feel ignored by advertisers, those over 65 often feel insulted, and all of them feel isolated, even though they buy 43 percent of all automobiles (the average Cadillac buyer is 57), frequently dine out or buy takeout, and spend more than any other group on recreation and travel.

Yet Madison Avenue continues to treat us as pariahs because they're absolutely convinced only younger people are willing to try new products. "We don't really need anyone over 50 years of age," commented 45-year-old Jamie Kellner, ex-president of Fox Broadcasting. "In four years," he added, to prove his point, "my number will no longer count with advertisers."

In an effort to find out if advertisers really are hostile to older consumers and their billions, I talked a while back with Fred Danzig, contributing editor of *Advertising Age*.

Fred Danzig is a tall, trim, easygoing family man who's spent more than thirty years with *Advertising Age* and said he had no plans to retire anytime soon. "Until fairly recently," said Danzig, "Madison Avenue was almost completely focused on consumers 18 to 34 years old, but now that's changing and the so-called youth movement is being superseded by the graying of America.

"In high-volume package goods such as chewing gum, soap, aspirin, and toothpaste, where advertisers don't think anything of paying $80,000 to run a 30-second commercial, they always go for high-volume sales when they plan their television commercials. In the case of toothpaste, they've tried to get young mothers to buy Crest, Colgate, Ultrabrite, etc. for their growing families. But now, perhaps imperceptibly, the creative approach is changing to commercials that aren't age-specific. They may not show people at all, but rather visual symbols reinforced with a voice-over. You'll see the tube of toothpaste being applied to a toothbrush, or diagrams of cavities, but you won't see just young mothers because they're trying to capture as many viewers as possible of all ages.

"As the aging process has taken hold in this country," said Danzig, "advertisers have recognized that retired people have a lot of money to spend on things like travel. So you may see an ad for a cruise line showing older couples strolling along the promenade deck of a ship with a young honeymoon couple walking right behind. This is part of Madison Avenue's effort to capture the older television viewer's attention—and money—while picking up a residue from the younger market.

"Then there are products such as denture cleaners that have been traditionally aimed at older consumers, but are now being advertised much more aggressively as the senior population has exploded. Not only that, but a steady stream of new products, from bladder control undergarments to battery-powered scooters, is now being heavily advertised to this fast-growing market.

"So older consumers are getting more attention from the advertising industry," continued Danzig, "whose leading figures are usually middle-aged themselves. Advertising industry banquets where awards for creative work are handed out are usually dominated by distinguished older people with great pedigrees, with people in their 20s and 30s peppered somewhere around the room. The young people coming in are working alongside older colleagues running the business, and are particularly good at doing things like TV commercials for youthful fashions, etc., with the quick cuts, the rock, and the rap, and all that.

"But it's dangerous for advertising people 50 and over if they're on the creative side," said Danzig, "because if they lose their jobs it's very hard for them to get back in the business. Advertising agencies are notorious—particularly during recessions—for saving money on payroll by giving high-salaried older people early retirement so they can go out and hire green people in their 20s.

"The older guy in his early 50s who's been let go figures he's got another ten good years left in him, so he bounces around with a wonderful portfolio of work. But he can't get a job because no agency wants to take on a high-salaried guy with costly fringe benefits. He's out of luck, so he becomes a creative consultant, does freelancing, or retires to the country and opens up an antiques store.

"The advertising industry hasn't yet recognized those of us 50 and older for the huge market we are today, and will be even more so tomorrow. Whoever eventually does is a shoo-in for the Advertising Hall of Fame."

Hunting for James Dean and I Love Lucy

T he television networks have at long last started appealing to older audiences—who watch a lot more television than youngsters—by bringing back such grizzled favorites as Ben Matlock, Perry Mason, and Lieutenant Columbo. These old-timers racked up substantially better ratings than a lot of jeans-and-jiggle shows targeted at young consumers. But since young viewers are known to be more willing to try new products than their elders, and since they represent tomorrow's adult consumers, television producers keep trying to create shows that will grab and hold their attention.

I wanted to learn more about television's attitude toward older viewers, so after leaving Danzig's office in The Daily News Building across from Grand Central Station, I walked up Fifth Avenue to the new Museum of Television & Radio to talk with its resident TV expert Ron Simon.

The museum is the nation's greatest repository of television memorabilia and the facilities to view it. Before we got down to what I wanted to talk about, Simon was regaling me with little-known but fascinating stories about the early history of America's most powerful mind-altering medium (the hosts of CBS's early morning *Today Show* even call their show "breakfast for your head"). Among Simon's more memorable historical gems:

➤ NBC launched commercial television right after the 1939 World's Fair in New York, but the only visual record that's survived is a program the museum found in an estate sale which someone just happened to film with a 16mm movie camera.

➤ Two television networks covered the first Super Bowl game on January 15, 1967 between the Green Bay Packers and the Kansas City Chiefs, but the programs were erased so the tape could be reused. Only a few minutes of TV news coverage exist today of this historic football game, in which the final score was Packers 35, Chiefs 10.

➤ Many early *Tonight Show* programs with Steve Allen, Jack Parr, and Johnny Carson were erased because they weren't considered important enough to save.

➤ Four Jackie Gleason programs with live *Honeymooners* segments were discovered in CBS's vaults, and then others were found in Gleason's vaults.

➤ The first *I Love Lucy* pilot program was located several years ago, and a Lucy movie which combined three of her early television programs has yet to turn up.

➤ The museum has the second *All In the Family* pilot program, but not the first. These programs are valuable because their originator Norman Lear used them to experiment with different cast members.

➤ The 1950s teen idol James Dean made three movies (*East of Eden*, *Giant*, and *Rebel Without A Cause*), but he also appeared in thirty television shows. "We have twenty of these shows," says Simon, "but ten are missing, including one where Dean plays opposite Ronald Reagan."

This seemed like the perfect spot to ask Simon what he thought about television's attitude toward older viewers. His response?

"You can really look at the history of television as appealing to a younger and younger group. The idea in the early stages of television," he said, "was to air programs like *The Goldbergs* and *The Ed Sullivan Show*, which had something for everyone.

"Then in 1959, ABC started going after growing young families willing to try new consumer products. In the late 1960s, CBS swept its schedule clean of programs appealing to older audiences such as *The Beverly Hillbillies*, Red Skelton, and Jackie Gleason, and replaced them with shows aimed at younger people such as *The Mary Tyler Moore Show*, which first aired in 1970.

"The target was housewives 18 to 34 (or even 49), and this continued until the 1980s, when Fox Broadcasting started going after single people in their teens and 20s. Fox shows like MTV and *Beverly Hills 90210* were carefully designed to attract this young, vibrant audience. This is scary because it represents a balkanization of the television market to appeal to this one group to the exclusion of everyone else."

I then asked Ron Simon if he thought the television industry, in cahoots with its advertisers, might lower their sights still further and go after, say, teenagers. His answer surprised me: He said the industry might now be ready to raise its sights and go after an older audience.

"Things are changing, and the Ross Perot campaign is a good example, because its impetus came from an older audience that's past 18 to 49 and is saying 'We don't like what's happening. We're going to get our own candidate. Our own product.'

Businesses are finally recognizing that "secure adults" are one of today's fastest-growing markets.

Here's a group of people that society has told is going to have to live out their lives as grandparents or something and they're not buying it.

"I think that's where television advertisers are right now, trying to bring back an audience they've splintered. So now the big question is what's going to be the great unifier, and whether there can be [one]."

Selling to Secure Adults

In recent years, a few businesses *have* wised up. They've begun wooing us seniors almost as aggressively as they do teenagers whose disposable incomes consist of their weekly allowance. Examples include:

➤ Spa Lady Health Clubs' fitness program for the "60 and Supple" woman.

➤ Levi Strauss' Actionwear jeans, which have elastic waistbands and are roomier than regular pants, to accommodate the mature figure.

➤ Kohler's walk-in bathtubs, which reduce accidents getting in and out of a bath or shower. They have a door on the side which you open, walk in, make yourself comfortable, and close before filling the tub. The instant the water is turned on, built-in sensors automatically start a pump that inflates a seal around the door, making it watertight.

➤ Fiskars' Softouch scissors, made of lightweight materials with a spring that reopens them after each cut for use by people with arthritis and other hand-crippling ailments.

➤ Xerox's device that reads printed documents out loud to people who are visually impaired, and Home Technology Systems' MainStreet Messenger telephone, which has big illuminated keys, visual and audible ringing, an Alert key which automatically dials 911 and other emergency numbers, and a hands-free speaker for two-way talk after an emergency number is reached. The American Society on Aging gave these two advances its top award for new products which can help improve the lives of older people.

One new product designed specifically for older homeowners who want to age in place, rather than be forced to move into a nursing home, is the prototype Friendly Home built in Chino, California. This home, which is a joint project of Lewis Homes

Management Corporation, the National Council on Aging, and the Southern California Gas Company, features levers rather than door handles; lowered light switches; raised outlets and phone jacks; grab bars by the toilet, bathtub and shower; contrasting colors to aid the visually impaired; and wide doorways to allow easy access by walker or wheelchair.

Stories abound about how seniors are loath to try anything new, including these high-tech homes designed with them in mind. But this is simply not true, says George Mochis, Director of Georgia State University's Center for Mature Consumer Studies. Mochis says that although older people are thought to shy away from technological advances, he's found they're perfectly willing to give them a try if they have some idea of how they work—and what's in it for them.

One way older consumers do differ from younger ones, says Mochis, is that they're less likely to complain when they're unhappy. Instead of telling a seller or supplier what's wrong, they'll simply switch to a competitor's product or service.

Since older people have money—lots of it—this avalanche of new products is expected to continue. Everything from powered scooters for those who have difficulty walking, to emergency-response systems that summon help with the push of a button (immortalized by the TV ad of an elderly woman plaintively intoning "I've fallen and I can't get up"). This heart-rending plea has inspired a manufacturer of T-shirts to introduce a hot-selling number emblazoned with "I've fallen and I can't reach my beer."

Portraying older folks as nice to be around, and on occasion even youthful and vigorous, may be an idea whose time has come, as illustrated by recent advertising campaigns for Coca Cola and Quaker Oats.

The Coke ads feature Art Carney (famous as Jackie Gleason's sidekick in *The Honeymooners*) having a wonderful time with his grandson as they enjoy Coca-Cola. The message comes through loud and clear: people of all ages are wonderful and so is Coke.

The Quaker Oats campaign stars well-padded and balding Wilford Brimley, who used to pitch oatmeal from the seat of a front-porch rocking chair. He now does it galloping along on horseback as an off-screen chorus energetically sings "Every day should feel this good."

These changes, said one advertising industry reporter, "underscore a broader shift in advertising aimed at older Americans. Portrayals of [them] resting quietly in God's waiting room are giving way to depictions of them as take-charge doers, almost as frenetically busy as their young professional children."

Automotive News has warned its car dealer readers not to patronize older customers by calling them senior citizens, retirees, or golden agers. A better name, it says, is "secure adults," which was dreamed up by Chester A. Swenson, president of a Los Angeles think tank called Marketing & Financial Management.

Swenson tells car dealers that selling to secure adults is "elusive, tricky, and one of the toughest nuts to crack in the history of modern marketing" since throughout their long lives they've been exposed to "media messages, hard sells, and junk mail." A better strategy, says Swenson, is to use "lifestyle marketing" by appealing to older customers' interest in prestige, quality, reliability, extended warranties, and a good service department.

It's worth the effort, Swenson concludes, because secure adults, who buy 43 percent of all new automobiles, prefer American-made cars and may "represent the last great bastion for the domestic auto industry."

Romancing older consumers is not without risk, however, as more than one company has found to its sorrow. Johnson &

Johnson's "Affinity" shampoo flopped until the company stopped promoting it as ideal for "brittle, hollowed-out older hair." And a Coty ad for its Sophia (Loren) perfume which poked fun at a trio of old ladies dressed in black got zapped by *Modern Maturity*. "Sophia, that's a poor choice," roared the magazine. Published by the American Association of Retired Persons for its 32 million members, *Modern Maturity* has the highest circulation in the country—certainly a formidable foe.

The Rising Cost of Modern Medicine: The Bad News....

As the miracles of medicine continue to proliferate—such as a new technique, called laparoscopy, that has slashed the time it takes to remove a gall bladder from one week in a hospital to one day as an outpatient—questions are being raised about their cost.

Hospital patients are babes in the woods when it comes to interpreting their bills, a staggering 99 percent of which contain overcharges, according to the federal government's General Accounting Office. One main reason for this is that hospital bills list dozens of incomprehensible charges like "PT-PTT" or "Apolipoprotein Al" whose cost is further inflated to cover the expense of caring for the hospital's indigent patients. And we haven't even touched upon the efficacy of all these hospital procedures.

Older people, for example, are prime candidates for the 300,000 coronary bypass operations performed in the United States each year at a cost of some $1.5 billion. Yet a study by the respected Rand Corporation found that more than 40 percent of these operations did little, if anything, to help the patient.

Questions are also being raised about the outpouring of hugely expensive new diagnostic machines such as the big-ticket trio of computerized axial tomography (CAT), magnetic resonance imaging (MRI), and positron emission tomography (PET). These scanning devices can peer inside the body to spot everything from sinus problems to brain tumors—at a cost of up to $2,500 per scan.

American hospitals and some private doctor-owned clinics have acquired these machines at great cost, and doctors often order their use to either protect themselves against malpractice suits, or because they own a piece of the clinic where the examinations are done. California Congressman Pete Stark wrote the law that makes it illegal for doctors to tell Medicare patients needing blood, urine, or similar tests to get them done at a laboratory in which they're part owners, and he's promised to expand the law to cover imaging centers as well.

Fraud committed by doctors and hospitals may account for up to $75 billion of annual U.S health care expenditures, according to the National Health Care Anti-Fraud Association. One example? A New York City doctor billed Medicaid for $50,000 worth of lab tests for a single older patient.

The bête noir of soaring health care costs, however, is the incredible—and apparently unstoppable—surge in administrative costs, which currently gobble up a record one out of every four dollars spent on hospital care. A recent study by Drs. Steffie Woolhandler and David U. Himmelstein of the Harvard Medical School revealed that on an average day in 1968, American hospitals employed 435,100 managers and clerks to care for 1,378,000 patients. By 1990, however, it took

1,221,600 administrative workers to look after only 853,000 patients.

Just who is taking care of whom?

....And the Good News

A nything that can slow the 14 percent annual rise in the cost of health care in this country, which hit just over $1 trillion per year in 1995, deserves a vote of thanks from old and young alike, since we are now spending a far greater share of our national income on health care than any of the world's other great nations. In early 1993, to mention just one unnerving statistic, the U.S. health care industry employed ten million people—a 43 percent increase in just four years.

One possibly hopeful sign is the boom in home medical care, heavily used by older people who are acutely ill or disabled. Only yesterday, many patients needing antibiotics, intravenous nutritional supplements, pain killers, anti-cancer drugs, and the like would have been hospitalized by their doctors at a cost—including ambulance service—considerably greater than the $200 or so per day required to look after them at home. Not to mention the fact that they will likely recuperate faster in familiar surroundings, while avoiding exposure to deadly hospital-based diseases.

Efforts to control the rising cost of caring for older Americans mirrors the situation with employee health care programs underwritten by U.S. corporations. Costs currently average $4,000 per worker, but could more than triple to $17,000 by the year 2000, according to Uwe Reinhardt, professor of political science at Princeton University.

Reinhardt made that hair-raising prediction during a Washington, D.C. Health Care Summit sponsored by *Business Week* and the accounting firm Deloitte & Touche. Other speakers were no less alarming. Judith Feder, codirector of the Center for Health Policy Studies and an adviser to President Clinton, warned business leaders that "If you do nothing, [your health care] costs will soar to $1.7 trillion during the 1990s, posing huge threats to the profitability and growth of your companies."

"To drive significant change in the health care system," added Robert A. Go, Deloitte & Touche's managing director of health care, "business leaders must learn more about health care, partner with the health care industry to rationalize delivery systems, and give employees appropriate financial and lifestyle incentives." Perhaps this will help control the seemingly inexorable rise in health care costs the accounting firm predicts could surpass $2 trillion in 2005.

Two companies that have learned this lesson are Xerox and Pepsico, whose health care costs have been rising at only a fraction of the national average. Their secret? "Aggressively directing employees and retirees to quality-driven health maintenance organizations," says Xerox's manager of health care strategy and programs.

Health maintenance organizations (HMOs) cover about half the U.S. population, and in recent years have succeeded in slashing the cost of medical care, from bandaging a cut to performing a heart transplant. All HMOs are eager for new patients, and both individuals and companies can examine the quality and cost of their care to see which one offers the best value for the dollar. Thanks largely to recent advances in health care, along with government and corporate pressure to reduce the cost of medical care, the amount Americans currently pay for medical care, according to the U.S. Labor Department, is the lowest it's been since 1973.

One problem that hit the headlines in 1996 is the effort of many HMOs to restrict what their doctors can tell patients to hold down costly procedures, such as bone marrow transplants for those suffering from cancer. Sixteen states, including California, New York, Pennsylvania, and Virginia had adopted such laws by mid-September 1996, and many more are expected to follow suit.

I recently signed up with an HMO, and have found the service quite satisfactory. My primary care doctor knows his stuff, and is willing to see me anytime. The nearby specialists he's sent me to are equally competent, as are their staffs. The HMO fee is automatically deducted from my Social Security check every month, plus a modest charge if I see a doctor or pharmacologist, or am admitted to a hospital. In conjunction with Medicare, my HMO saved me well over $15,000 (including a four-day hospital stay) within months after I joined, and hundreds more when I broke my arm while climbing Whiteface Mountain in North Carolina.

It is this kind of tough-minded, cost-containing service which appears to be bringing near-runaway U.S. health care costs to heel, even though some patient/provider conflicts still must be ironed out. "The very survival of America's health care delivery system is at risk," concludes Deloitte & Touche's Robert Go. "Accordingly, providers are now positioning themselves for fundamental change."

Yet the most obvious, if least discussed answer to reducing America's horrendous health care costs is to do everything possible to keep people from getting sick in the first place. Dr. Alexander Leaf of the Harvard Medical School, writing in the *Journal of the American Medical Association*, says "Medicine traditionally stands on two pillars: prevention and cure. For the past century, the profession has rallied almost exclusively under the banner of curative medicine," to the detriment of preventive medicine.

Dr. Leaf notes, for example, that "Blue Cross/Blue Shield and Medicare will pay $30,000 for coronary bypass graft operations and more than $100,000 for heart transplant surgery, but not for a $1,000 to $2,000 rehabilitation program. Medicare," he adds, "specifically eschews reimbursement for preventive measures."

The sharply rising cost of health care shows no sign of abating, but seems destined to speed up, exploding after 2010, when the huge baby boom generation begins turning 65. The burden both government and business have assumed in underwriting Americans' health care needs has already started to erode, and when coupled with accelerating provider costs, may degrade the level of health care so many of us enjoy today. Millions of people have already embraced money-saving health maintenance organizations, and millions more are turning to the curative powers of alternative medicine—acupuncture, chiropractic, and massage (more on these topics in Chapter 7).

But the best single way to enjoy good health, as we have seen, is to pursue a sensible lifestyle rich in the things that make us feel good.

Whither Social Security?

Quite a few specialists who study America's aging population are beginning to look at the growing perception that we're grabbing too big a slice of America's economic pie.

Today there are 44 million Social Security recipients getting monthly checks totaling more than $334 billion a year, or 22 percent of the federal budget. Steady increases in Social

Sun City, Arizona's Power Riders, including Beverly and Thomas Taylor (second and third from left) have been called "Geezers in Gear," but they're still burning up the highway like there's no tomorrow.

Security benefits and company pension plans, as we have seen, have significantly reduced the proportion of seniors living in poverty during the past thirty-six years.

This realization, however, is reinforcing the growing feeling that Social Security and other income-transfer programs are allowing us older people to live too high off the hog. Which helps explain why only 26 percent of nonretired Americans believe Social Security will be an important source of money when they retire, according to a recent survey by the Employee Benefit Research Institute and the American Savings Education Council. It is important that we seniors confront this reality head-on, since it could lead to conflict between us and younger members of our families.

An early sign of this unrest can be seen in a *Fortune* magazine article "The Tyranny of America's Old." The article stated, "By clinging to an outsize share of government goodies, the elderly are unintentionally forcing the nation to shortchange its young." Illustrating the article was a photo of a dozen or so older bikers beneath the caption, "Geezers in Gear: Seniors, like these Power Riders of Sun City, Arizona, don't look like Hell's Angels. But they sure can scare the folks in Washington."

Americans age 50-plus are ardent voters, possessing far more clout in Washington than younger people. This power makes them agents of political change, notes Princeton Survey Research President Andrew Kohuts. Young people aren't all that interested in voting, and have been going to the polls in declining numbers, even though what's happening in cash-strapped, tax-prone Washington will impact their material lifestyles for as far as the eye can see.

An obvious reason for this, quite apart from the slower growth of the U.S. economy, from which all blessings flow, is the aging of the U.S. workforce and the oldsters it supports through transfer payments. When the first Social Security checks were mailed out on February 13, 1936, there were thirty workers earning wages for every retiree. Today, it's 3.4-to-1, and by 2030 when the huge cohort of baby boomers will have retired it will be down to 2-to-1. To make matters worse, retirees are living longer and collecting Social Security checks for more years than any but the most optimistic demographers thought possible half a century ago.

While both the Democratic and Republican parties insist they can balance the budget in the years immediately ahead, less is said, let alone done, about the huge—and unsustain-able—future demands which will be placed on the Big Three entitlement programs of Social Security, Medicaid, and Medicare. These programs are financed by inexorably increas-ing income transfers from the pockets of working young people to their retired parents and grandparents, a majority of whom receive half their income from this government-mandated beneficence. One upshot of all this, says Treasury Department economist Francis X. Cavanaugh in his book *The Truth About the National Debt*, is that the average 70-year-old man now enjoys a level of total consumption 25 percent higher than that of his 30-year-old grandson.

So it's worth considering whether today's millions of comfortably fixed older folks, for whom Social Security, Medicare, etc. represent insignificant additions to their well-being, should take the lead in advocating a restructuring of federal entitlement programs to reduce the growing burden on young workers struggling to live decent lives in an America where average inflation-adjusted incomes have been falling for years. And as if that wasn't enough, their chance of receiving anything like the income support payments enjoyed by those already retired is evaporating before their eyes. The age at which American workers receive their full benefits has been under discussion in the House and Senate and seems likely to increase from 65 to 67 beginning early next century.

To make matters worse, the amount of money taken from a working person's income to cover Social Security payments to retirees is indexed to inflation. In 1947 the maximum contribution was $30 a year, whereas it was recently $4,245—with no place to go but up.

The pressure is going to be on delaying Social Security payments, while requiring seniors already getting monthly Social Security checks with built-in cost-of-living escalators to pull in their belts in order to leave more in the pot for future retirees. A variety of ways are being advanced to accomplish this, including:

> ➤ Encourage older people to keep working—and paying taxes—by ending the current docking of their Social

Security checks when they earn more than a certain amount.

➤ Raise the age at which older people can begin receiving major Social Security benefits to the already legislated 67, and as time goes by, perhaps even to 69 or 70.

➤ Cut the upward annual adjustment in Social Security benefits to reflect the true rate of inflation, rather than the overstated one many believe is currently being used.

➤ Allow workers to invest a substantial percentage of their Social Security deductions in common stocks instead of government IOUs, so they can earn a greater rate of return.

There's a good chance one or more of these changes will become law by the turn of the century, although Social Security is an explosive political issue and nothing is certain.

My guess is that overall, older people are more willing to reduce their financial dependence on future generations than is generally appreciated. Particularly since Uncle Sam's pension and health care programs are not need-based but available to everyone who reaches age 65—rich and poor alike.

The question, of course, is who will take the lead in selling older Americans on the idea of accepting less so their offspring can have more? Might it be an organization already in place, such as the American Association of Retired Persons? Or will a new lobbying group have to be built from the ground up? The only thing we know for sure is that this issue is going to command growing national attention in the years immediately ahead, and that it must be equitably resolved by us older folks for the benefit of those we love who are following along after us.

Are We Entitled?

While the Social Security program is solvent and will remain so until the baby boomers start retiring in droves, health care costs partially covered by Medicare and Medicaid are clearly out of control, with no remedy in sight.

"We are running out of ways to make savings and approaching the point where we will have to ration health care," says William B. Schwartz, a professor of medicine and medical economist at Tufts University in Medford, Massachusetts. Cuts in Medicaid and Medicare now seem all but certain, with only their size in doubt. Both the President and Congress seem committed to bringing the Federal budget into balance in the years immediately ahead.

One leading critic of U.S. entitlement programs is investment banker Peter Peterson, 71, founding president of the Concord Coalition (dedicated to building a constituency for fiscal responsibility), and chairman of Wall Street's Blackstone Group.

In a recent speech, Peterson said the federal government spends eleven times more per capita on the elderly who are approaching the end of life than it does on children who are beginning it (adding that money spent on elders is immediately spent on "consumption"), while dollars spent on children is "real investment." American politicians are far too gutless to adjust this disparity, says Peterson, since it would mean taking on America's all-powerful senior lobby.

This is not the case in Japan, he adds. "The Japanese Minister of Health called a commission to analyze the ballooning costs of their entitlement programs for their elderly in a society that is aging even more rapidly than ours. They concluded

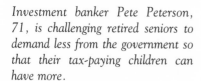

Investment banker Pete Peterson, 71, is challenging retired seniors to demand less from the government so that their tax-paying children can have more.

these programs were not only unaffordable but unfair to their children, so they reduced the future benefits by about 20 percent."

In his new book *Will America Grow Up Before It Grows Old?: How the Coming Social Security Crisis Threatens You, Your Family, and Your Country*, Peterson recommends slowing the growth in benefit levels, gradually raising Social Security deductions along with the retirement age, and limiting expensive terminal medical care that extends life for only a few days or weeks.

Among the least discussed plans for bringing entitlements under control is to equate them to actual need by ending them for the rich (for whom they're pocket change), cutting them—or their rate of growth—for the well-off middle class, and supporting everyone else on a need basis.

What has been ignored so far in all this, says Robert Eisner, Professor Emeritus at Northwestern University, and a former

President of the American Economic Association, is what is actually going on in the real world. While younger working Americans will have to give up a larger percentage of their incomes to support those not working in the future, says Eisner, writing in *The New York Times'* "Viewpoint" column, their paychecks will be so much larger they will still have far more spending power left over than they have today.

No sooner had Eisner's article appeared in the *Times*, than the newspaper printed a letter from a Dansville, New York physician taking him to task for believing that "economic growth will take care of everything" despite "the overwhelming consensus that Social Security and Medicare are facing an imminent demographic crisis."

Michael Boskin, a Stanford University economist, former head of the White House Council of Economic Advisers in the Bush Administration, and head of the independent five-member commission appointed by Congress to study the future of Social Security, predicts all-out war over budget-busting Social Security in his book *Too Many Promises: The Uncertain Future of Social Security.* "A confrontation between workers and retirees will arise [involving trillions of dollars]," warned Boskin, "that will create the greatest polarization along economic lines in our society since the Civil War."

Today's inflation-adjusted entitlements have been protecting us older Americans against economic and health care penury for decades, and nobody knows it better than we do. This protection will continue, but at a slower pace, which means we will have to accept a little less so that our taxpaying children and grandchildren can keep a little more.

Not a bad tradeoff, and one whose time has clearly come.

7

ADVENTURES IN
FUTURE WORLD

*The best thing about the future is that it comes only one
day at a time.*

—Abraham Lincoln

Change is inevitable, except from a vending machine.

—Bumper sticker

*I've gotten into enormous trouble. It cost me dearly in
school. It has helped me make out like a bandit in
technology, where the conventional wisdom changes
every five years.*

—Lawrence J. Ellison, multibillionaire founder of
software giant Oracle Corporation

It's a safe bet that most people in their early 20s didn't turn a
hair the first time they saw the ground-breaking television
commercial in which sexy singer Paula Abdul is shown talking
animatedly with deceased screen actor Cary Grant as he pours her
a Diet Coke, and dances with long-gone funny man Groucho
Marx.

These kids were born after July 20, 1969, when humans first
walked on the moon, and this kind of thing is simply part of

their world, like combined heart-lung-liver transplants, or satellites sending messages back to earth after they've left our solar system and are racing toward the far reaches of the Milky Way.

It's doubtful if anything has more power to isolate the old from the young than the incredible postwar scientific explosion—unless, of course, it's the often deadly realities facing today's young people compared to those confronting their parents or grandparents 50 years ago.

The seven top problems plaguing school children today, according to the California Department of Education and the Fullerton, California, Police Department are drug abuse, alcohol abuse, pregnancy, suicide, rape, robbery, and assault. Unbelievable as it now seems, the top seven back in the 1940s were talking out of turn, chewing gum, making noise, running in the halls, cutting in line, dress code violations, and littering. (Can you possibly wrap your mind around the fact that a "Top 40" tune in the 1930s was actually called "Little Old Lady," with lyrics "Little old lady passing by, catching everyone's eye. You have such a charming manner sweet and shy"?) But in an America where 7-year-olds bring tape recorders to class to capture their teacher's intemperate remarks, or a 6-year-old boy gets suspended for kissing a girl on the cheek, or a student is suspended for bringing an over-the-counter pain reliever to school, anything is clearly possible.

Young people are at ease in today's often hostile and fast-changing world. But to older people struggling to deal with hair-trigger security systems and genetically engineered tomatoes, it is more like an adventure in Future World. One we must embark on whether we like it or not, because it is impossible to quarantine ourselves from the increasingly high-tech world around us.

Computers, faxes, Automated Teller Machines (ATMs), video cassette recorders (VCRs), video telephones, on-line information services, video games, and interactive home shopping networks have long since transformed our daily lives. The new developments have even become the subject of humor—a sure sign of their vitality.

One magazine ad shows a young woman sitting at a computer keyboard. "The difference between my mother and me," she says, "is that she still thinks software is a nightgown." This is in a country that's actually discarding used computers at such a rate that Carnegie-Mellon University predicts the nation's landfills will hold 150 million computers by the year 2005, at a disposal cost alone of perhaps $1 billion. Not bad when you consider that more than 97 percent of the people on earth have never even *touched* a computer.

Yet this is only a glimpse of what's ahead in an era where parents are being urged to spend $129 on an attachment for the family computer featuring large keys marked with pictures instead of letters so babies can log on and get digital. A security analyst at the International Data Corp. says the benefits for 3-to7-year-olds, "can be extended to teenagers, to working single moms, and to the seniors market."

An example of the latter is IBM's recent announcement that it has developed voice-recognition software that enables radiologists to dictate their reports directly into a personal computer, rather than laboriously typing them in by hand. "What you see here," said a top IBM scientist, "is the first step toward the Holy Grail of continuous speech recognition by a machine."

Recently I visited my grandson's first-grade class in Alexandria, Virginia, and was overwhelmed by the amount of data these children will have to cram into their heads—or

know where to find on the Internet—compared to my generation. It is, as they say, "awesome." Yet these kids are taking it in
their stride, because they—literally—don't know any differently.

Clearasil vs. Preparation H

W hile some kind of loving relationship between youngsters and their grandparents is a given, the world outside
all too often reflects a self-imposed segregation between the
Clearasil and Preparation H generations. The high-energy, sex-
propelled, physically beautiful young cluster together amidst
their beer and boom boxes, while the slow-moving, increasingly asexual and wrinkled old retreat to their retirement
communities with planned activities and "Adults Only" signs
prominently displayed.

Or at least, that's how the stereotype goes.

"The two groups might as well be on separate planets," says
Jerald Carstens, assistant professor of speech communications
at the University of Wisconsin at River Falls, who's studied the
difficulties the young and old encounter when attempting
something as simple as talking to each other.

"When I asked retired people what they commonly talked
about and preferred to talk about," says Carstens, "they most
often mentioned topics such as funerals, illness, and medical
insurance. When I posed this same question to the young
people attending my classes at the University, I got answers
such as music, dates, work, and school. Seniors not only never
mentioned these topics, but said they had a strong aversion to
talking about music and dates in particular.

"There were, however, several areas where the interests of
the young and old overlapped such as current events, news, and

Some things will never change, like the joys of teaching a grandson how to fish—once you manage to separate him from his video games.

sports, including our local Minnesota Twins baseball team, which was a pennant contender when I did my survey.

"The trouble is that the old and young are really not all that interested in each other. They are like ships passing in the night, even though they do have areas of mutual interest."

One thing the very young and the old have in common is free time, so it's not unusual for, say, a 12-year-old boy and an old fellow down the block who's pushing 80 to enjoy a stroll to the fishing hole together, or even a conversation on the back porch, which can be an eye-opening experience for us seniors.

I was recently a Big Brother to an 11-year-old boy named Joey who had never known his father, and was always ready for my arrival at his house on Saturday morning to spend the day together swimming, fishing, hiking, going to the zoo, or playing video games. Joey had never heard of Franklin D. Roosevelt, Adolph Hitler, Dwight D. Eisenhower, or Shakespeare, but he was a grandmaster at playing video games whose names were equally unknown to me, like *Donkey Kong* and *Super Mario*.

The local Wal-Mart displayed an advanced version of Super Mario on the counter in its electronics department for anyone who wanted to try it out. Joey's idea of a perfect Saturday was for me to drop him off at the store so he could spend all morning playing Super Mario on the demonstrator. I couldn't help wondering if this was the way today's kids are unconsciously preparing themselves to earn a living in the computer-driven Information Age, just as I once spent weeks fixing up old jalopies—my generation's way of gearing up for life in the Industrial Age.

Dawn of a New Millennium

When we were kids growing up during the Great Depression, we played simple outdoor games like Hide and Seek, Pussy In the Corner, Red Rover, and my personal favorite, Boys After Girls. But no more. Today's youngsters are hunched over glowing CRT tubes engrossed, among other things, in shoot-'em-up computer games like "Heretic," in which a macho elf blasts monsters into oblivion.

As we seniors advance into the next decade, when we'll be among the first humans since the Chinese invented gunpowder to welcome in a new millennium, we'll be enveloped in an avalanche of change—everything from wearable machines to holographic lollipops. The latest Nintendo video games put as much power in the hands of an 8-year-old as a supercomputer generated ten years ago. And since the power of new computer chips is doubling every eighteen months, what takes a year to compute today will take about fifteen seconds in 2030.

Yet all this is run-of-the-mill stuff compared with the high-tech wonders which have recently arrived, or are bearing down upon us at warp speed. A small number of these new developments:

> Goggles containing a tiny television set in each lens which you can lay back and watch when you're on a long trip and somebody else is doing the driving.

> Microscopic machines so small they can be inhaled.

> Orchids infused with firefly genes so they'll glow in the dark.

> Electronic coins you can send across the Internet, or "smart cards" you can load with cash over your kitchen telephone.

> Molten-metal baths operating at 3,000 degrees Fahrenheit which can turn the most toxic environmental wastes into valuable raw materials.

> The twenty-four satellites operated by the U.S. Defense Department which continuously circle the planet and use atomic clocks and radio signals to pinpoint objects on earth within one centimeter.

> Luxuriously comfortable computer-guided trains flying along at 300 miles an hour on a cushion of air.

> CD-ROM programs such as top-selling *Automap, Map 'n' Go,* and *Tripmaker* which evaluate the best way to get from here to there for more than a million motorists. The programs cost about $39 and calculate the best way to go from start to finish, displaying on your personal computer screen driving distances and times, attractions, restaurants, hotels, places to buy gas, and interesting stopovers. (What the programs do not do, nor can they really, is draw your attention to

interesting little places down back roads that may appeal to you as an individual, such as an old civil war battlefield or a fishing hole revered by locals.)

➤ A new machine being developed by IBM, Toshiba, and Germany's Siemens will be capable of etching 600 million transistors on a computer chip. That's equivalent to drawing a street map of every town and city on earth on your fingernail.

➤ Surgeons such as Boston M.D. Ferenc Jolesz are investigating ways to detect breast cancer using real-time data from a nuclear-magnetic resonance machine, and to kill the cancer with ultrasound waves, leaving no marks on the body.

➤ Computer links enable yeshiva students in Riga, Lativa, where there's a scarcity of teachers of Judaism, to learn from religious scholars in Moscow, London, and Israel.

➤ Parallel processing computers will be capable of evolving their own programs for solving problems far beyond the capacity of the human mind (raising the question of where the dividing line between life and non-life actually lies).

One place where you'll really rub your eyes in disbelief is the new entertainment world of "virtual reality" which combines—in the words of its promoters—"the magic of film with the sensations of a[n amusement park] ride." Two seasoned ex-Disney executives are pioneering this theatrical revolution via their fast-growing new company Iwerks Entertainment.

One early film especially created for Busch Gardens in Williamsburg, Virginia, is *Haunts of the Olde Country* starring an American boy who unexpectedly stumbles across a friendly ghost while touring an ancient castle on the misty moors of Scotland. Theatergoers not only see the film in three dimensions, but actually feel the mist, fog, and cold air on their faces as the adventure unfolds.

The company has also developed a special film for theme parks based on the Hollywood hit race car movie *Days of Thunder*. Moviegoers sitting in a state-of-the-art, 74-seat simulation theater will be able to experience what it's like to drive a high-powered race car at speeds of up to 200 miles an hour, navigate dangerous curves, and engage in car-to-car combat with other drivers.

Another advanced attraction called Virtual Adventures is similarly destined to be a big-money attraction at the nation's amusement parks. Virtual Adventures will allow viewers to be visually transported into the fantasy world of their favorite movies and television shows. The company is readying films in which those in the audience—it calls them "riders"—will become part of the show. The first of these simulation films is *RoboCop: The Ride*, in which patrons will actually enter the movie so they can assist this metallic defender of law and order as he battles the forces of evil.

Says *The Plain Truth*, "Virtual reality offers the ultimate in escapism. It may soon be possible to spend many hours in a computer-generated environment, experiencing your own custom-designed fantasies. Most Christians will obviously decide to avoid virtual sadism and cybersex, just as we now resist pornography and fornication."

And again, even these developments are child's play compared to what 79-year-old writer Arthur C. Clarke sees awaiting our species a millennium from now. Clarke soared to fame with *2001: A Space Odyssey*, but in *3001: The Final Odyssey* he envisions a world so high-tech it must make even the Silicon Valley masters' heads spin. Clarke sees a mere one billion people inhabiting the Earth—and billions more living in the endlessly orbiting Star City, connected to our planet by four space towers that double as elevators. Snap-on brain caps contain all the skills and data needed to live a stimulating life, and keep nearly everyone on the straight and narrow: any miscreants are put in psychic straitjackets to live out their days as harmless servants. And when residents of Star City, with its controlled gravity, feel like a little R and R, they can pull on a set of physical wings and fly around through simulated landscapes from prehistoric forests crawling with dinosaurs to the beaches of Acapulco, crawling with gorgeous sunbathers in their birthday suits.

Sounds good to me!

Going Out with a Bang

Guru Timothy Leary (known for "tune in, turn on, drop out") and Gene Roddenberry, creator of the *Star Trek* television series, were among twenty-four people who probably put their affairs in order before taking their ultimate ride on April 21, 1997. Their cremated earthly remains were packed into cigar-shaped aluminum capsules and hurled into the heavens by a Pegasus rocket slung beneath a Lockheed 1011 jet.

This posthumous trip, called a commemorative space flight, cost $4,800 apiece, and the capsules will remain in a ninety-minute, 327-mile orbit above the earth at 17,500 miles per hour for up to ten years before reentering the atmosphere and burning up in a burst of light. Future flights for the departed are being booked by Celestis, Inc. of Houston, Texas—and it looks like a growth business.

This Pegasus rocket launches loved one's remains into orbit as part of a "space memorial service" costing $4,800 for a one-way ticket.

This is "a new and unique approach for honoring and remembering the spirit of a loved one," says Celestis, "while simultaneously helping to open the space frontier for all of us."

An Electronic Whirlwind

What's so extraordinary is that young and old alike are being caught up in an electronic synthesis of human and machine that's reshaping society so fast most of us don't have a clue as to what's going on. As a result, this movement has transformed the lives of millions of people practically in secret. The shift from big mainframe computers to ubiquitous desktop PCs has been called as profound a development as the move from gaslight to electric bulbs, trains to airplanes, or wired to wireless communications (via cellular phones).

One of the least appreciated fundamentals of the computer is that prosperity in America today is moving with lightning speed from the physical, in which we older Americans have lived most of our lives, to the informational, in which future generations seem destined to live theirs.

This really gets interesting when you combine the awesome power of computer networks to distribute facts and figures over existing telephone lines, with the appearance of high-definition, high-capacity television sets with the ability to receive one hundred or more channels over greatly expanded cable networks. This is fast transforming television from a medium long dominated by ABC, CBS, and NBC and their mass-appeal shows designed as enticements to sell their sponsors' products, to a veritable feast of new channels specializing in rifle-shot programming where attracting as few as 50,000 viewers is considered a home run.

The television industry has already launched channels specializing in real-life courtroom dramas, science-fiction and cartoons, and now it's beginning to deliver the Romance Classics Channel, two Game Show Channels, the How-To Channel, and if Ellen Orleans (author of *Can't Keep a Straight Face: A Lesbian Looks and Laughs at Life*) gets her wish, there will be a channel exclusively for women who are mad about other women.

A *TV Guide* team hopes viewers will realize that the good old days of spinning the dial aimlessly to find something they want to watch no longer makes sense, with potentially hundreds of channels clamoring for attention. So it is developing a system which will let viewers zero in on what they're in the mood to watch—sports, drama, game shows, movies, you name it—and will tell them everything that's available, plus how to find it, for a fee not unlike what they'd pay for their weekly

TV Guide. "The acid test," said one marketing executive immersed in making this new electronic system a paying proposition, "is would our 70-year-old mothers use it?"

Why not?—if it's as good as its backers claim. We seniors have all taken momentous changes in TV technology—from color to giant screens—in our stride, just as we're now getting ready to welcome TV screens a mere 4 inches thick that can be hung on the wall like a painting.

For those of us who were kids when Charles Lindbergh conquered the Atlantic, today's scientific and technological advances are astonishing. We are the major beneficiaries of today's life-saving and -prolonging drugs, government-financed safety-net income buoyed by a roaring high-tech economy, go-anywhere, anytime mobility, and many chances to hold the inroads of old age at bay through improved nutrition and exercise.

Dream Homes of Tomorrow

The marvelous thing about entertainment and travel is that once it's over, we can return to the cozy familiarity of our own homes—even though they too are being revolutionized by advanced technology.

Notable strides are being made in designing homes for people with disabilities of every kind. Julie Howard in *Aging Today* (November/December 1995) describes how a farmhouse just outside of Baltimore built in 1855 has been transformed into a home of the future to demonstrate how "assistive" technologies can help the disabled of all ages. Most of the house's systems are triggered automatically by infrared sensors. The curator of "Future Home" is David Ward, who became a quad-riplegic following a fall in 1977, and delights in showing visitors how the house can make life easier:

➤ Doors can be programmed to open automatically. Lights will turn on when a person enters a room, and switch off when a person leaves.

➤ Hearing-impaired people can be alerted to the ringing of a telephone or doorbell by flashing lights throughout the house.

➤ If no movement is sensed in the house for a specific period—possibly because the resident has lost consciousness and fallen to the floor—a motion detector will recognize what's happened and automatically dial a neighbor, relative, or security company to ask for help.

➤ An anti-wanderer detector can be alerted when an out-side door opens, followed by a computer voice asking how long the resident plans to be gone. This is designed to make people with Alzheimer's disease think through where they're going and how long they plan to be away. If they fail to return when they say they will, the system can automatically dial a neighbor or relative to alert them to what's happened.

It cost more than $500,000 to equip Future Home, includ-ing $65,000 for specialized equipment (which includes a $5,000 control computer). Yet David Ward, who shares his home with a full-time personal attendant, says most homes for the disabled can be refitted for well under $10,000, and provide a new free-dom. A specially-fitted home also means that the disabled homeowner's caregivers have the confidence to leave their charges for hours or longer at a time, knowing that their technological support system will help them through the day.

All Wired Up

On February 29, 1996, a team of Japanese and U.S. scientists in Tokyo succeeded in sending one trillion bits of information through an optical fiber in one second. That's equivalent to transmitting the contents of 300 years' worth of daily newspapers, or 12 million simultaneous telephone conversations in a single second.

New Jersey may become the first state in the nation to have a border-to-border fiber-optic telecommunications system, which is estimated to cost $1.5 billion and should be fully operational by 2010. New Jersey Bell is installing this network of hair-thin strands of glass capable of relaying billions of pieces of information anywhere in the state in seconds. This will give residents access to vast quantities of useful data, provide two-way links between physicians and patients (or teachers and students), and create the highway needed to turn megachannel TV reception into reality.

Tiny Blacksburg, Virginia, nestled in the foothills of the Blue Ridge Mountains, is already a highly computer literate community served by the Chesapeake & Potomac Telephone Company (C&P), owned by Bell Atlantic. The town is constantly looking for ways to increase traffic. C&P has joined with Blacksburg and the nearby Virginia Polytechnic Institute to install high-speed digital lines to apartment buildings primarily housing older VPI students, along with libraries and other public facilities.

This is one reason this tiny community of 37,000 is among the world's most heavily wired places—more than half of its residents are regular users of the Internet, to the tune of an hour a day sending and receiving electronic mail. Community organizations such as the town's senior center and Humane Society have noticed a surge in attendance at their meetings after they began using e-mail to alert members to upcoming events.

The Blacksburg Electronic Village system deals only in text, and will, for example:

> ➤ Allow voters to keep track of the time and place of various town meetings, peruse minutes of town council sessions, communicate with local government officials, and even hold referendums on key issues of concern to the community.

> ➤ Access thousands of computer bulletin boards.

> ➤ Use specialized software called *Gopher* to hunt for books, documents, and software scattered among thousands of computers in universities and government agencies.

In the meantime, cellular phones, which allow users to make calls from their cars, briefcases, handbags, you name it (despite claims they may cause cancer when held close to the head, allowing radio waves to enter the brain), are now being carried around by an estimated 40 million Americans. And the numbers are soaring: it is estimated that by 2004, a mind-boggling 125 million Americans will be using wireless phones.

Digital cellular and personal communications networks (PCNs), another form of wireless telephone, will be up and running in the next few years. They're expected to be no bigger than a pack of cigarettes or a fountain pen, and relatively inexpensive. You'll be able to use them practically anywhere including subways and elevators, and they'll work as both telephones and terminals to transmit data to computers or fax machines. When this happens, the telephone will be transformed from an office or household appliance to a personal accessory not all that unlike a wristwatch or ankle bracelet.

The telephone is also being used by older people as an emergency alert. Nearly half a million American have been carrying beeper-like personal emergency systems they can use to summon help simply by pushing a button. The new telephone-based system picks up this distress signal, automatically dials an emergency service, sends an identification code, and then transforms the telephone into a speakerphone so emergency personnel can talk to the elderly person who needs help.

But older folks are often hard of hearing, and many have their television sets on for hours at a time, making it difficult for the emergency voice on the telephone to be heard. Problem? Not anymore. A new device has been patented that will automatically turn down the sound of the TV set so the emergency worker's voice can come through loud and clear.

Still another means of communicating that's about to be transformed by advanced technology is sign language, which allows some 24 million deaf and hearing-impaired Americans to "talk" among themselves. The A.I. duPont Institute, a children's hospital in Wilmington, Delaware, has developed a personal computer system using a grant from the U.S. Department of Education, which enables a stripped-down form of signing to be captured by a television camera and sent over telephone wires to a receiving computer screen many miles away.

Other technology has revolutionary implications which are bound to dazzle and intrigue intellectuals for years to come. One example: within twenty years or so, translator telephones may be reduced in size, portability, and virtuosity to the point where you could speak English into one end and have any language you wish come out the other, enabling you to converse with foreigners all over the world.

A system developed by Japanese, American and German researchers already allows you to speak English into a phone in, say, Boise, Idaho, and have your words translated into Japanese or German by the time they reach your party in Kyoto or Munich. Think of how convenient this would be if you didn't know a word of French, but wanted to haggle with a non-English speaking antiques dealer in a Paris flea market. And scientists are already talking about the possibility of implanting a microchip directly in your brain giving you instant fluency in a foreign language, or in-depth knowledge of any arcane subject that happens to interest you—from free love to the Dead Sea Scrolls.

Conquering High-Tech Anxiety

One of the challenges of being a senior these days is that we're surrounded by technical wonders which weren't even conceivable in our day. Some of us simply avoid these developments, feeling that the automatic teller machine or credit-card-activated gasoline pump is just too scary. As an article in New Choices magazine put it, "Making a call on your brand-new Gadget-O-Phone has become an ordeal because you don't understand the 70-page manual that came with it. When you attempt to microwave a package of 'Macaroni in Moments,' it bursts into flame. Worse yet, your VCR endlessly flashes '12:00. 12:00. 12:00.,' signaling to all your friends that you're a technological dumbbell."

So we'll go inside the bank to make our deposit or withdrawal personally, or pay for our gas in cash at every fill-up. It may make matters worse that we're constantly being urged to forego contact with other human beings because it's cheaper for suppliers to serve us by machine. But it is important that we hitch up our courage and conquer today's technological advances, because—like that parking meter, TV remote control, and microwave oven we've learned to handle—they do make life a little easier. So herewith a few tips:

➤ **Don't be afraid to ask for help.** Bank tellers, filling station attendants, supermarket clerks, and others eager to be of service will be delighted to show you how their latest machines actually work. After all, they had to learn for the first time too. (Your relatives, also, may be a sympathetic source of assistance—especially the youngsters, who will be proud to show off their newly acquired knowledge.)

➤ **Plan to practice on the latest technology when there's the least pressure.** Computer terminals that have largely replaced library card catalogs, for example, are really quite simple, though they may look intimidating. Visiting the library at off-peak hours will give you the chance to feel your way through the computer's search and information programs at your own pace.

➤ **Try to buy high-tech products from responsible dealers who will take the time to show you how they work.** If you are purchasing unusually complex equipment such as today's top-of-the-line computers, which often have instructions that stump even the experts, it might be wise to have a knowledgeable person show you the ropes over several days or a week.

Dazzling changes will continue to bombard our lives. Which, if you think about it, isn't really a new thing at all—just think about how we got used to power steering, pop-top cans, self-winding watches, and disposable diapers. We seniors are tough. So bring on those glow-in-the dark orchids. We can handle anything.

Overselling the Future: A Word of Caution

To the old adage that the only two certainties in life are death and taxes, we might add one more—the guaranteed arrival of the future, filled with a cornucopia of marvels.

If you're over 60, you've lived in two of the three watershed periods in American history. The first was the great transformation from the Agricultural to the Industrial Age, followed by the equally epochal advance (following WWII) from the Industrial to our Information Age, now making the most of *mind* rather than muscle.

The Information Age has already remade America into a nation where 99 percent of all households have at least one television, 96 percent corded telephones, 88 percent VCRs, and 40 percent personal computers. This has helped the business of delivering information—which Microsoft's founder Bill Gates defines as "the reduction of uncertainty"—to grow at an amazing pace, leaving mature industries such as airlines and automobiles eating its dust.

The growth of the information business has been so extraordinary, and the profit opportunities so vast, that companies have been pushing products into the marketplace before we're ready for them. Electronic mail, video conferencing, debit cards, electronic banking, and TV telephones are all available, but underutilized for reasons ranging from excessive cost to often mind-boggling complexity—not to mention the human tendency to stick with the familiar until the advantages of the new are too obvious to ignore.

Big-name U.S. corporations have also invested hundreds of millions in state-of-the-art technology to improve their employees' and customers' efficiency, only to find it largely unused. One company spent close to $50 million on a home-shopping service which bombed. Video conferencing was touted as saving companies a fortune in travel costs, until it was discovered that many people *prefer* to talk to each other across a conference table, where they can pass papers back and forth and later go out to lunch. The seeming complexity of electronic mail and the World Wide Web intimidates many potential users, while video telephones have proven too expensive and effete up to now.

Advanced technology is also subject to disruption, as we saw when New York City's World Trade Center was shut down by a car bomb which exploded in its garage, and when a blizzard caved in the roof of a building in nearby Clifton, New Jersey, disabling 5,200 Automated Teller Machines used by a million bankcard holders nationwide.

A vastly more serious breakdown occurred in early 1996, when Pittsburgh International Airport's aging power systems shorted out, blinding air traffic controllers to the location of thirty-three planes circling the field. Fortunately, there were no deadly accidents. Yet as Joseph Fruscella, president of the National Air Traffic Controllers Association's eastern region told reporters, "There is not one day that goes by without our losing radar or radio communication with an aircraft. It compromises safety on a regular basis."

These events are of special interest because they beautifully illustrate the often cascading nature of the disasters hovering over today's increasingly high-tech world. Electronic Data Systems, which operated the ATM system that went down in New Jersey, thought it could quickly bring it back up by using a reserve computer site it had standing by for just such an emergency. Trouble was, this facility was already overflowing with computer users who only days before had been bombed out of their offices in the soaring twin towers of the World Trade Center.

If there's a downside to modernity, and there is, it has got to be the growing complexity and interdependence of the society in which we seniors will be spending our harvest years. This is a time when a single, often modest glitch can bring down a vast system vital to millions. And disturbing as this is, it seems fated to get worse in our increasingly computerized and networked society, moving ever deeper into the group think of the Information Age.

The Comeback of Unconventional Medicine

Advances in informational technology are being matched by renewed interest in something even older—unconventional or alternative medicine. Of course, patients are still seeing their family doctors (and if they're lucky enough to live in the province of New Brunswick, Canada, they can even dial-a-doc for $2.95 a minute for a consultation on what ails them). But far more family doctors are turning to what are still considered to be unconventional remedies such as acupuncture, herbs, homeopathic remedies, massage, aromatherapy, hypnotherapy, and megadoses of vitamins. Many of these "new" alternative healing techniques are actually ancient Eastern and native American remedies.

Acupuncturists, for example, use hair-thin needles and gentle finger pressure to relieve arthritis and other chronic pain, while herbalists base their prescriptions on the belief that certain plants can increase energy, alleviate some physical and mental ailments, and even strengthen the immune system.

Close to a dozen states currently license naturopathic doctors; Washington has the most. The Seattle county council has established the nation's first government-subsidized natural medicine clinic, and the city's Bastyr University specializing in natural medicine was awarded an $850,000 Federal grant to study alternative ways to treat AIDS. The state itself, as of January 1, 1996, began requiring health insurance companies to cover licensed natural health treatments such as acupuncture and massage therapy.

A detailed study by *The New England Journal of Medicine* has concluded that 34 percent of Americans use some form of alternative medicine, and that one-third of this number have visited a chiropractor, acupuncturist, or other specialist in nontraditional medicine. They also paid return visits to these practitioners an average of nineteen times a year, for a national total of 425 million visits. That's more than they made to their personal physicians and pediatricians *combined*.

Charles R. Halpern, president of the Nathan Cummings Foundation, which supports health programs, believes the medical industry has too long ignored these increasingly popular healing techniques. Although of proven benefit to millions of Americans, these methods, which emphasize the emotional and psychological side of illness, are still foreign to most physicians.

Witch-Doctor Medicine

S ome disgruntled physicians call the above approaches "witch-doctor medicine." Yet the National Institutes of Health (NIH) recently allocated $2 million out of its total budget (which exceeds $10 billion) to the newly formed Office of Alternative Medicine. The office is headed by Joseph J. Jacobs, M.D., who was trained in pediatrics—and is a very unusual fellow.

Dr. Jacobs received his medical training at Dartmouth and Yale, and holds an M.B.A. from the University of Pennsylvania's Wharton School. He was initiated into unconventional medicine by his mother, a full-blooded Caughnawaga Mohawk, and his father, who is part Cherokee. Jacobs spoke Mohawk as a child, and learned about nontraditional medicine from his mother, who often used it when a family member got sick, and was steeped in its practices again when he worked as a pediatrician for the Indian Health Service on a Navajo reservation in New Mexico.

During its first year of operation, the Office of Alternative Medicine used its meager budget to study everything from the application of imagery therapy in edenocystic carcinoma, to the study of hydrazine sulfate in lung and colon cancer, to the possible merits of using pulverized shark cartilage to treat tumors (based on the fact that sharks are resistant to cancer).

The NIH has already invited more than one hundred people from all walks of life to discuss strategies for evaluating alternative therapies. One of these people is Mike Culbert, Chairman of the Committee for Freedom of Choice in Medicine.

Culbert rejects what he sees as the medical profession's overly restrictive review policy for new ways of treating the seriously ill. "Business is booming right now in clinics in Mexico," says Culbert, "because the United States is so awful that it tells dying Americans that they have no right to therapies that may save their lives. You have to ask yourself, 'What is a proven therapy?' Disease-free survival time is all that counts, and if you're getting that from a so-called unproven therapy, so be it. The objective is still the healing of people."

Bionic Mice, Pigs, and Goats

Several years ago, when Harvard University patented a mouse predisposed to getting cancer, the government placed a five-year ban on issuing seventeen-year patents on new forms of animal life created in the laboratory. Now that the ban has been lifted, patent protection will encourage companies to invest millions to produce animals whose genetic makeup has been handcrafted to give them characteristics never before seen in the natural world.

In the years ahead we should see a rush to patent new forms of "transgenic" mice, pigs, goats, and even cows scientifically designed to assist in improving human health. Specially-bred mice will be used to study human illnesses such as Alzheimer's disease and AIDS. Goats will produce milk loaded with human proteins used in the treatment of heart disease. Cows may be genetically altered to give proteins normally found only in mother's milk for use in infant formula. And pigs will provide hearts, kidneys, and livers to terminally ill patients.

According to the United Network for Organ Sharing, close to 50,000 Americans are awaiting human organ transplants, and about 3,000 patients die each year while waiting. Another 100,000 or so aren't eligible, for reasons ranging from advanced age to already marginal physical condition. The private sector is rushing to remedy this situation by developing a special breed of pigs grown in antiseptic sties that produce immune-system proteins which allow their organs to be transplanted into humans. At first, these pig organs will be used to keep patients alive for a short time until human organs can be found. Eventually, however, it is hoped pig organs will approach human ones in their ability to keep transplant patients alive for years.

In the meantime, federal health officials are developing new guidelines for the transplantation of animal organs and tissues into human beings because of growing concerns about their potential for triggering outbreaks of both known and unknown diseases. The "xenotransplantation" of animal organs and tissues into humans is nevertheless gaining a lot of attention from the government and others because of their potential for treating a number of serious health problems, including:

➤ The use of insulin-producing pancreatic cells from pigs for diabetics.

➤ Fetal pig cells for treating Parkinson's disease.

➤ Genetically modified pig livers for treating the most severe form of liver failure.

➤ Implantation of adrenal glands from fetal calves to combat pain in the late stages of cancer.

Such developments, while they may seem to us foreign or even improbable, are greatly improving our chances of enjoying long and healthy lives.

Mother Nature's Number One Priority

M other Nature doesn't spend much time worrying about the fact that living creatures age and die. Her first priority is to see that we pass on our genes to the next generation. After that, as far as she's concerned, we're on our own.

Sometime after age 30, most of us have fulfilled our "biological destiny." Yet instead of perishing like most creatures in the wild from being eaten, dying of starvation, and so on, we humans are determined to live as long as we can after transferring our essence. So we hang on for dear life with whatever help the new science of biogerontology can give us.

Scientists are coming to believe that genes involved in aging are controlled by hormones, and when the hormones which act as chemical messengers to the genes are depleted, aging sets in.

As of today, most of the findings are tentative, although they're getting less so. Perhaps the most critical new discovery is that if you really want to live longer, consume fewer calories, since this seems to enhance the body's anti-aging chemistry. The National Institute on Aging is spending millions to see if such dietary restrictions actually work.

The work being done on extending the human life span, as we have seen, is considerably more exotic than the basics (proper diet and exercise). Through selective breeding, for example, University of California population geneticist Michael Rose managed to double the life span of fruit flies from 25 to 50 days.

The first true scientific attempt to reverse the aging process is believed to have taken place at the Milwaukee and North Chicago Veterans' Administration hospitals in 1989.

Twenty-eight elderly volunteers, including 65-year-old retired Waukegan factory worker Fred McCullough, were given weekly injections of genetically engineered human growth hormone. This substance is normally produced in the body but declines with age, finally disappearing entirely in one out of every three men.

Doctors had never seen anything like the results of injecting growth hormone into these old-timers—they believe the procedure reawakened certain anti-aging genes. McCullough's flabby skin tightened, and his muscles strengthened. Fat melted away. Internal organs shrunken by age resumed their youthful size and vigor. "I never felt so strong in my life," said McCullough. While the doctors stopped the hormone shots after a year as they prepared for the next phase of their research, some of the benefits still lingered among the original group which had received them. Hopefully, this is a portent of things to come.

Dr. Tomorrow—Today

N ow in case you're intimidated by any of these coming changes in the world around you, let me introduce you to 76-year-old Frank Ogden.

Ogden, who calls himself "Dr. Tomorrow," lives on a two-story houseboat in Vancouver, Canada packed with $30,000 worth of the latest high-tech gear, and earns $450,000 a year giving seminars around the world on the unfolding future— "with no academic qualifications whatsoever." His business card sports a full-color photographic scan of his brain, and he's

Right: Seventy-six-year-old Frank Ogden, a.k.a. "Dr. Tomorrow," probes the world via satellite and computer for insights into our future. Below: Ogden hang glides over the Grand Canyon—in virtual reality.

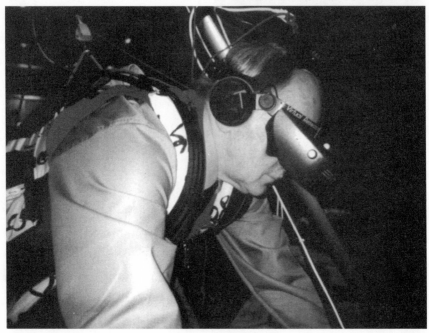

even had a writing pen filled with DNA-encoded ink, making it impossible for anyone to counterfeit his signature. "Flexibility is the key to tomorrow," says Ogden. "If I can adapt at age 76, anybody can."

Frank Ogden's latest book, *Navigating in Cyberspace: A Guide to the Next Millennium*, describes a wildly different tomorrow bearing down upon us: everything from ceramic houses to self-guiding cars that run on carbon monoxide. He even predicts talking billboards! Ogden claims that "information can lead to knowledge. Knowledge can lead to wisdom and wisdom can lead to power."

Dr. Tomorrow's information-driven world is one in which millions of computers communicate with each other, providing access to mushrooming global repositories of words, graphics, photos, and videos via the Internet. Harley Hahn, coauthor of *The Internet Complete Reference*, rhapsodizes over the "Net" as being "more impressive than the pyramids," "more beautiful than Michelangelo's David," and "more important to mankind than the wondrous inventions of the Industrial Revolution."

But before we all get carried away, it's worth noting that the Net is deluging us with irrelevant or purloined data, hardcore porn, and bothersome sales pitches that seem to be part of any new medium before society steps in and brings it to heel. Call it birthing pains.

The computerization of our daily lives has reached the point where it is providing a motherload of new material for comedians like 73-year-old Jackie Mason. In his one-man Broadway show "Love Thy Neighbor," Mason blasted corporate America's all-out drive to replace humans with computers in delivering information about their business. This includes airline flight schedules where "you have to press buttons for an hour" to get information a person could give you in seconds:

"Press 1 if you want to fly now, press 2 if you want to fly later, press 3 if you want to fly alone, press 4 if you want to fly with your sister, press 5 if it's your brother…if you want to press a pair of pants press 90…. You're pressing and pressing for an hour and a half and then you miss the plane."

8

SEARCHING FOR PARADISE

I have a feeling the next ten years, between 70 and 80, will be the most constructive of my life. I see the next century as a time when we civilize civilization.
— Reverend Robert M. Schuller

Each morning I wake up and say, "Dear Lord, I don't want anything better; just send me more of the same."
— Kitty Carlisle Hart

Paradise is where I am.
— Michel Eyquem, Seigneur de Montaigne

Bainbridge is a pleasant little place in the southwest corner of Georgia that's home to 13,000 friendly people, and is out to bag several hundred more to replace its young adults who've been flocking to greener pastures in the big city.

The town's main target of opportunity is the 35 million Americans who are expected to retire in the next ten years and are being aggressively wooed by dozens of picturesque villages across the country from Hot Springs, Arkansas, to Chewelah, Washington (not to mention assisted-living residences and nursing homes scattered from coast to coast).

Friendly Bainbridge, Georgia offers "some of the world's best hunting and fishing," along with the yearly Riverside Artsfest, shown here.

Older folks, it seems, are worth their weight in gold to communities which frequently have underutilized water, sewer, medical, and religious facilities, not to mention businesses like hardware stores and beauty parlors, and are genuinely fearful of becoming ghost towns.

So the welcome mat is out for seniors with their recession-proof monthly incomes from pensions, investments, and Social Security. Seniors also come with few, if any, kids to burden the public school system. They usually don't need jobs (but instead start their own businesses, or work free as volunteers wherever they're needed—the town library, the hospital, the day care center, the neighborhood association). Finally, seniors rarely misbehave themselves, which is a godsend to overworked local police departments.

Bainbridge, Georgia, like other towns courting retirees, sees itself as a kind of paradise where older people can move graciously from this life into the next. "Retire to the best of America. The way it was; the way it still is...." boasted a 24-page Retirement Guide which touted Bainbridge as offering:

➤ Apartments and rental homes available for $275 to $450 a month, while two- or three-bedroom houses average $70,000 (with property taxes and insurance "among the lowest in the nation for retirees").

➤ A cost of living that's nearly 8 percent lower than national average, and about a whopping 30 percent cheaper than San Jose, California, or Long Island, New York.

➤ "Some of the world's best hunting and fishing," a country club with golf and tennis, a new $3 million YMCA, a college offering classes to retirees at little or no cost, a bowling center, 125,000-book library, public tennis courts, and a small theater.

➤ An 80-bed hospital and medical center "with room and professional service rates a fraction of the cost of other cities," two nursing homes, and a Visiting Nurses Association.

➤ Plus a host of special events, from noontime Brown Bag Concerts at the bandstand in the city's downtown historic district, to a week-long Riverside Artsfest during May.

Sam Griffin, the ebullient publisher of Bainbridge's twice-weekly *Post-Searchlight* newspaper, generously invited me to lunch at a delightful waterside restaurant where he introduced me to two couples, one that had retired to this town from across the border in Florida, and the other from half a continent away in Marquette, Michigan on the shores of Lake Superior.

Joe and Deborah Clark had lived all their lives in Florida, but moved to Bainbridge after Joe retired from a big insurance agency in Tallahassee. "My father had a hardware store in Chattahoochee, Florida," says Joe, "and I began coming to Bainbridge with him to pick up supplies when I was a small boy. My father bought some attractive land near Bainbridge after World War II which I visited often and decided to build a house on after leaving the insurance business.

"It wasn't long after we settled in Bainbridge," Joe continues, "that I surprised the Executive Director of our local Chamber of Commerce by asking him 'Man, how about giving me something to do.'" Joe was soon involved with the Mentor Program in the Bainbridge High School, got interested in computers after his children gave him one as a gift, and was soon working toward a degree in computer science at a nearby college.

Joe has found a real home in Bainbridge, and so has his wife Deborah, although she admits most of her social life is still in Chattahoochee. "I think Bainbridge is a beautiful community," she says, "with plenty of activities from the Historical Society to the Candlelight Walk at Christmas. I was particularly proud of the way everyone came together during the Gulf War, with our churches holding special services to pray for the men who were fighting over there."

Don and Linda Skidmore retired to Bainbridge from their home in Michigan after deciding they wanted to go from "100 inches of snow in the winter to 100 degrees of heat in the summer." Don was a retired sergeant in the U.S. Air Force, and says he longed to relocate to a town "where I could play golf all year round."

"Our five children had left home," says Linda, a high school teacher, "so I started sending my résumé throughout Florida. I eventually accepted a job teaching physical science at

Bainbridge High School, and Don moved down here with me without ever having seen the town.

"I love this place," says Linda. "It's small enough so you know what's going on and can take a stand on issues which matter to you. I also like the variety of plants and wildlife here. I can grow orchids and cactus and they actually bloom. Don has even started rescuing injured box turtles, and we've incubated their eggs until they hatched. It's fantastic."

Adventuresome Retirees

There is no end to the variety of places beckoning older folks. New innovations appear all the time. Most people retire where they've always lived, among family, friends, and familiar surroundings. But more than half a million retirees move out of their home state every year to places such as the following:

➤ Sun City, Arizona welcomes older folks and holds young people at bay.

➤ Winslow Cohousing Group, located on an island 30 minutes from downtown Seattle, Washington, is a pedestrian-oriented community of some 70 people of all ages who live in attached houses and share everything from an orchard and recycling center to a large common house where communal dinners are served.

➤ Laghuna West, 12 miles south of Sacramento, California, describes itself as a new town "with an old-fashioned sense of place." The town offers walkable tree-lined streets, a village center where you can safely send your 10-year-old granddaughter to get a loaf of bread, and non-tract housing. "We want to get back to the way Grandpa used to live," says one local planner.

➤ Twelve communities located near military bases, for example Air Force Village West in Riverside, California, have been developed exclusively for retired military officers and their spouses (and for surviving spouses), whose average age upon entering is 72.

For the more adventuresome, the search for paradise finds us anywhere from being constantly on the road in a luxurious $250,000 recreation vehicle, to decorating a $500-a-month villa in Spain overlooking the Mediterranean.

Thousands of retirees are full-time Recreational Vehicle (RV) enthusiasts. Many belong to a group called the Escapees, whose outlook on life is summed up by the title of one of its founder's books: *Home Is Where You Park It.*

Sun-worshipping older folks can throw caution—and even their clothes—to the wind and live in one of America's mobile home nudist parks such as Florida's Cypress Cove.

Seniors struggling to survive on Social Security checks of, say, $700 a month can take off for places like Guanajuato, Mexico, where you can rent a two-bedroom apartment in a nice part of town for $140 a month, with $560 left over for nonstop partying.

If you want to live for a month or more in some exotic place, but don't want to spend a dime, you can exchange your home for someone else's fully-furnished residence in another country. San Francisco's Intervac International, which claims to be "the largest home exchange network in the world" can offer you some 8,000 houses, apartments, condos, villas, and even mobile homes in dozens of countries almost anywhere on planet Earth. You can find anything from palatial spreads complete with yachts, cooks, and chauffeurs to pop-up campers.

As a long-time newspaperman who thoroughly enjoys the fact-finding part of reporting a new story, I've always done a little bit of sleuthing before pulling up stakes and decamping someplace new. My decision to leave Princeton, New Jersey, and move down to Florida was made only after deciding that I would settle only for a new hometown that was:

> Mentally stimulating, and might hold out the possibility of keeping my hand in teaching entrepreneurship and communications.

> Friendly, with good amenities including schools, churches, heads-up police and fire departments, and knowledgeable and effective local government.

> Financially sound, with an equitable local and state tax structure.

I already knew I liked Florida's warmer year-round climate, and had spent enough time in the state, where I have friends and relatives, to get a good feel for the place.

So, having done my homework, I decided to move to Gainesville, home of the University of Florida, where I ended up doing some part-time teaching and hosting a public radio show called "Speaking of Business."

I've been living happily here in the Sunshine State ever since.

Dream Town—or Tourist Stop?

R etirees in search of a dream town should be entranced by the pastel beauty of Seaside, Florida, a professionally

The cozy post office (above) brings back the feel of the good old days, and a public pavilion's stairs lead elegantly down to the Gulf of Mexico in the planned community of Seaside: "The new town. The old ways."

planned community on the Gulf of Mexico in the western part of the Sunshine State. "The new town. The old ways," says an advertisement for Seaside, where all the homes sport picket fences and tin roofs, are painted in eye-stopping bright pinks, purples, yellows, and greens, frequently feature old-fashioned screened-in porches, and there is even a town commons, just like in the good old days when the horse and buggy ruled the roads.

Seaside has won just about every architectural award in the book. The town received extensive media coverage (including *House Beautiful* and *NBC Nightly News*), and has been praised by countless architectural critics, from H.R.H. The Prince of Wales to the *Boston Globe's* resident expert, who said flat out that "Seaside is perhaps the most important new piece of architecture in the country."

If there was ever a retirement heaven, this has got to be it. Nostalgic older folks should be flocking here—but they aren't. And the reason, according to an article in *Smithsonian* magazine, is that "More than a town, it became a model; more than a place to live, it became a place to visit. The whole town, summed up two architects, "became a hotel. Today, Seaside's houses are most often filled not with owners, but with renters— people who have come to see what the place is all about." When I asked one of Seaside's public relations people if there were any retired folks living there, she said the couple that runs the general store might be, but she wasn't sure.

While Seaside may or may not be the place for you, there is certainly no shortage of attractive new places awaiting older folks adventuresome enough—or perhaps bored enough—to crave something completely different.

The Adventures of Group Living

G roup living arrangements are one fast-growing option. Harvest House on Long Island, New York, for example, is a comfortable powder-blue clapboard home for six women and men, who pay just over $800 a month for rent, food, and utilities.

Group living is perfect for older people who prefer the camaraderie of contemporaries to being on their own, according to Margaret L. Harmon, Codirector of the National Shared Housing Resource Center in Burlington, Vermont. Harmon figures there are approximately 450 shared-housing programs in the United States today, up from 100 at most in 1981, with rents averaging between $350 and $400 a month.

I remember visiting a group home many years ago in Merchantville, New Jersey, run by the local Baptist church, and was impressed by how much its residents enjoyed the warmth and congeniality of the place. The thirteen residents lived in single and double rooms, ate their meals together in the dining room (they prepared their own breakfasts and lunches, but a cook came in to make dinner), and spent the day reading on the sun porch, having a singsong around the piano, shopping or attending community functions, and simply enjoying each other's company in a homelike family setting. One delight residents of this Baptist home did not share with those at Harvest House (which is nonreligious), however, is a drink before dinner.

Less elaborate alternatives to potentially lonely "independent" living range from several older people getting together in a condominium or apartment, to an older couple sharing their home with one or more young people who usually pay some rent, do a little work around the house, and provide a heightened sense of security.

In their 90s, distinguished psychologist Eric Erikson and his wife Joan, an artist, shared with others their rambling three-story Victorian house near Harvard Square in Cambridge, Massachusetts. At one time, the couple housed a graduate student, a professor of comparative religion, and a psychologist, with whom they often ate their meals. "Living communally is an adventure at our age," said Joan.

Today's rising cost of living, fear of crime, spreading urbanization, and memories of the beloved Andy Hardy lifestyle of youth should keep this exodus to retirement havens in high gear for some time to come. Aided along, of course, by the increasingly sophisticated marketing campaigns launched by communities eager to attract new blood.

Roadmaps to Paradise

Millions of older people, most of whom tend to be well educated and reasonably well off financially, go through their entire lives needing only minimal assistance from others until the very end. These lucky ones are able to pursue just about any lifestyle they please, including ending their days in the place of their dreams.

A sure sign that a new market is emerging in a particular field is when someone turns it into a business. This is already happening in the area of retirement real estate. One such entrepreneur is Tom Evons of Bend, Oregon, who publishes *The Small Town Observer: Rediscovering America's Heartland,* and claims he regularly talks with "thousands of people planning a major move."

While planning a place to retire, do your homework: that luxurious vacation spot may not be the best for year-round living.

Out of this new market has come a veritable galaxy of newsletters, books, magazines, and even computer software to help folks find their piece of retirement heaven here on earth. There are publications on retirement and recreation opportunities in Costa Rica, finding homes and businesses in the Caribbean, discovering "Where real estate will boom after the crash in suburbia." The answer: "in small, sleepy towns offering community, scenic splendor, historic roots, and a socially responsible lifestyle." These publications include "hundreds of practical, thought-provoking ideas you can use immediately to trade your business suit blues for blue jean dreams."

Retirement guides and resources, available in bookstores and libraries (and, increasingly, on the World Wide Web) can be helpful in researching the options—and avoiding possible pitfalls. Lee and Saralee Rosenberg, authors of *50 Fabulous Places to Retire to in America*, warn that the most common mistake people make in choosing a new home is thinking that a place where they had fun vacationing would be ideal for year-round living.

The Best Place in America if You're Old Old

"Old old" is defined as anyone who's 85 or older, and if you've arrived at that age there are few better places to call home than Iowa, which has more "old old" people than any other state—including Florida which ranks sixth.

The reason for this, according to an article in the *AARP Bulletin*, is that droves of young people deserted Iowa for greener pastures during the 1980s, while the old old stayed put. This triggered a 5 percent drop in the state's overall population but a 23 percent increase in the old old, so that today a remarkable 2 percent of Iowa's state's population is 85 and older—a proportion the nation as a whole won't reach until 2010.

Iowa has been looking after its old old in exemplary fashion. It began by recognizing that elderly people want to stay in their own homes. Then it brought together public and private services to help them do it at a fraction of the cost of ending their days in a nursing home.

"It isn't health services that keep people out of nursing homes," said Betty Grandquist, head of Iowa's Department of Elder Affairs, "it's the social services." This fact is impressively illustrated by the care received by 92-year-old Harold Mills of Cedar Rapids.

Mills got a weekly visit from home-health aide Nancy Hanson, who cleaned his house, gave him a back rub to alleviate a painful rash, took him grocery shopping, and ran errands—all paid for by the Linn County Department of Human Services Management. A private nonprofit firm called

Aging Services supplied Mills with a visiting social worker and an aide who cut his grass. He got a hot meal delivered at noon by a similar group called the Family Service Agency. And the Mercy Medical Center installed a response hookup in his house so he can call for help in case of emergency.

What's more, says the *Bulletin*, Iowa has augmented its case management system with other programs such as a home repair service and a respite-care initiative that trains volunteers to give regular caregivers a break from their duties. Some 80,000 Iowans, most of them 60 or older, also serve as volunteers giving their elderly neighbors a helping hand (even though most of the ongoing care for those 85 and older still comes from family members and friends).

Clients of Iowa's case management service are billed on a sliding scale according to their income, and those with the most modest resources pay nothing at all. The state doesn't know the exact cost, down to the last penny, of what it takes to keep its elderly citizens in their own homes. But whatever it is, it's a lot less than the average of $127 per day, or more than $46,000-a-year, for nursing home care, according to the U.S. Health Care Financing Administration.

Confronting Caregiver Burnout

Today, an estimated 10 to 12 percent of the U.S. work force is intimately involved in caring for a relative, and that figure will triple to around 33 percent by 2020, according to Andrew Scharlach, a University of California at Berkeley professor who is more aware than most that Americans are expected to live longer than any previous generation in the nation's history. One result is that upwardly mobile executives are turning down promotions attached to generous salaries because it would mean relocating far away from their elder relatives.

While most companies will not move "trailing relatives," a few will cover them if they're living with the employee it wants to relocate. One problem this presents, of course, is that the employee's spouse, who's usually in charge of the move, must suddenly include the oldsters in it. They must have a pleasant place to live, be introduced to community facilities from shops and physicians to houses of worship, and be helped to make new friends.

In about 80 percent of the cases, family members end up caring for their elderly relatives who have difficulty living on their own. And they do it even though they're seldom trained for the job, and often struggle to hold down full-time jobs while raising families of their own. Unfortunately, according to the National Family Caregivers Association in Kensington, Maryland, 49 percent of those looking after elderly family members have experienced prolonged depression. They're overcome by anger, severe anxiety, and clinical depression that often destroys their marriages, not to mention their careers.

It's this terminal caregiver burnout, this fear of jeopardizing their own physical and mental well-being, that often pushes even the most benevolent family members into putting their loved ones in a nursing home. This leads to the search for a pleasant facility with happy residents that's close by and reasonably priced. If such a home can be found, and more of them are appearing every year, everyone comes out ahead. The family can resume its own life, while the older folks embark on the secure, independent, and professionally managed homestretch of their lives.

Covenant Village in Plantation, Florida, run by the Baptist Church, is such a place. This retirement community looks like a resort with swimming pool, jacuzzi, flower gardens, libraries and so on, and offers three distinct kinds of living arrangements: regular condominiums for those who are completely ambulatory, an attached Care Center with round-the-clock medical staff (featuring condos upstairs for those who can get around with a walker), and hospital-type rooms downstairs for those needing constant care.

The greatest boon to older people living on their own is undoubtedly the assisted-living residence which can help them live comfortable independent lives without regimentation. The residences are typically bright and airy, with kitchenettes, bathrooms, and living rooms which guests usually decorate with furniture and accessories from home. They also offer amenities including beauty parlors, snack bars, sun rooms, and buses to take them into town, and a staff is on hand to help with daily needs such as walking, dressing, and bathing. Such costs usually run 25 percent less than skilled nursing care.

Real estate developers and big hotel chains, including Marriott International, have watched the demand for office towers, shopping malls, and hotels shrink in recent years, and are rushing to serve this lucrative new market in which demand currently far outstrips supply.

Wall Street is beginning to look at assisted living companies as interesting investments with upside potentials that rival drug companies (which also get a lot of their growth and profits from a rapidly aging America).

Every day of the week, new and improved living arrangements are being offered to seniors by savvy companies that recognize a golden investment opportunity when they see one.

A Nice Place to Visit, but ....

We all have our own ideas of paradise. But who in the world would name New York City as a haven for retirees? Just think of its sky-high living costs, over-crowdedness, and shooting gallery mentality. Or the young rappers who glorify mindless violence in lyrics such a "Throw ya' gunz in the air/And pop-pop like ya' just don't care," or "It ain't nothing you should laugh to/I'll shoot your moms if I have to."

Yet older people are not only staying put in New York, they're returning to the Big Apple from retirement hot spots as famed as Miami Beach and San Francisco. Innumerable explanations are offered for this remarkable state of affairs, from the city's abundance of museums, theaters, restaurants, and public transportation, to its high-quality medical care. But perhaps the wildest reason is one advanced by a tiny widow named Ada Bank, who's in her 90s, lives in a second-floor walkup apartment in Greenwich Village, and spends most of her time looking out her window at the goings-on in the street down below.

"This," says Bank, "is where the action is."

9

Into the Sunset

Death plucks at my ear and says "Live—I am coming."
                              —Helen Waddell

I shall die young, at whatever age the experience occurs.
                              —Ruth Bernard

*Some sigh for yesterday! Some for tomorrow! But
you must reach old age before you can understand the
meaning—the splendid, absolute, unchallengeable, irreplaceable meaning of the word "today"!*
                              —Paul Claudel at age 80

We humans have been scheming and conniving since time immemorial to hold the ravages of age at bay—or, as Dylan Thomas put it, to "Rage, rage against the dying of the light." Those who do the most—needless to say—are those who are best informed about the aging process, and have the most time and money to invest in going mano-a-mano with Father Time.

Long-time editor of *Cosmopolitan* magazine Helen Gurley Brown, author of *The Late Show: A Semiwild but Practical Survival Guide for Women over 50,* says in her book that at age 64, "I thought nobody, including me, would be able to tell I was older, because I was Doing Everything Right. I was a maniacal

*Helen Gurley Brown in her heyday
as* Cosmopolitan *magazine's editor-
in-chief.*

exerciser (I worked out for over an hour a day) and a nut case
dieter (I kept myself at a steady 105 pounds) making regular
'payments' to save the outside (silicone injections, face ex-
ercises, a little cosmetic surgery) as well as investing in the
inside (estrogen supplements, vitamins, veggies). So how could
I age?"

In her review of Brown's book in *The Washington Post,*
Barbara Raskin, author of *Hot Flashes,* says, "In 'hey-sailor' fashion, Brown recommends remaining a sexual 'player' at almost
any cost (including paying for it) throughout your 60s and 70s
because sex keeps you youthful." Raskin concludes her review
by hoping that Helen Gurley Brown will "...live to be 100 so
she can write and publish *Sex in your Second Century.* I'm afraid
I might need it."

All this may sound wild and off-the-wall, I know—but only
until you finally understand how absolutely wonderful one's
waning years can be. Or how many older people these days are

taking the final curtain in stride, in the certain knowledge that they've had one terrific time on dear old planet Earth.

Rethinking What It Means To Be Old

Since 1900, the average American's life expectancy has soared. As recently as the end of World War II, only 8 percent of us reached age 65. Today, nearly 13 percent or more than 31 million Americans are 65 or older, and by 2050—when today's teenagers start turning 65—a projected 20 percent of the U.S. population, or some 80 million people, are expected to be 65 or older.

The rapid aging of America is forcing us to rethink the idea of what it means to be old. Most of us continue to accept the conventional wisdom that we're old when we hit 65. But today that's obviously nonsense, since millions of us who have reached that age—and beyond—feel we're in the prime of life. This plain fact has led quite a few gerontologists, along with others who specialize in studying the aging process, to begin viewing it in stages rather than as a continuum.

Many gerontologists are now dividing our harvest years into two parts. The first is from 65 to 85, when most of us can look after ourselves—and then some. And the second part is from 85 on when most, but by no means all of us, need some help in managing our daily lives. Experts on aging call the years from 85 on the "Dreadful D's," since they are often marked by decline, deterioration, dependency, and eventually death.

The Dreadful D's, needless to say, do not apply to everyone. Some can even turn the whole concept on its head.

The *Florida Times-Union* recently reported on Arlue Francis, a 105-year-old African-American woman living in the small town of Hastings, Florida who is in such good shape she's able to help take care of her 76-year-old daughter Lizzie Lou Ross, a double amputee diabetic and stroke victim confined to a wheelchair. An aide from the local town council on aging comes in five days a week to help the two women with personal care, cooking, shopping, and household chores, and health care workers also visit regularly. But it's Francis who runs things.

"I look back and wonder how I made it, and I know nobody helped me out but Jesus," she told a reporter for the paper. "I know now that if he puts a burden on me, he's going to help me bear it. My strength is in the Lord, baby," continues Francis. "He's been better to me than I've been to myself."

A Philosophy of Aging

There's little doubt that more years, *good* years, will continue to be added to the human life span. Dr. Harvey B. Simon, who teaches at the Harvard Medical School and practices internal medicine at the Massachusetts General Hospital, says "Nine out of ten causes of death are preventable, and 75 percent of deaths in this country are needlessly premature."

But as we advance into great age and that final sunset, it's comforting to have a philosophy to help us through the inevitable loss of loved ones, youthful beauty, firm bodies, and physical strength, one that will help us preserve our optimism about the delights ahead.

American writer Marilynne Robinson gives one of her characters just such a philosophy: "…she conceived life as a road down which one traveled; an easy enough road through a broad country, and that one's destination was there from the very beginning, a measured distance away, standing in the

Famed psychologists Erik and Joan Erikson conduct a seminar for students and invited guests at Chicago's Erikson Institute in 1985.

ordinary light like some plain house where one went in and was greeted by respectable people and was shown to a room where everything one had ever lost or put aside was gathered together, waiting."

Famed psychologist Erik H. Erikson and his wife Joan, who lived into their 90s, spent decades developing a philosophy of aging which revolves around the need to feel a sense of completeness to help offset the despair which so often accompanies the physical disintegration of old age. Of course, "Wisdom and integrity are something that other people may see in an old person," said Joan Erikson, "but it's not what the old person is feeling. That's what ... roused me up to see what it was that old people do feel and what they have to face...."

More than forty years ago, the Eriksons identified distinct stages of the life cycle: Infancy, Early Childhood, Play Age,

Dr. Lee Salk, who was desperately ill with cancer of the esophagus, says he could not have survived without the knowledge that he was wanted, needed, and loved by his family. (Photo: Sigrid Estrada)

School Age, Adolescence, Early Adulthood, and Adulthood. If these earlier phases have been successfully negotiated, said the Eriksons, the struggle between completeness and despair can culminate in true wisdom. Joan Erikson believed wisdom "comes from life experience well digested." Old age is not synonymous with wisdom, she felt, but wisdom can only be achieved with age.

As we grow older, and one would hope wiser, we come to appreciate the central place in our lives of a loving partner, and of the family and friends who support us as we become less self-assured, and more vulnerable to the physical ills and accidents which accompany old age (not to mention the inevitable disappearance of those closest to us).

A heartfelt description of the importance of family in one's life is contained in the late Dr. Lee Salk's last book *Familyhood: Nurturing the Values that Matter.* Salk introduces his book with a description of how his family joined with his physicians in pulling him through a catastrophic illness eventually diagnosed as cancer of the esophagus. He was forced to undergo invasive and complicated surgery after which "just about everything that could go wrong did," from kidney failure and pneumonia to the surgical removal of most of his gangrene-ridden esophagus.

During this ordeal, Salk was surrounded by his family. His wife Mary Jane was by his side day and night, caring for him and offering him encouragement. Salk said that his son Eric, a medical student at the hospital, saw him "every morning when he came by just to touch me, kiss me, hold me." His daughter Pia flew in from her home in the Midwest and stayed with him throughout his hospitalization and beyond. His brother Dr. Jonas Salk, famed for developing a vaccine against polio, flew in from California to be by his side, as did his brother Herman, along with innumerable other family members and friends.

"I have been told by people who cared for me," said Salk after leaving the hospital to return home, "that my survival is amazing, a testament to phenomenal inner strength. I am a strong person, but beyond any doubt, the most powerful motivation to live comes from family. From the knowledge of being wanted, needed, and loved."

William Humphrey's novel *September Song* poignantly portrays "the terrible sadness" so many older people feel at the inevitable loss of those they once loved. One husband bursts into tears as he glimpses a bamboo back scratcher in a drugstore window: "He would have been lost without her, he used to say, and now he was lost." A 76-year-old woman, after 49 years of marriage, decides to run off with her lover and leave behind her old and ill husband, but in the end can't do it because "he could not look after himself."

One of the most agonizing cries from the heart at the end of an all-consuming love affair appears in *Genius*, a biography of the Nobel Prize-winning mathematical physicist Richard Feynman.

The book describes Feynman's celebrated contributions to science, including the one best known to the public: as a member of the presidential commission investigating the Challenger disaster, which took the lives of seven astronauts, Feynman demonstrated that the ship blew up because the frigid weather on launch day had destroyed its rubber rings, allowing hot gases to escape which consumed the space ship and its crew.

The great love of Feynman's life was his childhood sweetheart Arline Greenbaum, to whom he became engaged while he was a graduate student at Princeton. Not long afterward she developed lymphatic tuberculosis, and despite the violent objections of his family Feynman married her. He regularly visited her in the sanitarium, where she died four years later as he sat by her bedside. Feynman told a friend of the pure joy he experienced in caring for Greenbaum during the final years of her life. He grieved for her. And two years after her death, he wrote her a letter saying, "I find it hard to understand in my mind what it means to love you after you are dead—but I still want to comfort and take care of you—and I want you to love me and care for me.'"

All those who have been blessed by having a great love in their lives will know exactly what Feynman was experiencing. Like Feynman, those people will probably go on to other relationships and fulfilling friendships in the certain knowledge we weren't put here to live out our days alone.

Joan Erikson believed that older people who are fortunate enough to have had a long, committed, and hence intimate relationship are particularly blessed.

"You put such a stress on passion when you're young," she said. "You learn about the value of tenderness when you grow old. You also learn late in life not to hold, to give without hanging on; to love freely, in the sense of wanting nothing in return."

Suddenly You're the Family Historian

A rite of passage as we grow older is to wake up one morning and realize we're now the official family historian. The old-timer whom younger members of the clan will come to when they suddenly get curious about their ancestors.

No grandchild has yet asked me about our family's lineage, but when one does I'll be ready, thanks to a genealogy laboriously assembled by my late Uncle Herb going back to 1603. Among its revelations were that two of my forebears were soldiers in General George Washington's army—one died from exposure following the battles of Trenton and Princeton, near to where I was born and lived for many years. Just think of the thrill awaiting a grandchild hearing that news.

In years gone by, family histories were confined to the printed word. But today, many grandparents are capturing their reminiscences on tape recordings and film. It's a marvelous idea, and not unlike the personal histories of noteworthy men and women assembled for scholarly research at a number of our nation's major universities.

Older people remember an America very different from the one they live in today. It was somehow more gentle, caring, slower-moving, less materialistic, more family-oriented, and less infatuated with technology, which many of today's seniors want no part of. "I wouldn't have one of those microwave things," 97-year-old Gladys Carter of Elma, Washington, told the authors of *Quiet Pride: Ageless Wisdom of the American West.* "Anytime you can put a cold cup of coffee in something, take it out and the coffee's hot but the cup's cold, it's too spooky for me."

I remember my father, who was born in Philadelphia in 1896, telling me about spending evenings in the living room with the family huddled around a cat's whisker crystal set nestled in a metal mixing bowl which served as an amplifier. He'd move the whisker over the chunk of crystal, and with luck pick up Pittsburgh station KTKA in his earphones. We'd pass around the earphones so everyone could hear the miracle of music coming over the airwaves from hundreds of miles away.

My father was a big handsome guy, and he'd tell me how fellows and girls would attend Christian Endeavor meetings at church on Sunday night and then return to his house for a "sing song" around the piano (often interrupted by his mother entering the room, looking around at the girls wearing short flapper era dresses, and pulling down the skirts of any she felt were hiked up too far above their knees).

I once told my daughter a delightful story her grandmother often told me about an experience she had in 1916, during World War I, when she was a little girl living near Bristol, England: "One night our nanny came and got me and my two little sisters and rushed us to the window to see searchlights piercing the sky in search of German dirigibles shaped like big black sausages that had come to drop bombs on us. Just then a searchlight caught a dirigible and it exploded in flames after being hit by anti-aircraft guns. We three girls cried and cried because we thought the lovely men inside would be killed. But our nanny said "Don't cry, children, because the men will simply grease their bottoms and slide down the searchlight beam to the ground.' This comforted us, and we stopped crying."

The knowledge and experiences of grandparents are precious and irreplaceable. Says Rosamunde Pilcher, an American

Don't overlook your value as historian and teacher to younger folks: grandmothers can tell their granddaughters about everything from ice boxes to foot pedal-driven sewing machines.

writer, "That was one of the good things about getting old: you weren't perpetually in a hurry....There was time to stop and look, and, looking, to remember."

I'm sure all of you born during the 1920s, 1930s, and 1940s have your own memories which are worth writing down or tape recording, so you'll be ready if a grandchild climbs into your lap and asks what life was like before Barney and Big Bird.

Methuselah Here We Come

This book is dedicated to the proposition that there's never been a better time than today to be in the homestretch of one's life. We older people are healthier, stronger, more finan-cially secure, and certainly more attractive than any group of seniors in history.

If the latest research streaming out of the National Institute on Aging, major U.S. universities, and foreign study centers such as Sweden's national statistics office is any guide, millions of our offspring can look forward to living 85 years or longer, with millions more topping 100. Great age seems destined to become so common, in fact, that NBC's morning television program *Today* may have to reconsider showcasing people who've hit or surpassed the century mark: What now takes a minute or two could gobble up the entire two-hour show.

Census Bureau demographers predict the median age of Americans—that is, as many people above the age as below it—will increase from 33 today (the highest in our history) to 39 in 2035. But the real action, as we've seen, will be with "old old, " the 3.3 million people who are 85 and older today, and whose numbers will double to 6 million by 2010 and rocket to 19 million in 2050. Perhaps even more spectacular is the Census Bureau prediction that the number of people 100 and older will explode from 45,000 today to in excess of a million by 2050.

Not everyone, needless to say, agrees with this picture of a rapidly aging America. Some figure the Census Bureau's pro-jections are actually too cautious. Dr. James Vaupel, a leading population expert at Duke University who directed four critical research studies supported by the National Institute on Aging (NIA), believes that the average life span will be 94 for men and 100 for women by 2080, when he expects *72 million* Americans 85 or older to be alive, or nearly four times the Census Bureau's estimate. If he's right, these increased numbers would have a cataclysmic impact on retirement, pension programs, and Social Security, which—assuming it's still around by then—will look very different than it does today.

The Census Bureau's conservative view of the aging process is based on its belief that 85 represents the natural limit of the human life span, which has been increasing since the 1950s. This is now being questioned, however, by NIA studies conducted by scientists from the United States, Sweden, Denmark, and Finland, who say that there is no evidence to suggest the human life span is preordained.

So the great age debate rages on with no letup in sight. An item in *The Futurist* magazine, for instance, tells about a group in Houston, Texas called the Curing Old Age Disease Society. The society has posted a $100,000 prize to be awarded to the first scientist or group discovering a genetic cure for old age by the year 2000. The society, according to its president, believes old age can be cured by identifying and correcting defective genes, so that people can be returned from advancing age to their "normal adult condition." The society feels this would increase the number of people with mature minds and healthy bodies, who could then "evolve to preserve our precious planet."

So far, ruminations about stamping out old age and remaining forever young have stirred up remarkably little interest among older folks, compared with adding a few more healthy years to our already nicely lengthening life spans.

I've asked dozens of older people—a few well into their 90s—what they'd do if they were given the chance to turn back the clock and begin life anew without a trace of memory of their present lives and loves. They could be teenagers again, without a mark on them. In their 20s, feeling great, with energy to burn. In their 30s, just starting a family—or whatever stage of life they desired. An irresistible offer, right?

Wrong.

Renowned French writer Victor Hugo, shown here in a portrait from 1879, looked forward to his last great adventure with unabashed delight.

Only a handful of people I interviewed said they'd jump at the chance of being young again, including a 56-year-old woman with four daughters by a man she called "a cheap yap-yapping jerk," whom she divorced shortly after their last child was born. "I'd have children again," she says, "only this time I'd make sure they were with a good man I loved who would take care of us." But almost everyone else I spoke with wanted no part of exchanging the life they'd had for a completely new one. The very thought of giving up years of joy, sadness, even tragedy with loved ones with whom they have shared their lives was more than any of them could bear. They were all quite content to let their lives draw to close and move on, to turn out the lights at the end of their earthly journey, and simply bid adieu. Immortality might sound good on paper, but the reality—as countless stories from Greek mythology warn—might be something we don't really want.

There are many stories of well-known figures who accepted their final days with grace, good humor, and courage.

Famed French poet, playwright, and novelist Victor Hugo, who published his last great work at age 81, is quoted as saying toward the end of his days "I am old. I am going to die. I shall see God. See God! What a tremendous event. What shall I say to Him? I often think about it. I am getting ready."

Stephen Foster, who composed well over a hundred songs, wrote the following lyrics just a few days before his death, when he dreamed of waking up in the arms of God:

> Beautiful Dreamer, wake unto me.
> Starlight and dewdrops are waiting for thee.
> Sounds of the rude world heard in the day,
> Lull'd by the moonlight have all passed away.

World-renowned French physicist Marie Curie, winner of two Nobel prizes for discovering radium and radioactivity, was finally confined to her bed at age 66 from a lifetime of exposure to high levels of radiation. "On the morning of July 3 [1934]," her daughter wrote, "for the last time Madame Curie could read the thermometer held in her shaking hands and distinguished [the] fall in fever which always precedes the end. She smiled with joy."

Even Oscar Wilde, author of the hugely successful 1895 London play *The Importance of Being Earnest* and other famous works, died in disgrace in a cheap hotel room he could barely afford. Still, he apparently met death with characteristic wit. His last words were reported to be "It's the wallpaper or me— one of us has got to go."

And American artist John Marin, confined to New York Hospital and nearing death at age 82, picked up the hospital syringe used to give him his daily injection, filled it with black ink, and sketched the view outside his hospital window.

Journey's End

A s the years pile on, it's difficult not to think about the end of life and what may lie beyond. As late as 1960, most Americans died at home, but today that number is only one in five. The rest end their days in institutions, often surrounded by overworked doctors and nurses and expensive high-tech machines designed to keep us going until the bitter end.

If that end is within sight, as it so often is, then the best place to bid adieu may well be the "hospice," a word dating back to medieval times, when it meant a place of shelter and rest for weary or sick travelers on long journeys. Today, according to the National Hospice Organization (NHO) in Arlington, Virginia, the word means a special kind of care designed to provide support for people in the final phase of a terminal illness. Two out of three hospice patients are at least 65 years old, 84 percent were diagnosed with cancer, 4 percent with AIDS, and 3 percent with cardiovascular disease.

Hospice care seeks to enable patients with a life expectancy of six months or less to carry on an alert, pain-free life and to manage other symptoms so that their final days may be spent with dignity and quality at home, or in a home-like setting, where they can wear their own clothes rather than a hospital gown, enjoy familiar foods in warm atmosphere rather than on an antiseptic hospital tray, and experience their last days surrounded by family, friends, and caregivers sharing this last great adventure.

According to the NHO, the overwhelmingly nonprofit hospice movement began in 1974, and is now "one of the fastest-growing segments of the healthcare industry." Nearly 2,000 programs in all 50 states serve close to 250,000 patients, and are growing at 12 percent a year. The NHO says what it gives patients and their families differs from other types of healthcare in that:

➤ **Hospice offers comfort-oriented rather than curative treatment.** Sophisticated methods of pain and symptom control prescribed by a physician enable the patient to live the fullest, most comfortable life possible under the circumstances.

➤ **Hospice treats the person, not the disease.** An interdisciplinary hospice team of trained professionals made up of doctors, nurses, counselors, therapists, aides, and volunteers address the medical, emotional, psychological, and spiritual needs of patients and their families.

➤ **Hospice emphasizes quality, rather than length, of life.** It neither hastens nor postpones death, but rather affirms life and regards death as a normal process.

➤ **Hospice considers the entire family, and not just the patient as the "unit of care."** Both patient and family are included in the decision-making process, and bereavement counseling is provided to the family after the death of the loved one.

➤ **Hospice offers help and support to the patient and family on a twenty-four-hour-a-day, seven-days-a-week basis.** Patients routinely receive periodic in-home services of a nurse, home health aide, social worker, volunteer, and other members of the hospice team who, if suddenly needed, are just a phone call away.

➤ **Hospice care is frequently less expensive than conventional care during the last six months of life** because it uses less high-cost technology, and more family, friends, and volunteers to look after the patient.

➤ **Hospice care is covered under many programs, although payments rarely cover its full cost.** This includes private insurance plans, Medicare, Medicaid (in some states), the military's CHAMPUS program, and the NHO says it is working closely with the Veterans Administration Hospital System to make hospice care available to those who have served their country.

The most disturbing problem facing the National Hospice Organization, according to its president John J. Mahoney, is that a recent Gallup Poll found that far too few people have actually heard of hospice care. "We're encouraged that the results support our belief that people want to die at home and prefer to be cared for by relatives and friends," says Mahoney, "but are concerned that the apparent confusion and lack of knowledge about what hospice care is may keep some people from considering it as an option if they or family members are faced with a terminal diagnosis."

The Secret of Immortality

As we think about the new reality of living far longer than anyone else in human history, it's worth remembering that true immortality comes not only through our descendants, but from our life's work, if it leaves something of value to those who come after us.

In her book *Matisse and Picasso: A Friendship in Art*, Francoise Gilot talks about how "Matisse came to the notion of trends and families of artists, in the sense of traditions handed down from generation to generation, not through genetics but through oral teaching linking one artist to the next, as from Perugino to Raphael or from Verrocchio to Leonardo da Vinci."

Gilot quotes Matisse as saying, "As long as some painters continue to be interested in our ideas or our works, we will not be dead. That does not prevent each new artist from being entirely different, but he or she must also entertain a dialogue with the dead and keep them alive within himself or herself."

"All of a sudden," Gilot says, "I understood what he meant and what he was after: a permanent metamorphosis, yes, but also each artist being nourished by his love and understanding of the pilgrimage of his predecessors. Similarities, meanderings, zigzags, and contradictions all bringing a new leaf to the tree of life."

It seems all artists have their own concepts of posterity. Irish writer James Joyce believed that his great works, culminating in *Ulysses*, will keep his memory alive forever. "I've put in so many enigmas and puzzles," Joyce once said, "that it will keep the professors busy for centuries arguing over what I meant, and that's the only way of insuring one's immortality."

A less sanguine view is espoused by modern American artist Jasper Johns, 66, who professes, "It seems to me one can never make a comprehensive statement. One just continues to do things—this, that and the other—and then it stops." Poet Barbara Guest has said, "Some things are never completed. You just leave off."

To one distinguished cultural historian, Jasper Johns' attitude is nothing but a cop-out, since it sidesteps what he calls the most important unresolved dilemma facing concerned seniors today. Thomas R. Cole, director of the graduate program at the Institute for the Medical Humanities on the

University of Texas campus, discusses this dilemma in his Pulitzer Prize-nominated book *The Journey of Life: A Cultural History of Aging in America.*

In the American Society on Aging's newspaper *Aging Today,* Cole discussed his book at length, beginning his examination of aging by asking himself these questions: "Is old age the culmination or the dreary denouement of life's drama? Is there anything important to be done after children are raised and careers completed? Has death always cast its shadow over old age? What are the rights and responsibilities of older people? What are the virtues of old age? Has there ever really been a 'good' old age?

"Since the mid-19th century," Cole continues, "Americans have come to view aging not as a fated aspect of our individual and social existence, but as one of life's problems to be solved through willpower, aided by science, technology, and expertise."

While Cole says he applauds "the contributions that gerontology and geriatrics have made to the health and well-being of older people." He insists, "We need a cultural reorientation as well. For all its accomplishments, the cultural hegemony of science intensifies the pathos of aging in a society devoted to the limitless pursuit of individual health and wealth."

What we've failed to do, says Cole, is confront what he calls "the 'demeaning' of aging rooted in modern culture's relentless hostility toward decay and dependency. In the late twentieth century," he concludes, "later life floats in a cultural limbo. Old age remains a season in search of its purposes."

That said, and knowing the clock is ticking, how come so many of us old timers are zestfully celebrating our harvest years? Is it because so many of us are living longer, feeling great, enjoying our new-found financial security, firing up our imaginations, and doing things the over-the-hill gang in years gone by could only dream of? The presumed desolation of old age is old thinking. What's new is *us*. And ain't it grand?

While stepping down as president of the Southern Christian Leadership Conference and pastor of Atlanta's historic Ebenezer Baptist Church at the age of 75, the Reverend Joseph E. Lowery offered some advice on the subject of immortality. "If you can take care of the internal," said this visionary, who had walked shoulder-to-shoulder with Reverend Dr. Martin Luther King, Jr. and Reverend Ralph D. Abernathy, "you can easily take care of the external. Then you can avoid the infernal and latch on to the eternal."

Drawing Nigh

In so many instances it is young people who suffer the most at the loss of someone who has been part of their lives for as long as they can remember. They grieve over that loss and the sudden realization that they too are aging, and must increasingly look to their own growing family for the comfort and sense of belonging they once got from their parents, aunts and uncles, and grandparents.

I've told those I love who will be there to witness my departure not to shed too many tears for me, as I've had one hell of a life. It's been a marvelous trip. Couldn't ask for anything more. So kids, celebrate the old man. Raise a glass or two to his memory. Remember the good times, even the funny times, and if you want to make a joke—as TV comic Joan Rivers did at the loss of her husband Edgar—nothing would give me a bigger kick.

"The first Edgar joke I did," said Joan, "was about five or six months after he died. I said 'He asked to be cremated and have his ashes scattered in Neiman-Marcus, because that way I would visit him every day.' I had to say to the audience, in effect, 'I know that you know, and we've dealt with it, and it's now gone.'"

One critical obligation every conscientious oldster should handle before it's too late—yet which two-thirds of all Americans neglect to do—is getting legal assistance in putting together written instructions for the handling of your estate. Important steps include ensuring that you have:

1. A valid up-to-date will naming an executor (to insure your estate is properly administered) and your beneficiaries.

2. A durable power of attorney authorizing someone to act on your behalf if you are unable to manage your own affairs.

3. A "living will" spelling out your wishes as to what life-prolonging measures you want provided or withheld if you are unable to communicate those wishes for yourself.

4. An informal letter of instruction telling your executor how you want to wrap up your affairs, that is, everything from funeral instructions to an inventory of your assets and where to find them.

You can breathe a lot easier once this is done since it means your heirs will receive your estate with a minimum of red tape—certainly a nice way to be remembered.

Evensong

In the meantime, millions of older people are simply getting on with their lives. Doing what they love to do. Reveling in the moment. And hoping there will be many more of them before it's time to move on.

John Barrymore, Sr. said "A man is never old till regrets take the place of dreams." This quote was running through my mind the other day as I got down on bended knee at age 70 and asked a lovely lady of 64 to be my wife.

Older couples like us who have raised their families, are financially secure, and in reasonably good health are marrying or living together in record numbers. We're looking forward to years of happiness just like young lovebirds a fraction of our age.

My new wife is a trim blonde whose great-great grandfather helped launch the Western Union Telegraph Company and later founded Cornell University. We're enjoying a marvelous new life as a couple again, which, among other things, is a joy to our children and grandchildren.

My wife's son is a Lt. Colonel in the U.S. Army who was commanding a battalion of troops in Panama when he called to congratulate his mother on her imminent wedding. "But," he added, "I've go to ask you a question, Mom, and I hope you'll give me a straight answer. Are you pregnant?" "Of course not, silly," she replied, "we're not even getting married until next week."

Sharing one's life with someone new late in life is different from a committed relationship when one is young. Older couples simply have more time to enjoy each other, to do what pleases them from volunteer work with community organizations, to spending quality time with their children and grandchildren, to finally getting around to seeing the stately homes of England, the palaces of India, or the cafés of Paris.

I'm constantly amazed at the happiness my new wife and I enjoy when simply reaching out to one another under the covers as the sun comes up. Having a leisurely breakfast as we plan our day, walking around the garden, feeding the ducks on the pond, comparing notes on the latest books we've read, dining at sunset at our favorite restaurant on the ocean, watching the nightly news on television, and then slowly drifting off to sleep in each other's arms until another wonderful new day begins.

One perhaps surprising side of a late-in-life marriage is that it's possible to remain friendly with one's former spouse. My wife's ex-husband sent her a letter of congratulations when he heard our news, and we often get together with my ex-wife and her new husband, who live just a few miles away.

Since our wedding, we've been doing all we can to bring our single friends together so they, too can revel in the delights of a vintage love affair. Usually it's the simple joys of sharing one's everyday life with someone, and rejoicing in the love of friends and family.

My wife and I were married in a little church chapel with two of our closest friends at hand. Outside there was a lovely garden with flourishing grass, trees, flowering shrubs, and a fountain. We asked the pastor about the garden and he told us we could begin our final journey there side by side.

Two lovers, no longer young, looking forward to being together forever.

A PPENDIX

Resources on Aging

Countless organizations offer older people help with their
health, the law, travel, opportunities to assist others,
finances, housing taxes, and the like, both in the United States
and abroad.

Many of these organizations can be found right in your own
community, and you can locate them by talking with friends,
inquiring through your church, fraternal organization, or city
hall, chatting with someone at your senior citizens' club, looking through the yellow pages in your local telephone directory,
reading about happenings of interest to seniors in your local
newspaper, or by perusing the giveaway weekly publications targeted at older folks that are springing up around the country.

There are hundreds of organizations serving seniors on the
national level, and you can find out about many of them by
stopping by your local library and consulting a guidebook such
as the Encyclopedia of Associations. This three-volume publication has sketches of dozens of groups of interest to seniors, as
diverse as The National Indian Council on Aging (Albuquerque,
New Mexico), American Society of Retired Dentists (Boca
Raton, Florida), Old Lesbians Organizing For Change (Houston,

Texas), National Council on Black Aging (Durham, North Carolina), National Senior Citizens' Law Center (Los Angeles, California), and the Council of Religious Volunteer Agencies (Chicago, Illinois).

To give you an idea of some of the services available to seniors, here are capsule sketches of several of varying interest, and a list of contact addresses for additional resources mentioned in the book, followed by a rundown of sources of information on investing.

American Association of Retired Persons (AARP)

601 E St. NW
Washington, DC 20049
(800) 424-3410
www.aarp.org

The AARP offers many services and publications for older people. Membership is $8 for one year, $20 for three years, and $45 for ten years, and includes subscriptions to both *Modern Maturity* magazine and the AARP *Bulletin*.

The *AARP Guide to Internet Resources Related to Aging* lists and describes Internet sites of interest to older people and those concerned with aging-related issues, including researchers, policy makers, service providers, caregivers, and students. You may order a copy of the guide by calling the AARP's toll-free number.

American Society on Aging

833 Market Street
Suite 511
San Francisco, CA 94103-1824
(415) 974-9619; Fax (415) 974-0300
www.healthanswers.com

This membership association of professionals covers all aspects of growing older through its bimonthly newspaper *Aging Today* (the price of which is included in members' annual dues, or $30/year for nonmembers), and its quarterly journal, *Generations* (priced at $38 for nonmembers). ASA also holds an annual three-day meeting in various parts of the country, with themes such as *Aging: The Next Generation*, featuring sessions on several hundred topics by experts in their fields. ASA's membership dues are $100/year, or $25/year for those with incomes under $25,000 a year.

America's Pharmaceutical Research Companies

1100 Fifteenth Street, NW
Washington, DC 20005
(800) 862-4110
www.phrma.org

This group offers a free series of health guides on topics such as heart attack, stroke, breast cancer, menopause, prostate problems, and mental illness.

Elderhostel

75 Federal Street
Boston, MA 02110
(617) 426-8056
www.elderhostel.org

A "nonprofit educational adventure group for older adults looking for something different, from Maori culture to the Roman Forum ... Viking shipbuilders to London theater ... from Ecuador to Egypt, Jamaica to Japan, Poland to Portugal." More than 300,000 Elderhostel students 55 and older are expected to have a learning adventure in 1998 through a network of 1,800 participating institutions offering two- or three-week programs ranging from an average of about $350 in the United States for lodging, meals, and education, to $5,500 or so in Australia (including transportation). Elderhostel publishes thick catalogs four times each year for those Elderhostelers in the United States, Canada, and abroad, plus one for seniors looking to be of service to others. Elderhostel will send you catalogs free for the first year, and will continue sending them free if you participate in one of its programs, or for $10/year.

Environmental Alliance for Senior Involvement
8733 Old Dumfries Road
Catlett, VA 20119
(540) 788-3274
www.easi.org
This alliance of organizations, from the Nature Conservancy to the U.S. Environmental Protection Agency, reaches "... 1,000,000 seniors a day to facilitate their involvement in causes for the betterment or our environment."

Habitat for Humanity International
121 Habitat Street
Americus, GA 31709-3498
(800) HABITAT or (912) 924-6935; Fax (912) 924-6541
www.habitat.org
Habitat for Humanity is a nonprofit, ecumenical Christian housing ministry. Habitat works in partnership with people in need throughout the world, building simple, decent shelter that is sold to them at no profit, through no-interest loans. Funds, building materials, and labor are donated by individuals, churches, corporations, and other organizations which share its goal of eliminating substandard housing worldwide. Habitat for Humanity International is at work in 53 countries and is approaching the completion of its 60,000th house worldwide.

Health After 50, *the Johns Hopkins Medical Newsletter*
  P.O. Box 420235
  11 Commerce Boulevard
  Palm Coast, FL 32142-0235
  (800) 829-0422
  www.enews.com/magazines/jhml
Articles by Johns Hopkins University School of Medicine doctors. Covers subjects from Alzheimer's Disease to pain relief for arthritis. Subscription $28/year.

National AFL-CIO Committee on Political Education Retiree Program
  815 16th Street NW
  6th Floor
  Washington, DC 20006
  (202) 637-5124
The program helps retired union members learn about the political process from the viewpoint of organized labor and assists in getting out the vote among union members, retirees, and their families.

National Center on Rural Aging
  409 3rd Street, SW
  Suite 200
  Washington, DC 20024
  (202) 479-1200
This center develops social and public policies addressing the needs and interests of older people living on farms and in rural communities. The center does everything it can to upgrade services for rural areas by working directly with national groups and government agencies at all levels. It also provides guidance to community support groups, including service methods that

have worked before in rural areas, along with training those helping seniors to live better lives.

The center is part of the National Council on the Aging (Membership Services, Department 5087, Washington, DC 20061-5087; (202) 479-6606/6605; Fax (202) 479-0735; www.ncoa.org), which helps professionals better serve the needs of older Americans.

National Institute on Aging Information Center
P.O. Box 8057
Gaithersburg, MD 20898
(800) 222-2225
www.senior.com/npo/nia.html

This center offers free information about diseases, disorders, conditions, health promotion, disease prevention, medical care, medications, planning for later years, and other health-related topics.

The Plastic Surgery Information Service
(800) 635-0635
www.plasticsurgery.org

This is a recorded answering service that will send you a list of five board-certified plastic surgeons in your area. Leave your name, address, and telephone number.

The Web site for plastic surgery is sponsored by the American Society of Plastic and Reconstructive Surgeons (ASPRS, 444 E. Algonquin Rd., Arlington Heights, IL 60005; (847) 228-9900) and the Plastic Surgery Educational Foundation (PSEF). The membership of ASPRS comprises 97 percent of all plastic surgeons certified by the American Board of Plastic Surgery.

Third Age Media
>620 Folsom Street
>Suite 310
>San Francisco, CA 94107
>(415) 908-6900; Fax (415) 908-6909
>www.thirdage.com

Third Age Media provides news and feature stories of interest to older readers via its Third Age News Service, carried by more than 200 newspapers across the country. Third Age also publishes special reports of interest to seniors, and has its own site on the World Wide Web which offers (among other things) breaking news stories, columnists, and a chat line where subscribers can meet and "talk."

Travel Companion Exchange
>P.O. Box 833
>Amityville, NY 11701
>(800) 392-1256

Serves "single, divorced, and widowed travelers" with its *Travel Companions* newsletter, which contains information on places to go, travel tips, listings of "single friendly resorts," and its VIP membership, which lists older men and women in search of travel companions. A one-year subscription to the newsletter costs $48; a VIP membership (which includes the newsletter) is available for $159 a year.

United Seniors Health Cooperative
>1331 H Street NW, #500
>Washington, DC 20005
>(202) 393-6222
>www.ushc-online.org

A nonprofit consumer organization advising seniors and caregivers on health issues through its *United Seniors Health Report*

($5/five issues a year), *Long-Term Care Planning: A Dollar and Sense Guide* ($15, about options available for financing extended care), and a series of *Eldergames* booklets such as *It's a Woman's World* (featuring 200 questions and answers about famous women, from Martha Washington to Ann Landers).

Additional Resources

The organizations listed below, mentioned at various points in the book, provide services and information that you may find useful. Many of these organizations, including Big Brothers Big Sisters, the American Red Cross, Meals on Wheels, and the Salvation Army have local branches that are listed in your telephone book.

Big Brothers Big Sisters of America (BBBSA)
National Office
230 North 13th Street
Philadelphia, PA 19107
(215) 567-7000
www.bbsa.org

Dancin' Grannies
c/o 714 Vista Del Mar Drive
Aptos, CA 95003
(800) 433-6769; (408) 684-9550

Find People Fast
P.O. Box 20190
St. Louis, MO 63123
(314) 638-4700; Fax (314) 631-5785
www.fpf.com

Global Volunteers
375 E. Little Canada Road
St. Paul, MN 55117-1628
(800) 487-1074; Fax (612) 482-0915
www.globalvlntrs.org

Good Samaritan Project/
The National Association on HIV Over 50
3030 Walnut
Kansas City, Missouri 64108
(816) 561-8784; Fax (816) 531-7199

Infoquest ("We can locate anyone, anywhere.")
101 North 4th Street
Suite 105
Sandpoint, ID 83864
(800) 562-7547 or (208) 263-4548; Fax (800) 793-3463

Meals on Wheels
See your local telephone directory for listings.

National Health Care Anti-Fraud Association
1255 23rd Street NW
Washington, DC 20037
(202) 659-5955; Fax (202) 833-3636
www.nhcaa.org

National Hospice Organization
1901 North Moore Street
Suite 901
Arlington, VA 22209
(703) 243-5900; Fax (703) 525 5762
www.nho.org

Old Friends Information Services
1 Camino Sobrante
Suite 21
Orinda, CA 94563
(800) 841-7938 or (510) 254-3646; Fax (510) 254-0700
www.oldfriendsinc.com

The Salvation Army
(800) SAL-ARMY
www.salvationarmyusa.org (National Headquarters)
www.salvationarmy.org (International Headquarters)
You can also find your local Salvation Army center in your phone book.

United States Peace Corps
1990 K Street NW
Washington, DC 20526
(800) 424-8580
www.peacecorps.gov

Sources of Information on Investing

Amazing as it seems at first glance, a majority of Americans have money invested in securities, and a majority of those are 50 or older.

It's also safe to say that older people are the most market-savvy investors, since we have the money, hard-won experience, and the time to work on fattening our portfolios now that we've graduated from the nine-to-five rat race.

How many seniors begin their days poring over *The Wall Street Journal* or *Investor's Business Daily*, switching on

CNBC-TV's non-stop investing program, driving down to their brokers' offices to get caught up on the latest stock tips, dashing to the library to spend a little time with Standard & Poor's massive investment guides, attending the regular evening meeting of their investment club, and then (before hopping into bed) checking how the markets are opening in London and Tokyo?

More than 51 million Americans own shares of stock, and more than 100 million participate in the market indirectly through investments in pension funds, insurance companies, universities, and banks—and this doesn't include billions sunk into bonds, commodities, precious metals and other investments.

As good luck would have it, there is a mother lode of valuable investment information available at no charge from the U.S. Securities and Exchange Commission, New York Stock Exchange, National Association of Securities Dealers, Inc., Chicago Mercantile Exchange (specializing in commodities), and some 8,000 independent securities dealers.

For example, The New York Stock Exchange (11 Wall Street, New York, NY 10005) offers these booklets: "Getting Help When You Invest," "Understanding Stocks and Bonds," "Understanding Financial Statements," "Glossary" (of words and phrases related to investing), an easy-to-understand booklet for young and old called "You and the Investment World," and the impressive "Marketplace: A Brief History of the New York Stock Exchange."

Fidelity Investments, the world's largest mutual fund company with more than $500 billion under management, also has a bevy of booklets, including several of particular interest to those approaching retirement, including the "Retirement Planning Guide" and the "Fidelity Mutual Fund IRA." Many of the more than 8,000 other mutual funds offer free guides to senior investing, and it's well worth asking your broker about those you are considering using.

American Association of Individual Investors
    625 N. Michigan Avenue
    Chicago, IL 60611
    (312) 280-0170
    www.aaii.org

The American Association of Individual Investors (AAII) is an independent, nonprofit organization formed in 1978 to help investors—particularly experienced ones "with substantial sums to invest"—become better managers of their money. The AAII provides seminars, home study texts, and educational videos to its 175,000 members. Local chapters throughout the country focus on investing and investment techniques.

A one-year membership costs $49 and includes a subscription to the *AAII Journal*, published ten times a year, which contains interviews with leading mutual fund managers, portfolio strategies, stock and critical analyses, and financial planning (all written by experts), along with the *Individual Investor's Guide to Low-Load Mutual Funds*.

The AAII also offers a galaxy of investment publications, software, videos, and an interactive on-line site, providing information on everything from investment basics to portfolio management. A 24-hour phone line gives access to real-time, undelayed, last-sale quotes on exchange-listed and over-the-counter securities and mutual funds, not to mention investor seminars abroad and luxury cruise ships such as the Holland-America Line's *MS Veendam*.

The Chicago Mercantile Exchange
   30 South Wacker Drive
   Chicago, IL 60606
   (312) 930-1000
   www.cme.com

The Chicago Mercantile Exchange is where very sophisticated traders, operating on their own or through their brokers, buy and sell agricultural commodities, such live cattle or lean hogs, foreign currencies such as the British pound or Japanese yen, financial paper bearing interest rates as with 90-day U.S. Treasury bills, or investments based on financial indices such as the Standard & Poor's Stock Index.

Traders, often moving at lightning speed, either sell a contract on one of those investments hoping to buy it back later at a lower price, or buy a contract hoping to sell it later at a higher price. Investing in futures contracts is a very fast track, and it's a good idea to know what you're doing before putting your money down.

The exchange offers a wide range of publications, videotapes, and computer software that describe investing in its various products, and you can get a pamphlet listing them by calling the phone number listed above. A copy of "The Merc at Work: A Guide to the Chicago Mercantile Exchange" is also available at (312) 930-1000.

Merrill Lynch
Check your local telephone directory for the location nearest you, or visit the Web site www.merrill-lynch.ml.com.

Merrill Lynch is the nation's largest broker, and local offices offer a wealth of investment information. Three publications of particular interest to older investors are "Planning For The Future: How Americans Save For Retirement And Other Goals," "Retirement Management Service," and "IRA Sourcebook: Merrill Lynch Retirement Plans."

The National Association of Securities Dealers, Inc. (NASDAQ) Stock Market
  1735 K Street NW
  Washington, DC 20006
  (202) 728-6964
  www.nasdaq.com

NASDAQ is the largest and fastest-growing securities market in the United States, and deals with the stocks of more than 5,500 leading companies in computers, data processing, pharmaceuticals, telecommunications, biotechnology, and financial services, along with initial public offerings of firms whose stocks are just beginning to trade, as well as international companies.

Well known companies such as Microsoft, Intel, American Greetings, Fuji Photo Film, AB Volvo, Northwest Airlines, and Tyson's Foods are traded on NASDAQ, which is a wholly owned subsidiary of the National Association of Securities Dealers, a national securities association registered with the U.S. Securities and Exchange Commission.

What sets NASDAQ apart from the New York and American stock exchanges is that it has no frantic trading floor with brokers shouting and waving their arms at each other. Instead, trading is conducted entirely via computers that post the best prices brokers are willing to pay to buy or sell stocks, which other brokers can then act on by completing orders from their customers.

You can get more useful information on this market, such as "Investor Insight or the NASDAQ Backgrounder," by contacting the Office of Individual Investor Services at the telephone number above.

National Association of Investors Corporation (NAIC)
  711 West Thirteen Mile Road
  Madison Heights, MI 48071
  (248) 583-6242
  www.better-investing.org
The NAIC is a not-for-profit educational organization founded in 1951 whose main goal is to help educate its members about investing and to encourage them to put money into lifetime financial programs. The organization achieves its goal by suggesting people join with ten or twenty others to form a club to learn investment principles and exchange information with the help of NAIC materials.

The NAIC has an extraordinarily wide range of services, including various types of membership, some twenty books on investing, computer software on investing programs, and more than ninety regional councils coast to coast.

Individual club memberships cost $39 a year and include a year's subscription to its monthly *Better Investing* magazine, a copy of its *Official Guide*, and a low-cost plan for getting started in building your personal or investment club portfolio.

The Securities and Exchange Commission (SEC)
  Office of Investor Education and Assistance
  Mailstop 11-2
  450 5th Street NW
  Washington, DC 20549
  (202) 942-7040; Fax (202) 942 9634
  www.sec.gov

The SEC's Office of Investor Education and Assistance offers free publications on investing and suggests the ones of greatest interest to older people are:

➤ *"What Every Investor Should Know"*: The essentials of investing in securities.

➤ *"Invest Wisely: Advice From Your Securities Industry Regulators"*: How to choose a broker, pick an investment, and look out for trouble.

➤ *"Invest Wisely: An Introduction to Mutual Funds"*: How mutual funds work, factors to consider before investing, and how to avoid pitfalls.

The SEC also offers other kinds of free investor information and special reports, available from (800) SEC-0330.

INDEX

A

A Dud at 70, a Stud at 80 (Johnson), 93
AARP Bulletin, 239-40. *See also*
    American Association of Retired
    Persons
Achenbaum, W. Andrew, 147-48
Acupuncturists, 217
A Dance with Death (Noggle), 134
Adler, Stella, 143
Age and Achievement (Lehman), 8
Age discrimination, 146-48
Age Discrimination in Employment
    Act, 146
Age-related research, national, 86-88
Age Wave (Dychtwald), 123
Aging Services, 240
Aging Today, 207, 264
Aging
    and advertising, 170-74, 180
    and artistic achievement, 7-9, 137-
      39
    and careers. *See* Careers
    and costs of health care, 181-86
    and diet. *See* Diet
    and disease, 77-84, 274
    and education, 3, 5, 17-19
    effects of, 58-60
    and exercise. *See* Exercise
    and financial matters, 159-93
    and good health, 55-93, 245-46
    and health maintenance tips, 89-90
    income and, 162-67
    is not a disease, 57
    and life expectancy, xiii-xiv, 247,
      255-57
    and love, 95-126
    and mental performance, 1-19. *See*
      also Mind
    philosophy of, 248-49, 264-65
    poverty rate, 160
    and prescription medication, 78,
      83-84, 181-86
    research on, 86-88
    rethinking, xi-xiii, 77, 247-48
    and retirement. *See* Retirement
    reversing the process of, 91, 221-22,
      257
    and sex. *See* Sex
    and technology. *See* Technology
    and work, 5, 127-58, 188
AIDS (Acquired Immune Deficiency
    Syndrome), 77, 81-82, 115-17, 135,
    217, 219, 260
Alexander, Daisy, 168
Alternative medicine, 216-19
Alzheimer's disease, 6, 47, 77, 80, 208,
    219, 273
America Online, 45
American Association of Retired
    Persons (AARP), xiii, 18, 35, 50,
    121, 142, 181, 190, 270
American Institute of Stress, 74
American Society on Aging, 264, 270-
    71
American Visionary Art Museum, 25
Anatomy of an Illness (Cousins), 127
Andenauer, Conrad, 10
Andrus Foundation, 50, 121
Angelou, Maya, 8
Anti-aging genes, 222, 257
Apple Computer's Worldwide
    Disability Solutions, 48
Art collecting, 27-29
Assisted-living residences, 227, 242
Assistive technologies, 207
Automated Teller Machines (ATM),
    212, 215-16

B

Baby boomers, 140, 145, 171, 188
Baltimore Longitudinal Study of Aging,
    57

Barnet, Will, 135
Barrymore, John, 267
Beckwith, Pete, 117
"Becoming a Better Grandparent," 50
Bell, Alexander Graham, 10-11
Biogenetics, 79-80, 91, 219-22
Bird watching, 27
Blair, "Banana" George, 28-29
The Body is a Clear Place (Hawkins),
    139
Bolles, Richard, 136
Bolter, Elliot, 29
Borgnine, Ernest, 139
Bortz, Dr. Walter M. II, 92
Boskin, Michael, 193
Bound for Good Health (NIH), 89
Breast cancer, 85, 157
Brier, Barbara, 9
Brimley, Wilford, 180
Bronte, Dr. Lydia, 134-36
Brown, Helen Gurley, 245-46
Bulcroft, Richard and Kris, 100
Burns, Dr. David, 119
Burns, George, 91
Bush, George, xi, 10, 39, 154
Butler, Dr. Robert, 97
Byrd, Admiral Richard E., 21

C
Calment, Jeanne, xvii-xviii
Cancer, 12, 77, 125,185, 220, 251, 260,
    271
  breast, 85, 157
  death rates from, 79
  prevention, 63-64, 89
Caneel Bay resort, 34
Capa, Cornell, 152
Capital Holding Corporation, 163
Capps, Dr. John, 15
Careers, 127-58
  artistic, 137-39, 262-64
  in entertainment, 140-42
  Explorers, Homesteaders, and
    Transformers, 135-36
  new, 152
  post-retirement, 152-53, 155-56

self-employment, 154-56
  vintage achievers, 133-37
Caregiver burnout, 241
Caring for elderly relatives, 241
Carney, Art, 179
Carstens, Jerald, 198-99
Carter, President Jimmy, 39
Casals, Pablo, 127-28
Castelli, Dr. William, 63
Cavanaugh, Francis X., 189
Census Bureau, 160, 162, 256-57
Center for Creative Retirement, 19
Center for Mature Consumer Studies,
    179
CHAMPUS program, 262
The Change (Greer), 121
Channing, Carol, 142
Chaplin, Charlie, 160
Cherekin, Alvin, 154
Child, Julia, 73, 127
Churchill, Winston, 10
Clark, Clifford, 3-4
Clark, Joe and Deborah, 230
Clarke, Arthur C., 203
Clinton, President, 39, 184
Cohen, Dr. Gene, 5
Cole, Thomas R., 263-64
Committee for Freedom of Choice in
    Medicine, 218
Common Cause, 136
The Commonwealth Fund, 143
Communication between young and
    old, 198-200
Computers, 44, 197, 200, 202, 206,
    209, 213, 224. See also Internet,
    World Wide Web
  America Online, 45
  emoticons, 44
  netiquette, 44
  online Elders Group, 44
  senior cybernauts, 44-48
  textual poachers, 44
Conner, Dennis, xvii
Corey, Irwin, 168-69
Cort-Van Arsdale, Diana, 120
Cosmetic surgery, 75-77, 91, 274

Cousins, Norman, 127-28, 136
Covenant Village, 242
Crews, McKinley, 130
Criminal Justice Services, 36
Crimmins, Dr. Eileen, 133
Cronyn, Hume, 135
Crown, William H., 162
Culbert, Mike, 218-19
Curie, Marie, 259
Curing Old Age Disease Society, 257
Cybersex, 203

D
Dancin' Grannies, 61-62, 65, 276
Danzig, Fred, 172, 174
Dating, 110, 118
Dating services, 107, 123
Days Inn, 143-44, 156
De Mille, Agnes, 138
DeBakey, Dr. Michael, 134
Debernardis, Frank, 13
DeCrow, Karen, 96
Dennis, W., 8
Depression, 7, 118, 157, 241
Diabetes, 69, 78, 102, 220
Diet, role in maintaining good health,
    xiii, 62-70, 78, 92, 221
*Directory of Learning Opportunities for
    Older Persons* (AARP), 18
Diseases, age-related, 77-84, 274. *See
    also names of individual diseases*
Dodson, Betty, 103
Dr. Spock's Baby and Child Care
    (Spock), 159
Dr. Tomorrow, 222-24
"Dreadful D's," 247
Durdik, Dr. Herb, 14
Durwood, Stanley, 140-41
Duyn, Mona Van, 134
Dychtwald, Ken, 123

E
Ear implants, 78
Early retirement, 142, 173
Ecotourism, 34
Edison, Thomas Alva, 10, 161

Education, 3, 5, 17-19
Eisner, Robert, 192
Elderhostel, 19, 271-72
The Elderly as Modern Pioneers, 15
Employment, 5, 127-58, 188
Empty nesters, 96
Engler, Governor John, 148
Entertainment, careers in, 140-42
Environmental Alliance for Senior
    Involvement (EASI), 35, 272
Erikson, Eric and Joan, 237, 249-50,
    252
Estate handling, 266
Estrogen hormone replacement, 85-86
Evons, Tom, 237
Exercise, xiii, 60-62, 65-70, 78, 91-93

F
*50 Fabulous Places to Retire to in
    America* (Rosenberg), 238
Family histories, 253-55
Familyhood (Salk), 250
Fasano, Mary, 18
Favaloro, Dr. Rene G., 134
Feder, Judith, 184
Feeling Good (Burns), 119
Feigenbaum, Armand "Val" and
    Donald, 130
Feynman, Dr. Richard, 252
Finance, 159-93, 278-84
Find People Fast, 125, 276
Fine, Sidney, 147-48
Fisher, Helen, 98
Florida, 233, 239
Ford, President Gerald, 39
Forsythe, John, 136
Francis, Arlue, 247
Frank, Barney, 114
Freud, Sigmund, 12
Friends, 124-26, 252, 278
Frost, Robert, 7
Fruscella, Joseph, 215
Fry, Art 13
Furlong, Mary, 46
Future Home, 208
Future Shock (Toffler), 149

G

Gardner, John, 136
Gates, Bill, 149, 214
"Geezers in Gear," 187-88
Gemigniani, Beverly, 60-62, 65, 276
Gene therapy, 79. See also Aging,
    reversing
Genius (Feynman), 251
Geriatrics, 86-88, 264
Gerontology, 15, 247, 264
Gerontology Research Center, 91
Getty, J. Paul, 161
Ghandi, Indira, 10
Gilot, Francoise, 262
Global Volunteers, 37-39, 277
Go, Robert A., 184-85
Goethe, Johann Wolfgang von, 126
Goldenage Web site, 46
Golf Begins at 50 (Rodriguez), 152
Good health. See Aging, and good
    health
Good Samaritan Project, 117, 277
Gorney, Dr. Mark, 77
Grace, J. Peter and W.R., 135
Graham, Martha, 137-39
Grandparents
    babysitting and child-rearing, 48-51
    as family historians, 253-55
    single and two parent families, 49
"The Grandparent Role: A Double
    Bind," 49
Grandquist, Betty, 239
Greer, Germaine, xii, 121-22
Griffin, Sam, 229
Group living, 236-37
    Guest, Barbara, 263
Guinness Book of World Records, xvii, 29

H

Habitat for Humanity International,
    39, 272
Hahn, Harley, 224
Hale House, 135
Hale, Mother Clara, 135
Halpern, Charles R., 217
Hamburger, Rose, 153

Hammer, Dr. Armand, 137
Handel, George, 9
Hardy, Joseph A., 160
Harmon, Margaret L., 236
Harvard, oldest person to earn a degree,
    19
Haunts of the Olde Country, 202
Hawkins, Erick, 139
Health. See Aging, and good health
Health After 50, 88, 273
Heart disease 58, 77, 260
    implants, 78
    preventing, 64, 92
    and Procardia, 84
    risk factors for, 68
Heart Letter (Harvard University), 103
Hefner, Hugh, 96
HIV (human immunodeficiency virus),
    77, 116-17. See also AIDS
HMOs (Health Maintenance
    Organizations), 184-85
Homes for people with disabilities, 207
Homosexuality, 112-15
    discrimination against, 113
    equal rights for, 113-14
    teenagers, 114
Hospice care, 260-62
Hot Flashes (Brown), 246
Howard, Julie, 207
Hudson, Rock, 116
Hugo, Victor, 258-59
Humphrey, William, 251

I

Iacocca, Lee, 137
Impotence, causes and treatments, 101-
    102
Inactivity, effects of, 68
Inflation, 189
Infoquest, 125, 277
Information Age, 214, 216
Insomnia, 71-73
Institute for Learning in Retirement,
    19
Internet, 44-48, 90, 224. See also World
    Wide Web

The Internet Complete Reference, 224
Investing
    after retirement, 165
    fixed-income, 165
    sources of information on, 278-84
    strategies, 166

J

Jacobs, Dr. Joseph J., 218
The Janus Report on Sexual Behavior
    (Adams), 115
Javacheff, Christo, 32
Jefferson, Thomas, 27
Johns, Jasper, 263
Johnson, Helen, 152
Johnson, Magic, 81
Johnson, Noel, 93
Jolesz, Dr. Ferenc, 202
The Journey of Life (Cole), 264
Joyce, James, 263

K

Keller, Helen, 11-12
Kennedy, President John F., 7, 41, 165
Kimball Farms retirement community,
    17
The Kinsey Institute for Research in
    Sex, Gender, and Reproduction, 122
Klausner, Dr. Richard, 64
Klieman, Dr. Charles, 14
Koch, Bill, xiv
Kurosawa, Akira, 147

L

Labor force, reasons for reentering,
    142-46
LaMorte, Michael F., 2
Land, Edwin H., 161
Lappert, Walter, 153
Lasker, Emanual, 9
The Late Show (Brown), 245
Late-stage learning, 17-19
Lauer, Jeannette and Robert, 96
Laundromats, and singles, 110
Le Figaro, 116
Lear, Frances, 156-58

Leary, Timothy, 204
Lehman, Harvey, 8
Leibowitz, Professor Yeshayahu, 4
Leigh, Douglas, 131-32
Lemelson, Jerome H., 161
Lesbian/Women (Martin), 112
Lewis, Michael, 164
Lewis, Myrna, 97
Life expectancy, xiii-xiv, 247, 255-57
Lifestyle marketing, 180
Link Resources, 148
Living will, 266
Llinas, Dr. Rodolfo, 16
Loneliness, 117-18
The Long Careers Study, 134
The Longevity Factor (Bronte), 135
Longino, Charles F., Jr., 162
Loss, coping with, 265
Lou Gehrig's disease, 77, 80-81
Love and Sex after 60 (Butler, Lewis), 97
Love, 95-126, 267-68
    of family, importance of, 250-53
    of friends, importance of, 124-26
Lowe, Ed, 30-31
Lowery, Reverend Joseph E., 265

M

MacDonald, Ernie, 92
Magnetic Source Imaging (MSI), 16
Mahoney, John J., 262
Mandell, Johnny, 141
Marin, John, 259
Marquez, Gabriel Garcia, 119
Martin, Dean, 25
Masloff, Sophie, 129-30
Mason, Jackie, 224-25
Matisse, Henri, 263
McClintock, Dr. Barbara, 135
McCoy, Amelia B., 154
McDermott, Trish, 107
McGinty, Andrea, 109
McGowan, William, 66
The McLaughlin Group, 2
McLaughlin, John, 2
Mead, Margaret, 86
Meals on Wheels, 126, 277

Median age of Americans, 256
Medicaid, 182, 191, 262
Medicare, 182, 185-86, 189, 191, 262
Medicine
   rising cost of, 181-86
   scientific advances in, xiii-xv, 14,
      77-81, 202, 219-22
Meditourism, 34
Meeker, Richard, 131
Meir, Golda, 10
Memory, 6, 9, 14-16
Menopause, 85-6, 121-22, 271
Mental performance of older adults. See
   Mind
Michelangelo, 9, 224
Mills, Harold, 239
Mind, of older adults, 1-19. See also
      Memory
   and education, 17-19
   functioning of, 5-7
   keeping it trim, 14-16
   and learning new skills, 5
   and longevity, 59-60
Mochis, George, 179
Modern Maturity, 157, 181, 270
The Money Game (Lewis), 164
Money market funds, 166
Monroe, Bill, 129
Monroe, Marilyn, 161
Moore, Patricia, 107
Morley, Robert, 67
Morris, Dr. John, 3
Morse, Harley, 55-57
Moses, Grandma, 9
Moses, Herb, 114
MTV, 140
Murdoch, Rupert, 140

N
Nathan Cummings Foundation, 217
The National Association on HIV
   Over 50, 117, 277
National Cancer Institute, 64
The National Council on Aging, 179
National Family Caregivers
   Association, 241

The National Golf Foundation, 152
The National Health Care Anti-Fraud
   Association, 182, 277
National Hospice Organization
   (NHO), 260-262, 277
National Institute on Aging (NIA), 5,
   23, 57, 89, 221, 256-57
National Institutes of Health (NIH),
   91, 218
National Organization for Women, 96
"The Nature and Functions of Dating
   in Later Life," 100
Navigating in Cyberspace (Ogden), 224
Near Changes (Van Duyn), 134
Neugarten, Bernice, xii
New Choices: Living Even Better After
   50, 44
Newhouse, S. I. "Sam," 131
Newman, Phyllis, 120
Newspaperman (Meeker), 131
Nickelodeon, 140
Nicklaus, Jack, 152
Noggle, Anne, 134
Nudist parks, 232
Nureyev, Rudolf, 116
Nursing homes, 227, 240

O
Office of Alternative Medicine, 218
Ogden, Frank, 222-24
Old Friends Information Services, 125,
   278
Older consumers, 179-80
Older Women Make Better Lovers, 111
Older workers, 5, 127-58
Olsen, Ken, 2
One Hundred Years of Solitude
   (Marquez), 119
Operation Lifeline, 36

P
Palance, Jack, xiv
Palmer, Arnold, 90
Parkinson's disease, 77, 80-81, 220
Partners-in-Travel, 34
Passions (Witkin), 104

The Patricia Moore Group, Inc., 106-109
Pavarotti, Luciano, 69-70
Peace Corps, 39-42
Penn, William, 35
Perot, Ross, 10, 176
Personal ads, 110-11
Personal Communications Networks (PCNs), 210
Peterson, Peter, 191-92
Phelps Stokes Institute, 134-35
Philanthropy, 35, 164
Phillips, Ed, 123
Phillips, Susan Elizabeth, 43
Picasso, Pablo, 9, 55
Pilcher, Rosamunde, 254
Player, Gary, 152
Plisetskaya, Maya, 139
Plum, Dr. Fred, 79
Policy Center on Aging, 162
Political clout of older Americans, 188
Polygamy, 123
Procardia, 84. See also Heart disease
Products for older adults, 177-81
Protease inhibitors, 81-82. See also AIDS

Q
Quiet Pride: Ageless Wisdom of the American West, 253

R
Rabut, Peggy, 38
Raffray, Andre-Francois, xvii
Randall, Tony, 96
Rapoport, Dr. Stanley, 5
Raskin, Barbara, 246
Reading as a pastime, 42-44
Reagan, President Ronald, 10, 65-66, 150-52
Recreational Vehicles (RVs), 232
Red Cross, 126, 276
Reinhardt, Uwe, 183
Reis, Al, 7
Remes, Gary, 76
Respite-care initiative, 240

Restak, Dr. Richard, 7
Retired military officers, 232
Retirement. See also AARP
    age, 142, 192
    and computers, 44-48
    communities, 17, 198, 231-35, 242
    deciding against, 142-46, 148, 150-56
    educational programs and, 17-19
    guides, 229, 238
    and hobbies, 25-30
    income, 167
    and the Internet, 44-48
    locations for, 227-43
    mandatory, 22, 148
    publications on, 238
    surprising delights of, 25-29
    and withdrawing from the world, 14, 24
Reverse mortgages, 163
Reversing the aging process, 91, 221-22, 257
Riley, Matilda, 23
Rivers, Joan, 265-66
Roach, Dr. Paul J., 74
Rockefeller, Lawrence, 34
Roddenberry, Gene, 204
Roloff, Dr. Michael E., 118
Romance, 96-100, 106-11
Roosevelt, President Franklin Delano, 132
Rose, Michael, 221
Rosenberg, Lee and Saralee, 238
Rowan, Henry W. and Betty, 164
Rubenstein, Arthur, 9
The Road Ahead (Gates), 149

S
Sadow, Sue, 41
Salk, Dr. Jonas, 136, 251
Salk, Dr. Lee, 250-51
Salvation Army, 126, 278
Santmeyer, Helen Hooven, 12
Schaie, Dr. Warner, 17
Schindler, Dr. Robert A., 78
Schnell, Dr. Lisa, 79

Schriver, Sargeant, 41
Schwab, Dr. Martin E. 79
Schwartz, William B., 191
Scientific advances in medicine. *See*
   Medicine, scientific advances in
Scott, Robert, 17
Sealey, Peter, 141
The Second Seduction (Lear), 156
"Secure adults," 177-81
Seibert, Muriel, 154
Self-employment, 154-56
Selye, Dr. Hans, 73
Senior citizens. *See* Aging
SeniorNet, 46
September Song (Humphrey), 251
Serving the Ageless Market (Wolfe), 57
Sex, 59, 97-98, 100-106, 111, 115, 246
Sexual revolution, 115
Sicker, Martin, 142
Simon, Dr. Harvey B., 248
Simon, Herbert and Melvin, 164-65
Simon, Roy, 174, 176
Simplot, J.R., 130
Skidmore, Don and Linda, 230
Sleep Disorders Center, 71
Sleep, effects on health, 71-73
Smith, Dr. T. Burton, 65-66, 150-52
Smyslov, Vassily, 9
Social Security, xiii, 160, 163, 185-93,
   228, 232
Solitude, 117-20
Sophocles, 9
Spock, Benjamin, 159-60
Spratt, Donald, 38
Stages of the life cycle, 249
Stark, Congressman Pete, 182
Steineck, Lavina, xvii
Sternberg, Robert, 97
Stress, 73-75
Strictly Business, 2-3
Summer camp, for grandparents and
   grandkids, 48
Surgery, cosmetic, 75-77, 91, 274
Swenson, Chester A., 180
Szymborska, Wislawa, 134

T

Tandy, Jessica, 135
Technology, 148-49, 195-98, 200-16,
   219-25
   benefitting seniors, xiii, 44-48, 207-
      209, 211, 219-22
   conquering fears of, 212-14
   downside of, 214-16
Telecommunications, 44-48, 148-50,
   209-12
Telecommuting, 148-50. *See also*
   Computers, Internet
Television industry, 174-77, 206-07
Testosterone patches, 102
Thayer, Nancy, 124
Theresa, Mother, xiv
Third Age Media, 46, 275
Thomas, Dylan, 245
Thomas, Professor Jean L., 49
Thurmond, Strom, 129
'Til Death Do Us Part (Lauer), 96
Time Dollars, 167
Toffler, Alvin, 149
Tolstoy, Vera, 51-54
Too Many Promises (Boskin), 193
Transgenic animals, 219
Transitions (Newman), 120
Translator telephones, 211-12
Transplants, 184-85, 196, 219-20
Travel, 33-34, 39-42
Travel Companion Exchange, 34
Travis, Doris Eaton, 3
Troiseme Age, 46
Trout, Jack, 7
The Truth About the National Debt
   (Cavanaugh), 189
Turnkovsky, Antonina, 129
Twomey, Jerry, 26

U

Uhse, Beate, 111
U.S. Savings Bonds, 166

V

VanBarringer, John, 32
Vaughn, Norman, 21-24

Vaupel, Dr. James, 256
Verdi, Giuseppe, 9
Veterans Administration Hospital
    System, 262
Virtual reality, 202, 223
Vitamin supplements, 63-65
Vogel, Dorothy and Herbert, 27-29
Volunteering, 35-42, 128, 240, 267
Von Zedtwitz, Waldemar, 9

W
Walking, 67-68, 93
Wallace, Mike, 146
Walters, Barbara, 97
Walton, Sam, 137
Ward, David, 208
Weight-training, 91
Weissman, Samuel, 44
What Color Is Your Parachute? (Bolles),
    136
*What's on Your Mind?: A Quiz on Aging
    and the Brain* (NIA), 5
White House Doctor, 65, 150
Whitkin, Dr. Georgia, 104
Wilde, Oscar, 109, 259
*Will America Grow Up Before It Grows
    Old?* (Peterson), 192
Williams, Dr. T. Franklin, 92
"Witch-doctor medicine," 218
With Byrd at the Bottom of the World
    (Vaughn), 22
Wolfe, David B., 57
Wolman, Bill, 1
Woodruff, Robert W., 164
Woods, Tiger, 90
Woopies, 171
Work, 5, 127-58, 188
World Wide Web, 45, 215, 238. *See
    also* Internet
popular sites for seniors, 45-47
Wright brothers, 11

X
Xenotransplantation, 220

Y
Yanovitch, Joe, 69-70
Yeltsin, Boris, 134
"You Can Afford the Lifestyle You
    Want...," 167
Youth
    in dating, 108-109
    educational problems of today's, 196
    interests of, 198-200
    overemphasis on, xi-xii, 77
    turning back the clock to, 257-58

Z
Zartman, Barbara 40

ACKNOWLEDGMENTS

This page constitutes a continuation of the copyright information at the beginning of this book.

The publisher gratefully acknowledges the permission of the following to reproduce the photographs in this book:

P. 8: © Steve Dunwell, by permission of Wake Forest University; p. 11: Courtesy of Alexander Graham Bell Association for the Deaf, Inc.; p. 28: Courtesy of Banana George, Inc., Box 122, Cypress Gardens, FL 33884; p. 31: Courtesy of the Edward Lowe Foundation; pp. 37, 38: Courtesy of Global Volunteers; p. 40: Courtesy of Peace Corps/Barringer.; p. 45: Courtesy of Third Age Media, Inc.; p. 49: Courtesy of Camp Sagamore; p. 51: Courtesy of Vera Tolstoy; p. 56: © Wayne Replogle; p. 61: Courtesy of Beverly Gemigniani/Dancin' Grannies; p. 69: Courtesy Florida Times-Union, © 1997 Florida Publishing Company; p. 90: Courtesy Arnold Palmer Enterprises; p. 121: © Knopf/Jerry Bauer; p. 132: Courtesy of Douglas Leigh; p. 138: © Cris Alexander, courtesy of *Goddess: Martha Graham Dancers Remember* (Limelight Editions, 1997); p. 151: Official photograph of the White House, Washington, courtesy of T. Burton Smith, M.D.; p. 157: © Knopf/Michel Comte; p. 160: © 1991 Henry David Teller, courtesy of Mary Morgan and Benjamin Spock; p. 169: Courtesy of Lustig Talent Enterprises, Inc.; p. 187: Courtesy of Beverly and Thomas Taylor; p. 192: © John Maguire, courtesy of Peter G. Peterson; p. 223: Courtesy of Contemporary Communications/National Speakers Bureau/Frank Ogden; p. 205: Courtesy of Celestis, Inc.; p. 228: Courtesy of Bainbridge *Post-Searchlight*, Inc.; p. 234: © Steven Brooke, courtesy of Seaside; p. 246: Courtesy of Cosmopolitan International Editions; p. 249: Courtesy of Erikson Institute; p. 250: © Sigrid Estrada, courtesy of Simon & Schuster.

The publisher also wishes to thank the following for permission to reproduce copyrighted material in this book:

Excerpt from *White House Doctor* (Madison Books, 1992) by Carter Henderson and T. Burton Smith, M.D. reprinted by permission of Madison Books. Excerpts from "Goodbye, Professor Chips?" by Andrew Achenbaum reprinted by permission of *LSA Magazine*/University of Michigan. Excerpts from The Long Careers Study (later published as *The Longevity Factor* [HarperCollins, 1993]) © Lydia Bronte, reprinted by permission of the author. Excerpt from "Smart House" (*Aging Today*, November/December 1995) by Julie Howard reprinted by permission of *Aging Today*.